D1203413

GOLEM

Golem

Modern Wars and Their Monsters

Maya Barzilai

NEW YORK UNIVERSITY PRESS

New York

NEW YORK UNIVERSITY PRESS
New York
www.nyupress.org

References to Internet websites (URLs) were accurate at the time of writing. Neither the author nor New York University Press is responsible for URLs that may have expired or changed since the manuscript was prepared.

Library of Congress Cataloging-in-Publication Data
Names: Barzilai, Maya, author.
Title: Golem : modern wars and their monsters / Maya Barzilai.
Description: New York : New York University Press, [2016] | Includes bibliographical references and index.
Identifiers: LCCN 2016017269 | ISBN 9781479889655 (cl : alk. paper)
Subjects: LCSH: Golem. | War.
Classification: LCC BM531 .B37 2016 | DDC 296.3/827—dc23
LC record available at https://lccn.loc.gov/2016017269

New York University Press books are printed on acid-free paper, and their binding materials are chosen for strength and durability. We strive to use environmentally responsible suppliers and materials to the greatest extent possible in publishing our books.

Manufactured in the United States of America

10 9 8 7 6 5 4 3 2 1

Also available as an ebook

For Shuli and Eli Barzilai

The resemblance of [the golem of Prague] to the golems of our nuclear age staggers the imagination. While we attempt to surpass our enemies and to create new and more destructive golems, the awful possibility is lurking that they may develop a volition of their own, become spiteful, treacherous, mad golems. Like the Jews of Prague in the sixteenth century, we are frightened by our golems. We would like to be in a position to erase the uncanny power we have given them, hide them in some monstrous attic and wait for the time when they too will become fiction and folklore.

—Isaac Bashevis Singer

CONTENTS

ACKNOWLEDGMENTS

Golem creation is a dangerous undertaking, but so too is writing books about golems. Both activities require total immersion and can entail the creator's own destruction. I have managed to emerge unscathed from the lengthy and arduous process of molding what has finally become this book only because of the ongoing support of mentors, colleagues, friends, and family. They prevented me from being crushed by my own creation, and it is to them that I owe this book.

At the Hebrew University, Ruth Ginsburg and Shlomith Rimon-Kenan initiated me into the academic world and challenged me to read carefully and deeply. The gift of their intellectual mentorship and personal friendship still nourishes me to this day. At UC Berkeley—where I first began to think and write about the golem as a figure of war—I had the fortune of engaged and supportive advisors whose work continues to enrich my own. Robert (Uri) Alter unfailingly backed my intellectual pursuits and shared his wealth of knowledge about Hebrew literature and S. Y. Agnon in particular. Chana Kronfeld's invaluable and generous feedback on my work has not only greatly enhanced my writing but also provided me with a role model of passionate mentorship and rigorous scholarship. Anton (Tony) Kaes's Weimar film seminars at Berkeley shaped the way I think about the (moving) image, and I am grateful to him for innumerable thought-provoking conversations, for his savvy advice, and for his help with the book's arguments and title. I am also grateful for the stimulating intellectual environment that other faculty and students at Berkeley provided, in particular, Michael André Bernstein, Daniel Boyarin, Yael Chaver, Naomi Seidman, Kaja Silverman, Naomi Brenner, Katra Byram, Lital Levy, Noam Manor, Sabrina K. Rahman, Allison Schachter, Shaul Setter, and Zehavit Stern.

At the University of Michigan, I have been blessed with welcoming chairs and exceptional colleagues to whom I could turn for advice. Deborah Dash Moore always had her door open and helped me navigate the academic publishing world. She also provided valuable comments on portions of the book. In addition to branding "golem studies," Geoff Eley engaged my work and offered his friendship and support. Jonathan Freedman has shared my fascination with all things on the borders of Jewishness, providing sharp feedback and heartening advice. Mikhael Krutikov has been an amazing resource on Yiddish culture, taking an interest in my work and offering incisive feedback on chapter 2. The erudite Shachar Pinsker provided crucial references and shared his insights into the writing process. Rachel Neis believed in me and in the project from day one. I cannot thank her enough for her brilliant feedback, her willingness to answer calls at all times of the day (and night), and her keen sense of humor, which has kept me afloat. Anita Norich has been the finest mentor a young faculty member could ever hope for. She guided me through every aspect of the writing and publishing process, commenting on numerous drafts of the project. Her encouragement, wisdom, and warmth have made Ann Arbor feel more like home.

Other colleagues at Michigan have contributed to this project, and I feel fortunate to work in their midst. Levana Aronson, Kathryn Babayan, Carol Bardenstein, Kerstin Barndt, Sara Blair, Sigrid Anderson Cordell, Deirdre de la Cruz, Elliot Ginsburg, Gottfried Hagen, Doron Lamm, Christi Merrill, Piotr Mikhalowski, Joshua L. Miller, Johannes von Moltke, Regina Morantz-Sanchez, Ellen Muehlberger, Yopie Prins, Anton Shammas, Scott Spector, Jindrich Toman, and Jeffrey Veidlinger all offered helpful advice and many words of encouragement. Eitan Bar-Yosef, a visiting fellow from Ben Gurion University, has been a valuable interlocutor and celebrated important milestones with me.

My year as a fellow at the Frankel Institute for Advanced Judaic Studies, under the energetic leadership of Jonathan Freedman, was influential for the formation of this book. It was there that I had the mental space to reconceive the project and the opportunity to workshop my writing. I thank my cofellows Lois Dubin, Harvey Goldberg, Kathy Lavezzo, Tatjana Lichtenstein, Jessica Marglin, Ranen Omer-Sherman, Meera Schreiber, Andrea Siegel, and Orian Zakai for their intellectual honesty and inspiring remarks. Laurence Roth went beyond the call of duty to provide me with perceptive feedback on chapter 4; Jennifer Glaser was a shrewd interlocutor on all matters of American Jewish culture; Lisa Silverman helped me untangle a knot of theoretical issues.

Colleagues at other institutions generously read my work and supported my endeavors. I thank Brad Prager for his many kindnesses and insightful feedback on chapter 1. Steve Choe and Joel Rosenberg generously allowed me to read their own manuscript drafts. Ilana Pardes's work has always been a source of inspiration for me, and I am grateful for her feedback on my Agnon materials. Zoe Beenstock wisely commented on the prospectus, and Ofer Ashkenazi has been a helpful resource on all matters of German cinema and German Jewish culture.

Many other programs, institutions, and archives have made the research for this book possible and even enjoyable. The Berlin Program for Advanced German and European Studies generously supported my research on German cinema and Paul Wegener. I am grateful to the Berlin Program 2007–2008 cohort of fellows, and especially to Freyja Hartzell, for their feedback and cheer. I also thank the patient and helpful archivists and librarians at the Deutsche Kinemathek in Berlin, the Deutsches Filminstitut, Frankfurt am Main, and the YIVO Archive in New York. The immensely knowledgeable Raphael Weiser of the National Library at the Hebrew University assisted my research on S. Y. Agnon's German period. A summer grant from the National Endowment for the Humanities enabled me to conduct archival research in New York. A 2015 semester of research leave for junior faculty at the University of Michigan allowed me to complete the manuscript.

Throughout my studies and research across three continents, I have enjoyed the continuity of lasting friendships and intellectual exchanges. Catherine Rottenberg has been my pillar of strength and love, supporting my endeavors from afar and always finding the time to comment on my work. Yosefa Raz and I have shared an incredible journey from Jerusalem to Berkeley (and back), and I am forever grateful for her keen eye, wise comments, and steadfast friendship. Na'ama Rokem has been an enthusiastic "partner in crime," always ready to read, comment, and collaborate: the field of German-Hebrew studies has greatly benefited from her intellectual generosity. Naama Hochstein, Avia Pasternak, and Sharon Tamir have stood by my side for decades now, taking a keen interest in my work and well-being. In Ann Arbor, Zarena Aslami, Ilana Blumberg, John Carson, Dan Cutler, Uljana Feest, Mark Jacobson, Christi Merrill, Polly Rosenwaike, Yael Stateman, Daphna Stroumsa, and Cody Walker have extended their kind friendship and support.

Several research assistants and editors have diligently helped me bring this project to completion. I am grateful to Alexandra (Sasha) Hoffman and Yaakov Herskovitz for their energetic research skills and for uncovering many hidden gems in the Yiddish press. Nadav Linial assisted me with his eye for detail and probing observations. David Lobenstine has been my most ardent critic and enthusiastic supporter, helping me mold this book into its current shape. I cannot thank him enough for his brilliant editorial work and for helping me develop my style as a scholar. I am also grateful to Polly Rosenwaike for her careful editing, elegant style, and speedy delivery.

At NYU Press, my editor, Jennifer Hammer, believed in this project and offered invaluable advice and support, making sure that I wrote the strongest book possible. It has also been a pleasure to work with Constance Grady, Ulrike Guthrie, Dorothea S. Halliday, Andrew Katz, and the entire marketing and design team, and I am grateful to Jennifer and the press for the smooth and conscientious process from submission to publication. The book's reviewers gave up precious time to carefully read the manuscript, and I thank them sincerely for their insights and helpful suggestions. Parts of "S. Y. Agnon's German 'Consecration' and Miracle of Hebrew Letters," *Prooftexts* 33, no. 1 (2013): 48–75, are reprinted in chapter 3 with the kind permission of Indiana University Press Journals.

My immediate and extended family have tolerated my absences and appreciated my commitment to this project. I thank Janet, Ed, Nick, Alan, and Brenda for their loving support and interest in my work. My German family—Andrée, Werner, Ludwig, David, and Tamara—welcomed me with open arms and supported my research endeavors in Germany. My sister, Sarit, has been my intellectual role model and devoted ally, ready to offer words of wisdom and constant encouragement. My mother, Shuli, has spoiled me rotten by always agreeing to read my work and never failing to note my achievements. I am also grateful to Eli, my father, for not allowing me to kvetch and for listening, instead, to the arguments of the book. Whenever needed, he also filled the role of technical and research assistant, forever available and helpful. My parents' abiding love, support, and involvement have accompanied this project from day one, and I therefore dedicate the book to them with profound respect.

Amalia and Guy are younger than this book and yet so much wiser. They have inspired me to tell better stories and imagine different endings. After long days at my computer, I could look forward to their laughter. My deepest gratitude goes out to Russell, the most dedicated reader of all. This book bears the imprint of your careful attention, poetic sensibility, and punning wit. And even when you claimed to be my golem, toiling through endless drafts, you knew that in fact you resembled Rabbi Loew, always there to share in the wonders of creation.

NOTE ON TRANSLITERATION AND TRANSLATION

For Hebrew, I use the Library of Congress system with some modifications. I have dispensed with the final *h* for the Hebrew *he sofit*—except in the case of established biblical and rabbinic Hebrew terms—and with the *e* for *shva na* (e.g., *dvarim*, not *devarim*). For Yiddish, I use the YIVO transliteration system. For foreign proper names in both Hebrew and Yiddish, I defer to the most common English form and to the author's preferred translation. When Hebrew and Yiddish proper and geographical names appear within titles, I transliterate them according to the systems stated here. For translations, I quote from existing English translations where available and amend when necessary. Unless otherwise noted, all translations from German, Hebrew, and Yiddish are mine.

Introduction

The Golem Condition

On January 28, 1922, a severe storm descended on Washington, D.C.; in some parts of the capital, snow mounted twenty-eight inches high. That day, at the seventeen-hundred-seat Knickerbocker movie theater, the accumulation of snow collapsed the theater's new roof during a sold-out screening of a silent comedy. Ninety-eight people died, and many more were injured. As reported in the *Washington Post*, following a moment of "applause and laughter" in response to a funny bit on screen, there was a "crash . . . and then, after one concerted groan, there was silence— and Crandell's Knickerbocker theater, previously the temple of mirth, had been transformed into a tomb."[1]

The theater's collapse bore an uncanny resemblance to one of the central scenes in Paul Wegener's film *Der Golem, wie er in die Welt kam* (*The Golem, How He Came into the World*), released in Germany in 1920 and first screened in the United States only a few months prior to the Washington catastrophe. In the film, Rabbi Judah Loew of Prague arrives at the court of Emperor Rudolph II together with his creation, the magical clay giant referred to as the "golem." Asked to entertain the Emperor and his entourage, Rabbi Loew projects onto the wall of the palace "moving images" of wandering Jewish ancestors and warns the courtiers not to laugh at the spectacle. But they do nonetheless. An explosion follows, and the ceiling of the hall begins to collapse. Panic ensues as debris tumbles down, and people fling themselves out of the windows. The rabbi orders the golem to hold up the ceiling beams, saving the lives of the courtiers. But he demands something of the Emperor in return: to annul a recent edict that ordered the expulsion of the Jews.

FIGURE I.1. Paul Wegener in *Der Golem, wie er in die Welt kam*, 1920. (Courtesy of Deutsches Filminstitut, Frankfurt am Main)

While the collapse of the roof at the American theater was an unexpected disaster, it became symbolic of the destructive nature of modern technology, particularly as this technology served the growing mass entertainment industry. The Russian-born Zionist writer and journalist Reuven Brainin (1862–1939) published in the pages of the Yiddish New York daily *Der tog* (The day) an article titled "The Golem (Concerning the Theater Misfortune in Washington)." He metaphorically evoked the clay monster to address the Washington tragedy and offer a critique of technological progress. Brainin drew on the popular golem story to portray modern mechanistic society as soulless, frivolous, and destructive. He even suggested that the theater in Washington was itself constructed "like a golem" since it eventually collapsed and killed those who consume modern entertainment, just as the golem, in some story variants, grows too large and, when deanimated, collapses on its maker.[2]

The association of the golem with cinema and technology at large is a modern, twentieth-century development, but we find that throughout the long and complex history of the golem, it has been linked with the different linguistic and material "technologies" of human artificial creation. The Hebrew word *galmi* (my golem) first appears in Psalms and later in the Midrash. There, *galmi* refers to the unfinished and unformed human shape prior to receiving a soul.[3] Centuries later, in the medieval and Renaissance periods, the golem was an object of Jewish mystical speculation and interpretation that drew on the ancient Hebrew mystical treatise *Sefer yetsira* (*The Book of Creation*). In the early modern period, stories of artificial creation ascribed to particular historical figures began to emerge, often composed by Christian authors. By the early twentieth century, there existed several variations of the golem story that located the golem either in central or in eastern Europe. What they all had in common was the presence of a rabbi who artificially molds a clay anthropoid and magically brings it to life through Hebrew writing, either engraved on the body or on parchment. Though it exhibits extraordinary strength, its lack of intelligence and its inability to speak mark the golem as inferior to the human being. From here, the Yiddish term *goylem* figuratively came to denote an idiot, fool, or clumsy fellow. Created to serve the rabbi or, in twentieth-century narratives, to protect the Jewish community against anti-Semitic attacks and redeem it from oppressive conditions in the diaspora, the golem ultimately runs amok and attempts to destroy its surroundings, causing "a good deal of damage."[4] To animate and maintain a golem is therefore a dangerous enterprise. The rabbi risks his own life and that of his community when he imitates the act of divine creation.

Although golem stories began circulating in Europe beyond the Jewish world during the seventeenth century, it was not until the late nineteenth and early twentieth centuries that the golem enjoyed mass appeal. In this later period, the golem became more commonly known and seemed representative of both the wonders and the burdens of our modern human condition. The ascendance of the golem into the sphere of popular culture took place during World War I, an unprecedented historical event in terms of both the enormous loss of human life and the new technologies that enabled such loss. The golem was a wartime celebrity, particularly in Germany but also worldwide. The war era witnessed a proliferation of golem texts and films; Gustav Meyrink's 1915 *Der Golem* (*The Golem*) became the *Da Vinci Code* of its day, and Paul Wegener released three distinct cinematic adaptations of the golem story between 1915 and 1920. Meyrink's mystical thriller sold approximately 150,000 copies during the war and close to 200,000 copies by the early 1920s. It also appeared in a special pocket edition intended for soldiers on the front lines.[5] The wartime fascination with the golem story was further augmented, as in Meyrink's rendering, through its perceived connection to Jewish mysticism and occult practices. This connection rode the wave of fascination with spiritualism and "unmodern" or "myth-ridden" phenomena "in the midst of a war representing a triumph of modern industrialism, materialism, and mechanism."[6]

The Galician-born Chajim (Chayim) Bloch spurred the wartime interest in the mystical golem, publishing his serialized tales in 1917 while serving as a soldier, and the book *Der Prager Golem* (*The Golem: Legends of the Ghetto of Prague*) in 1920. It was a German rendition of Yudl Rosenberg's popular Hebrew and Yiddish chapbook about Rabbi Loew and his golem, *Nifla'ot Maharal* or *Seyfer nifloes Maharal* (*The Golem and the Wonderous Deeds of the Maharal of Prague*), published in 1909.[7] In Bloch's first preface to *Der Prager Golem*, signed in a prisoner-of-war camp where he was stationed, he notes that in the preceding few years, the golem had risen to European "stardom." Having emerged from the confinement of the (Jewish) ghetto, the legendary golem figure was now familiar to the entire Western world. Moreover, the world itself had become golem-like (*vergolemt*) in its wartime rampage. A "dreadful golem-atmosphere rages and demolishes everything," writes Bloch, "and no wise Rabbi Loew can be found who might calm the golem down."[8]

In the immediate post–World War I period, the Polish-born Yiddish writer Israel Joshua Singer claimed that the "tragedy of the world" was encapsulated in the conflict "between creator and mass, between spirit and golem." For Singer, the golem embodied both the soulless masses that could be manipulated and crushed and the world at war: he imagined World War I as a giant golem that destroyed everything in its way.[9] In the piece on the Washington catastrophe, Brainin maintained that while the golem of lore was animated using the ineffable name of God, the "modern world-golem," a fully technological being, has lost its connection to the divine and, with the name of God removed, clumsily carries out its work of destruction. World War I incarnated this modern-world golem, for "he used to once be made of clay—now he is made of steel." The steel golem of war is no Messiah figure; it can no longer bring about redemption.[10] Brainin's deliberate conflation of the technologies of war and entertainment through the figure of this clay monster and its destructive tendencies is paradigmatic of the golem's larger evolutions and shifting relevance in early twentieth-century Western culture.

The World War I years thus marked a significant shift in the circulation of golem stories and in the interpretation of their significance. The mute monster became a means to reflect on how battlefield technologies have altered human lives, as well as a way to experiment with the visual and verbal expression of war's chaos. In 1917, the philosopher Martin Buber evoked the golem tale in an address to his "Prague friends," Jewish residents of the city who might find themselves in "danger" or in "captivity." As long as Europe is still at war, he declared, "the Sabbath has not arrived yet! First we must remove the name from under the tongue of the golem." In other words, while the golem story evoked the threat and violence of war, as experienced also by Jewish populations, it also pointed to the route for resolving the condition of warfare and ushering in a peaceful era (Sabbath)—that is, by deanimating the golem.[11] In 1921, the Yiddish writer H. Leivick published a lengthy poem, *Der goylem* (*The Golem*), in which he dramatized the tension between the "two sides of the messianic event" in Jewish thought: catastrophe and utopia.[12] Leivick's Rabbi Loew molds a powerful redeemer that, he hopes, will usher in brighter days. Instead, the rabbi is confounded by the golem's misery and ultimate violence. In this postwar text, as in other works of the world-war period, the golem represented an apocalyptic unleashing of destructive forces, but its aggression was also associated with the (failed) promise of messianic deliverance.

This association of the golem with technology and violence is not an obvious one, however, even though it has become increasingly prevalent over the past century. Whereas traditionally the golem figure is made of a decidedly "low-tech" substance—clay or earth—and brought to life through the manipulations of written letters and/or spoken language, rather than through any scientific, chemical, or physical processes (in contrast to, say, the monster in Mary Shelley's *Frankenstein*), many twentieth-century writers remolded the golem in the image of war. It was now made of lead or metal rather than clay, facilitating its resignification as a mechanical weapon on the modern battlefield.[13] Even when portrayed as a monster fashioned from earth, the twentieth-century golem often exhibited a toughened exterior, as though its entire body were a shield. The golem's growing association with war technology literally reshaped this monster and its narrative of creation and animation, enabling it to express the horrors of trench warfare and, later, of nuclear warfare.

While the golem was made of clay, it was also imagined, especially in the twentieth century, as an automaton, "a machine that mimics a living being."[14] Already in the industrial era, machines no longer operated in a harmonious manner but "came to be regarded as a superhuman entity of enormous and sometimes mysterious force," explains Minsoo Kang. Post–World War I depictions of automata revealed the "destructive, dehumanizing, and maddening aspects of modern technology," cementing thereby the link between the figure of the golem and that of the automaton.[15] Both are human-like machines that could turn against their creators and human society at large, wreaking immense havoc. In a 1924 satirical piece, "Dem Golem auf der Spur" ("The Golem"), the

Czech journalist Egon Erwin Kisch's narrator compares the golem to a "robot" or, literally, a "humanautomaton" (*Menschautomat*) that has been subordinated to the will of others and forced to work for foreign benefit. In view of the mistreatment of human beings in industrialized societies, God wills that this golem-automaton remain irretrievably buried.[16] From here, it was only a short step to compare the golem with the robot, a term first used in the 1920 play *R.U.R.* (*Rossums Universal Robots*) by the Czech Jewish writer Karel Čapek.[17]

A combination of equal parts astounding creation and wanton destruction, the golem has come to epitomize the contradictory condition of modern human life. And yet the golem's transnational significance and its role as a cultural image of wartime violence have not yet been thoroughly explored. Instead, scholars have tended to focus on the evolution of different golem narratives across literary genres and aesthetic movements, oftentimes neglecting the historical and social contexts that have made the golem story a relevant and popular one.[18] While in *The Golem Returns: From German Romantic Literature to Global Jewish Culture, 1808–2008*, Cathy Gelbin has convincingly unraveled the ethnoreligious construction of the golem primarily in the German-speaking world, she has not dealt with the specific prevalence of this figure in the context of warfare and its cross-cultural import. In the lay imagination, moreover, the golem continues to nostalgically represent only the Jewish communities in central and eastern Europe.

By contrast, this book examines the ways in which the newly visualized and widely disseminated golems of the twentieth century have enabled artists to explore the violent uses of technology, particularly in the framework of modern warfare. This association of the golem with war and its technologies can explain, in part, the figure's strong and long-lasting grip on the popular imagination. Commenting on the spread of the golem story and its ability to traverse linguistic and national borders, Brainin proclaimed, "Modern culture shouts: the golem is coming! And he comes with gigantic steps."[19] Whereas previously the golem was confined to certain genres (Jewish chapbooks published in central Europe or Romantic German folktales), the golem's first gigantic steps were entwined with the new media and art forms that so profoundly came to shape the twentieth century, as well as with their new modes of circulation. The myriad of recent golem renditions—in belletristic writing (*The Amazing Adventures of Kavalier & Clay, The Golem and Jinni*), television (*The X-Files, Supernatural,* and *Sleepy Hollow*), film (*Inglourious Basterds*), comic books (*Breath of Bones*), and even video games such as Minecraft and Assassin's Creed—attests to the ongoing relevance of this narrative of artificial creation.

The spread of mass visual culture, whether in the form of the moving image or that of the printed comic book, was one of the main catalysts for the globalization of the golem story and its newfound significance. Paul Wegener's 1920 cinematic adaptation made its way across the Atlantic and was screened in New York, exerting its influence on local Jewish American culture in Yiddish. During World War II, Paul Falkenberg (the editor of Fritz Lang's *M*) and Henrik Galeen (the screenplay writer of Wegener's 1914 golem film) developed a film treatment in which Jews in the ghetto mobilized the fear of the golem to combat the Nazis.[20] Then in the post-Holocaust period, particularly in the 1970s, the golem resurfaced in American popular culture, specifically in comic books, as an all-powerful monster that could vanquish Arab and German enemies alike. Less human than Superman and his successors such as the Hulk, the golem was imagined as a deterrent avenger—a thuggish weapon—rather than as a full-fledged superhero.

The modern golem narrative has been adapted and readapted, written and rewritten by Jews and non-Jews alike, evolving into a kind of multivalent palimpsest of Western cultures. In order to understand these modern incarnations of the golem, this book begins its historical and cultural analysis with the surge of the golem's popularity during World War I. We then will see how in its "travels" from Europe to the United States and to Israel, the golem figure continued to offer insight into the perils of war and the dilemmas of the human condition throughout the bloody twentieth century. In Israel/Palestine, the golem attained a dual and even contradictory significance: on the one hand, the Hebrew-language press of the pre- and immediately poststatehood period mobilized the clay monster as a metaphor for the new nation's enemies. On the other hand, Israeli writers cast the golem as a wounded soldier, using the story to evoke the state of living death caused by war.

In examining versions of the golem story across twentieth-century cultures, languages, and media, this book focuses on the story's continual reshaping in the context of modern, as well as postmodern, warfare and its implications for Jewish populations and nations.[21] While the figure's clay substance linked it metonymically to the mud of the trenches during World War I, more broadly and metaphorically, the golem lent itself well to wartime and postwar depictions of the violence and injury associated with technological power. In the post–World War II period, the golem continued to be linked with mass destruction and the threat of nuclear weapons, as well as with cybernetic systems, both disembodied computers and hybrid cyborgs. In the pages that follow, we will see how intercultural contact and exchange, through literature, film, and print media, enabled the "golem epidemic" to spread, rendering this figure an emblem of modern destruction.

Monstrous Metaphors

Especially around World War I, the golem fulfilled in the European popular imagination the ideal of an infallible, all-powerful war machine. In contrast to the "inapt" and "docile" body of the modern soldier that, according to Michel Foucault, must be plied and mastered, rendering it more machine-like and automatic, the golem is already created an apt and powerful soldier. Although both soldier and golem are molded out of the same "formless clay," in Foucault's own metaphor, and are meant to be transformed and used by others, the artificial golem epitomizes a triumphant and vital militarism, an ideal body far from the weak human soldier who requires constant training.[22] Thus, one of the reasons for the appeal of the golem story during times of war was that, unlike the "docile" body of the soldier, this clay "machine" could be constructed easily and was not constitutionally delicate. Formed in the image of the human, the golem is a double that also functions as "an extension of man," able to perform tasks that go beyond ordinary human capacity.[23] Already in the 1940s, an Israeli journalist imagined that golem-like weapons would soon render the human soldier redundant on the battlefield. People would control these "golems" from a safe distance, with the actual fighting playing out between masses of robotic machines—not unlike our use of drones today.[24]

In tandem with the idealization of the golem as a war machine, the narrative of an artificial creation that goes awry and must be put to rest or terminated also reminded readers and audiences of their mortality and self-destructive powers. Meyrink's 1915 novel portrays the golem as a ghostly and menacing presence, rather than a stolid clay giant, that returns to wreak havoc in the ghetto every thirty-three years. In Wegener's films, the golem's existence is precarious, controlled by others, and ultimately short-lived. In this respect, the golem resembles the soldier who is intensely exposed to his own mortality and that of others. Writers from divergent backgrounds, the Galician S. Y. Agnon, the Russian H. Leivick, and the Czech Egon Erwin Kisch, all used the golem story to explore the ways in which war and civil strife ravage the fragile human body and psyche, resulting in states of psychosis or else utter immobility and apathy.

From these contradictory impulses emerges what I call the "golem condition": the golem forces us to recognize that the fantasies of expanding our capacities and transgressing our natural boundaries are always curbed by the inborn limitations of human existence. Hence, in most golem works created during or after a period of conflict, the strong protector turns into a violent destroyer, a rebellious monster that exposes its fallibility and the vulnerability of those who created it. The golem as artificially "born" and controlled by others might appear at first to offer the promise of escaping the most basic human condition of birth and death, as described by Hannah Arendt in 1958. However, in its living-dead state of artificial existence, the golem collapses natality and mortality into one event, embodying a lack of spontaneity and constantly reminding us of our own mortality.[25] At the same time, the golem's (often) erratic behavior when misused makes it both a test case for the rebellion against our mortal limitations and a cautionary tale. The golem condition thus describes the dire repercussions of focusing our human activities and endeavors on murderous wars and their technologies.

The golem figure has run amok in the twentieth century in part by exceeding the realm of a literary tale and becoming a metaphoric embodiment of our technologies, specifically advanced weapons technologies. As the Yiddish American writer Isaac Bashevis Singer commented in 1984, on the occasion of a new production of Leivick's 1921 *The Golem* at the Delacorte Theater in New York, the "golem drama of our epoch" forces us to wonder whether we are capable of exerting our free will to stop the nuclear menace and whether we can divest the golem monster of its all-too-real contemporary powers, reducing it back to "fiction and folklore."[26] Such sentiment is not new to the nuclear age, however. Brainin, for one, had already expressed such anxiety in 1922 when he wrote that "the golem is now no longer a legend but reality. A golem epidemic."[27] Be the fear one of technological tyranny or of nuclear extinction, the problem is the same: as an embodiment of technology, the golem can easily be re-created and refined, but it cannot be fully controlled. For many thinkers, the soulless golem is a metaphor turned all too literal. In 1965, the scholar of Jewish mysticism Gershom Scholem proposed to name one of the first computers constructed in Israel "Golem Aleph." In the inauguration speech for the computer, he exhorted this "golem" and its creators, "Develop peacefully and don't destroy the world."[28] The enduring link between the golem and modern technology offers a frightening analogy: the golem, like some of our greatest technological creations, has the power not only to enhance but also to destroy our world.

The success of the metaphor depends on the golem's conceptualization as an inherently malleable entity, one that has been molded and remolded, animated and deanimated throughout modern cultural history. Victor Turner reminds us that metaphors in general work as a "species of *liminal monster . . .* whose combination of familiar and unfamiliar features or unfamiliar combination of familiar features provokes us into thought, provides us with new perspectives."[29] Not surprisingly, monsters such as the golem and the zombie have become master metaphors in Western culture and beyond. As in the case of the rebellious Frankenstein, the golem metaphor may itself "rebel" and become too literal.[30] Through the golem, the violence of the metaphoric yoking of tenor and vehicle is further concretized, as is the tension between progress and destruction. If the resemblance between the Prague golem and the golem of the nuclear age "staggers the imagination," it is because of the folkloric golem's "uncanny power" and its uncontrollability.

Whether adapted by Jewish or non-Jewish artists, the golem narrative has predominantly dealt with Jewish-related subject matters, so that the general "golem condition" needs to be framed within this specific cultural and social context. During World War I, the golem came to stand for the real and imagined contact zone between western and eastern European cultures. The encounter with eastern European Jews on the front lines "dramatically enlarged the scope and magnitude of the cult of the *Ostjude*" amid German Jews, according to Steve Aschheim. They imagined the culture of eastern European Jews as spiritual, premodern, and whole.[31] Bloch, for example, endowed his golem tales with an aura of authenticity and a folkloric appeal by attributing them to a Polish Jew from Chelm whom he met at the prisoner-of-war camp. In supposedly transposing the Yiddish text of these stories into "western European" German, he claimed to have retained the "simple" and "heartwarming" language of the original.[32] Reviewers of Wegener's first 1914 film similarly associated the golem with eastern European Jewry, a poor, servile, and abject people who seemed to live in the past of their old traditions, including the "esoteric doctrine" of medieval kabbalah, as allegedly taught by Rabbi Loew, creator of the golem.[33]

Hence, despite the fact that World War I mobilized Jews on both combatting sides, molding them into soldiers in much the same way as the rest of the population, the Jews of eastern Europe functioned in the popular imagination as the transmitters and mediators of the "golem cult." They were perceived as a source of "authentic" Jewish culture but were also derided for their mystical inclinations, as manifest in these narratives of artificial creation.[34] In this sense, the golem functioned as the powerful weapon of a powerless people. Precisely because Jews were an often-persecuted minority, especially with the rise of racially inflected anti-Semitism in Europe and the early twentieth-century pogroms in eastern Europe, they appeared to need a strong protector of fantastical proportions.

The indeterminate golem, in my reading, is a form of reverse "ethnic drag": rather than heighten the performativity of *Jewish* identity, it constitutes an exaggerated enactment of the Jewish ability to transform into the *non-Jewish* masculine ideal. The hypermasculine golem alerted readers and viewers to both the enormous potential and the danger of such border crossings.[35] Performed on behalf of Jewish populations but not by Jews themselves, the golem's violence evokes anxieties concerning the refashioning of Jews into more powerful, bellicose combatants. Even when suggesting a revitalized, combative Judaism and Jewish masculinity, the golem was inevitably associated with diasporic Jewish culture. For this reason, Israeli writers and artists often spurned the golem as an exilic myth in the early to mid-twentieth century.

Yet the discourse of the "new Jew" or "muscle Jew," encapsulated in the Zionist leader Max Nordau's famous call for a Jewry of muscles to counter stereotypes of male effeminacy and degeneration, only partially accounts for the twentieth-century popularity of the golem story.[36] According to Judith Halberstam, "monsters are meaning machines": their bodies represent a variety of categories, commenting on constructions of gender, class, race, nationality, and sexuality. Their monstrosity derives from the ability to "condense as many fear-producing traits as possible into one body."[37] Because it destabilized and confused conceptions of ethnicity, gender, and religion, the indeterminate golem was able to facilitate reflections on the purposes, justifications, and aftereffects of both Jewish and general forms of mass violence. Embodying both the fantasy of war and its failure, the golem was simultaneously a product of Jewish society and a marker of the shifting borders of Jewishness: at one extreme, this creature even came to represent German soldiers blindly obeying their Nazi leaders.

Whether imagined as Jewish or non-Jewish, Israeli or German, human or robotic, the golem of war persistently appears as a masculine being and, oftentimes, an object of female attention and attraction. Female golems do exist in both Jewish and Christian scriptural and literary sources, from the German Romanticist Achim von Arnim's *Isabelle von Ägypten: Kaiser Karl des Fünften erste Jugendliebe* (Isabella of Egypt) (1812) through the American novelist Cynthia Ozick's *The Puttermesser Papers* (1997) to Helena Wecker's *The Golem and the Jinni* (2013).[38] But the works I discuss in this book feature masculine-appearing golems because of the overwhelmingly predominant male service in the front lines of twentieth-century wars. In the 2013 comic book trilogy *Breath of Bones: A Tale of the Golem*, a Jewish grandfather molds a golem to combat a German attack on his village during World War I, informing his grandson, "it will only work if you give it strength." The next panel shows the boy's clenched fist, covered in mud, underscoring the direct connection between male physical "strength" and the resulting clay monster.[39] As we shall see, when writing about a cyborg created to defend a futurist Jewish community, the author Marge Piercy claims that "he must be male, the golem," since it needs to fulfill the archetypal male roles of "killer" and "protector."[40] Performing an exaggerated form of male aggression—or else of male vulnerability in the case of the injured, living-dead soldiers—the inherently indeterminate golem figure served writers and artists in varied cultural contexts to criticize the militarization of society but also to give free rein to fantasies of (Jewish) revenge.

Violent Precursors

The golem narratives and images that developed around World War I and have continued to circulate since World War II do not, by any means, constitute a complete break from past imaginings of this anthropoid. The golem's violent tendencies were already present in seventeenth-century renderings of the tale, though this motif attained additional war-related meanings in the twentieth century. The destructiveness of the golem figure in pre-twentieth-century writings was thus an important precondition for this new twist in the evolution of the golem theme, and twentieth-century writers and artists drew heavily on precursor stories.

Since at least the seventeenth century, the golem has been associated with Polish Jewry, specifically with the figure of Rabbi Eliyahu Ba'al Shem of the city of Chelm. An influential Latin letter written by Christoph Arnold to the Christian Hebraist Johann Christoph Wagenseil in 1674 took up such a narrative about a Polish Jewish community. Arnold's version tells of a clay anthropoid animated by an amulet inscribed with the Hebrew word for truth, *emet*. This golem performs domestic tasks for its master, the Polish Ba'al Shem. But when the golem grows extremely tall and strong, threatening its creator, the Ba'al Shem has the golem bend over so he can erase the letter aleph, transforming the word *emet* into *met*, meaning "dead." In the process, the deanimated golem falls over his maker and crushes him.[41] This story was translated into German in 1689 and used as alleged proof of Jewish sorcery, so that, according to Gelbin, it was now "filtered through the lens of Christian writers and imbued with the stereotypes that their time held regarding Jews."[42] The golem's destructive aspect needs to be understood from within this intercultural and interreligious framework, the result of Jewish-Christian interaction.

In 1714, the Christian Orientalist Johann Jacob Schudt, drawing on Arnold's letter and other sources, compiled a lineage of tales concerning the golem. His aim was to prove that Jews performed sorcery and abused the name of God. Schudt's text served as the basis for Jacob Grimm's golem tale of 1808, a rendition that inspired the rewriting of the story among a number of Christian German nineteenth-century Romantics, such as Ludwig Achim von Arnim and E. T. A. Hoffmann. In Grimm's succinct version, the Polish Jews who create the golem verbally pronounce the explicit name of God ("*Schemhamphoras*") in order to bring the anthropoid to life, and they use it as a servant until it grows threateningly large and ultimately crushes its creator. Grimm universalized the narrative by omitting the specific site of Chelm in Poland and the figure of the Ba'al Shem. He also reconfigured the golem story as a "minimal folkloric report" rather than a fairy tale written in the style of his famous *Children's and Household Tales*.[43]

In response to these Christian variants, particularly to the Grimm tale, Jewish writers sought to reattach the golem story to a specific place (Prague of the Jewish-tolerant monarch Rudolph II) and to a historical figure (Rabbi Loew).[44] The "migration" of the legend from eastern to central Europe occurred in the 1830s and 1840s, with the appearance of written versions that associated the clay figure with Prague and its Rabbi Judah Loew ben Betzalel, also known as the Maharal (Our Teacher) of Prague. Edan Dekel and David Gantt Gurley explain that precisely because the historical Rabbi Loew was *not* known as a practitioner of kabbalah, he could lend Jewish mysticism more authority, in contrast to the Christian view of kabbalah as "some kind of Jewish thaumaturgy." Even more so, the Jewish Prague versions emphasized the holy written word, the act of writing the secret name and animating the golem in this manner, unlike the Christian account of verbally performed magic.[45] The drama of the Prague variant, initially recorded in an 1836 text by Ludwig August Frankel and, later, in an 1841 work by the journalist and folklorist Franz Klutschak, still revolves around the threatening nature of the golem: when the rabbi forgets to deanimate his creation on the Sabbath eve, the golem becomes mad and begins to destroy the rabbi's house.[46] Likewise, Wolf Pascheles's 1847 German-language collection of Jewish tales, *Sippurim*, included the influential Prague story by Leopold Weisel, in which "the magic servant became enraged, tore down the houses, threw rocks around, uprooted trees, and thrashed around horribly in the streets."[47] An "instant success," Weisel's narrative went through many reprintings and became "the standard for the rest of the century," until the publication of Rosenberg's more elaborate tales sixty years later.[48]

Significantly, the Maharal of Prague emerges unscathed in these nineteenth-century Jewish versions, rather than being crushed by his gigantic servant. He manages to subdue and deanimate the golem before the Sabbath, thereby preserving the sanctity of the Jewish ritual. The story of the Prague golem may therefore be understood as a corrective to Arnold's and Grimm's texts, in which no such heroic affirmative ending is to be found.[49] In the Prague tale, the golem runs amok when Rabbi Loew forgets to remove from the creature's mouth the animating "formula" with God's name; but order is subsequently restored, and the rabbi returns to perform the Sabbath ritual. Moreover, in Pascheles's *Sippurim*, Rabbi Loew appears as an enlightened philosopher, and the golem narrative is treated as "a well-known story" that does not require lengthy elaboration.[50] Yudl Rosenberg's 1909 *Nifla'ot Maharal* continues this trend of praising the Jewish creator of the golem and harnessing the golem's strength toward successful Jewish ends. His golem is a God-sent protector of the Jewish community from Christian persecution. Although the golem uses physical violence to round up Christian agitators and deliver them to the police, in Rosenberg's text, it does so only for the sake of communal self-protection and preservation.[51]

By contrast, in the decades before the publication of Rosenberg's chapbook, two prominent Jewish writers, Isaac Leib Peretz and Sholem Aleichem (Sholem Rabinovitch), wrote short narratives in which the golem carries out its role as protector of the Jewish community in a highly problematic manner. It is worth pausing and reflecting on these stories, first, because of the degree of violence found in them and, second, because they foreshadow the ways in which relations between Jews and non-Jews become a central component of the golem narrative, starting in the late nineteenth century and continuing through the twentieth.

For both Peretz and Scholem Aleichem, the protective function of the golem devolves into senseless and uncontrollable violence, so that the stories ultimately warn their readers against the hubris of Jewish creation and the attempt to bring about, via the golem, a significant rupture between the Jewish and Christian worlds.

In Peretz's brief tale, written in Yiddish and first published in 1893, the Maharal animates a golem in order to protect his community from rape and slaughter, but then, at the mere threat of violence, this monster is preemptively sent outside the ghetto to thrash the enemies of the Jews. Once set into motion as a mass murderer, the golem never tires, and Prague becomes "filled with corpses." As in Rosenberg's later text, Peretz's golem directs its violence outward, toward the Christian world, rather than crushing its Jewish creator to death or destroying his home and the Jewish ghetto at large. The Jews finally complain to their leader, "The golem is slaughtering all of Prague! Soon there won't be any Gentiles left to heat the Sabbath ovens or take down the Sabbath lamps."[52] The Maharal therefore summons the golem by reciting the Sabbath Psalm and deanimates it, although he retains the clay remains in the attic of the Prague synagogue in case future generations of Jews might need the golem's help.

Peretz's tale ironically conflates the golem's servitude with its violent rampage, as described in the nineteenth-century Frankel and Weisel versions. Rather than interrupting the Sabbath Psalm in order to subdue his servant, the rabbi utters the Psalm as a means of bringing the slaughter of Christian Prague to an end. Peretz thus marries the revenge narrative to a critique of (religious) Jewish hypocrisy. The amorality of the Jewish community and its leader comes to the fore in the motivations for calling off the slaughter. It is not so much that the Jews mind the killing of Christians as that they still need their *shabbes-goys*, Christians who are willing to work on the Sabbath. If Jews are to maintain their particularity, the golem must be stopped, since they are dependent on others for the observance of their religion.

In 1901, Sholem Aleichem published a similar narrative, most likely inspired by Peretz, in *Ha-dor* (The generation), a Hebrew weekly published in Warsaw and edited by David Frishman. This text was swiftly translated into German and appeared in the more widely read Viennese weekly of the World Zionist Organization, *Die Welt* (The world). In Sholem Aleichem's narrative, said to be adapted from a "Jewish folktale," the persecution of the Jewish community also precedes the golem's creation and justifies it, since before the golem, "the blood of the innocent flowed like water." Rabbi Loew forms out of clay a robust humanoid with "iron-strong hands" and places it on the bridge over the Moldau River; whenever a Christian seems about to harm a Jew, the golem throws him into the river. Soon the river begins to fill with "countless human corpses," symbolically balancing the scales of justice. But, as in Peretz's story, the Jewish population is not pleased; through the loss of important mercantile relations, the golem has caused more harm than all the foes of the Jews past and present, they claim.[53]

The depiction of the golem as a mass murderer in both texts is startling: it draws on the theme of the sorcerer's apprentice that circulated in German literature starting in the late nineteenth century but pushes it to an extreme. Instead of a flood, we witness a bloody massacre, an overflowing of corpses that cannot be stopped until the rabbi utters the word. In this respect, these tales caution against the Jewish abuse of power, even while they give free rein to a fantasy of mass retribution against Christian populations. Such turn-of-the-century renditions, Rosenberg's included, use the revenge fantasy to transform the story of the Prague golem from a mere "corrective" to negative Christian depictions of Jewish sorcery into a compensatory spectacle of Jewish aggression executed by a monster figure that nonetheless cannot be fully identified with its Jewish creator. Leivick's *The Golem* likewise grapples with the issue of the golem's violence, although Leivick is most interested in the golem's destructive impulses toward his creator and the Jewish community. The themes of Peretz's and Sholem Aleichem's stories reemerged in full force only in the second half of the twentieth century, after World War II. In the popular medium of comics, for instance, the golem was imagined as a figure of revenge that expressed the Jewish desire for physical and technological power.

In writing these ironic cautionary tales, Peretz and Sholem Aleichem were also reflecting on the significance of Jewish folklore amid the rise of Zionism and the rush to secularize and modernize. Even while retelling the golem narrative and so assisting its spread and continuity, these writers imply that such a tale is perhaps irrelevant at a time when Jews no longer believe in their God and when the integrity of the community can hardly be preserved in the face of the forces of capitalism. In this context, the golem story also becomes a parable for the overdependence of Jews on their surroundings and the need to instill a new sense of national and cultural independence. If controlled properly, such a nationalist "superhuman" could be harnessed for the good of the Jews, even when it appears as a double-edged sword or weapon in the framework of traditional, observant Jewish society. As we shall see, carrying over this issue into the twentieth century, Israeli writers such as S. Y. Agnon and Yoram Kaniuk, as well as Americans such as Michael Chabon and Marge Piercy, have used the golem story to comment on the dangers of militaristic nationalisms that harness technological force to protect their enterprises.

To sum up, starting in the seventeenth century, the modern history of the golem story is one of intercultural negotiation over the significance and uses of artificial creation. The Jewish creator of lore has the power to bring an inanimate object to life through his belief in a divine force, and this power can be presented in a negative light (as in the early Christian sources) or in a more positive one. But rather than consider the golem story as a site for the projection of pro- or anti-Jewish notions and images, this genealogy reveals that the golem's violence was productive on an intercultural level, generating an ever-growing body of renditions and adaptations that enabled critical reflections on Jewish-Christian relations in modern times. What marks many twentieth-century versions, starting with the turn-of-the-twentieth-century narratives just discussed, is a more extreme vision of the violence perpetrated by Jews, albeit in self-defense, and an ambivalent position toward golem creation as an act that marks Jewish separatism. The brutal precursor golems depicted in both Christian and Jewish sources of the seventeenth through nineteenth centuries paved the way for such new associations in the twentieth century.

A Brief User's Manual

The focus of this book on twentieth-century rewritings of the golem story and its metaphoric uses has led me to select texts that address the dilemmas of the "golem condition." Through this specific lens, the book traces the golem's appearances both within particular national frameworks of cultural production and across cultures, revealing the golem to be a powerful means of transnational exchange regarding the monstrosity of war. To investigate this exchange, the book deals only with those works that cast the golem as a figure of war-related violence. By situating these texts, films, and productions in their respective historical and social contexts, and by uncovering unknown sources and suggesting fresh juxtapositions, my discussion offers new insights into the sheer pervasiveness of the golem narrative. Since "the traditional division of high and popular cultural has been a political division rather than a defensible intellectual or aesthetic distinction," my aim has been to reveal the constant cross-fertilization between "highbrow" and "popular" works, both visual and literary.[54]

If ever a monster was created perfect for the task of revisiting the very notion of the "popular," it is the golem, since, as Gelbin maintains, "modern Jewish popular culture . . . reveals the heterogeneous nature of all popular culture, particularly because it is not tied to one particular language or national context."[55] The golem not only became a highly transportable figure that traversed national, religious, and ethnic boundaries; it was also transformed by the emergence of new media and of modern publication and exhibition practices. The intense cultural work that the golem performed in the context of twentieth-century wars can be located in the works themselves, at their borderlines, through prologues and scores, and in reviews and advertisements. The reconstruction of the golem's diverse resignification as soldier and weapon can take place only through a comparative and intermedial approach that brings the more well-known works—Paul Wegener's *The Golem, How He Came into the World*, S. Y. Agnon's *To This Day*, H. Leivick's *The Golem*—into dialogue with the lesser-known but equally pervasive golem metaphors and texts of their day.

Chapter 1 concerns the popularization of the golem figure in World War I Germany through Wegener's three films of 1914, 1917, and 1920. With the help of Wegener's wartime diary and his unpublished letters and notes, I argue that his approach to the golem materials and their aesthetics underwent a pronounced shift after he returned from fighting on the front lines, where he came very close to death and experienced the killing and wounding of many others. If, in 1914, the cinematic golem is a ready-made object dug up, sold, and employed for mundane, familial purposes, Wegener's 1920 golem, a product of Jewish mystical and astrological practices, is a heroic figure used to teach the Christian emperor and his courtiers a lesson in empathy toward the Jews. The cinematic golem, however, is not merely a weapon that defends Jews from the threat of expulsion; it is also an animated, evolving being that ultimately attains a semblance of humanity. Drawing on early twentieth-century film theory by the Hungarian writer Béla Balázs, I show how Wegener and the architect Hans Poelzig designed expressive and animated cinematic spaces that enhanced the vivacious quality of cinema itself and pointed to the need for national recovery and reanimation.

In the summer and fall of 1921, Wegener's third golem film was screened in New York to much acclaim, accompanied by a new musical score and live theatrical prologue, orchestrated and performed by Jewish artists. These American framing devices, reconstructed for the first time in chapter 2, underscored the status of the Jews as a persecuted and expelled minority in Europe and posited the golem as a fantastical savior figure. In the context of the deteriorating status of German Jews around World War I and the violent pogroms against eastern European Jews during this period, the American golem "cult" addressed some of the pressing issues of the day: the quotas placed on Jewish immigration to the United States and the responses of Jews to anti-Semitic violence. Wegener's film sparked a wave of popular American golem performances, including Max Gabel's 1921 Yiddish production *Der goylem: Muzikalisher legende in dray akten mit a prolog* (The golem: A musical legend in three acts and a prologue). Gabel replicated Wegener's costume as the golem, but he also drew inspiration from the film's American prologue and, likewise, depicted the creation of the golem as a response to the condition of Jewish homelessness. This chapter juxtaposes Gabel's forgotten operetta with Wegener's famous film and Leivick's modernist poema, published in New York in the same year, to reveal that these works all contend with the contemporary issue of Jewish uprooting and immigration. "Permitted to shed blood" in defense of the Jews, Leivick's golem is unique, however, as an utter outcast, a disposable defender and abject being that violently turns against the Jewish community.

In comparison to the American enthusiasm for the golem story, in both the pre–and post–World War II periods, its relative lack of popularity in Israel/Palestine is noteworthy. Chapter 3 shifts to this particular geopolitical arena, showing that while Zionist culture did not take up the golem story with the same "cultish" zeal as in Germany and the U.S., it nonetheless evoked the figure in the context of twentieth-century wars, both external and internal. The Hebrew-language press of the 1940s used the golem metaphor primarily with reference to the enemy other, whether Nazi or Arab. No longer bearing the name of God, these metaphoric golems were mere mechanical monsters (German pilotless airplanes) or else artificial creations (the Arab League), formed to deter the small Israeli army.

Only in post-1948 Hebrew literature was the golem story rewritten as a tale of war injury, in which the dichotomies of us and them, friend and foe, break down in the face of the overall devastation of war. In *To This Day*, the Israeli writer and Nobel Prize winner Agnon responded to the German golem "fad" in its various manifestations, recasting the clay being as a brain-injured German veteran. Through this apathetic soldier, Agnon criticizes the wartime desire—which he sees in World War I Germany just as in his own Israel—to produce an infallible military man and demand self-sacrifice for the sake of the nation. In the 1966 novel *Ḥimo, melekh yerushalyaim* (*Himmo, King of Jerusalem*), the Israeli writer Yoram Kaniuk similarly uses the golem moniker to refer to a war-injured soldier, in this case one severely disabled in the battles of 1948. Setting this golem narrative in a makeshift military hospital in Jerusalem, Kaniuk focuses on the Israeli home front to reveal the internal tensions between Jews and Christians, as well as between local Sephardic Jews and recent Ashkenazi newcomers. Over and against the Zionist rejection of the (diasporic) association of Jews with the golem figure, these Israeli works convey the ongoing relevance of the golem for narratives related to the founding of Israel and its militarized society.

In contrast to the internally directed destruction of Leivick's golem and the bifurcation of Israeli golems into evil enemies and injured, living-dead soldiers, American popular culture of the post–World War II period provides us with full-fledged fantasies of Jewish retribution, particularly for Nazi persecution. Chapter 4 traces the motif of the golem as a violent avenger and deterrent weapon both in comic books of the 1970s and in millennial works of art and fiction. The latter include Michael Chabon's novel *The Amazing Adventures of Kavalier & Clay*, Quentin Tarantino's film *Inglourious Basterds*, and James Sturm's graphic narrative *The Golem's Mighty Swing*. This chapter shows that a Jewish revenge fantasy undergirds many of these popular American rewritings of the golem story, with the Holocaust serving as a common backdrop. The superheroic golem is no longer bound by any ghetto walls and, drawing on its imagined nuclear power, can beat Nazis to a pulp. Yet the link between Jewishness and vengeance was apparently too unsettling to be fully developed, even by Jewish cartoonists proficient in spinning popular lore. The American ambivalence toward the golem as an icon of retribution is evident in its typical portrayal as an inhuman, all-too-powerful figure, susceptible to transmogrifying into a destructive, even evil, monster. Only in the irreverent *Inglourious Basterds* does Tarantino give full rein to the fantasy of an unleashed Jewish power, linking his character of the murderous "Bear Jew" with the golem as an "avenging Jew angel."

Chapter 5 takes the association of the golem with technology, war, and destruction into the Cold War age of cybernetics. It discusses how the golem was used to grapple with the ethics of new and intelligent computational machines put in the service of governments and their armed forces. The chapter pairs Norbert Wiener's philosophical *God and Golem, Inc.* (1964) with the Polish writer Stanislaw Lem's *Golem XIV* (1981), and Donna Haraway's "A Cyborg Manifesto" (1983) with the American writer Marge Piercy's *He, She, and It* (1991), to explore how the golem story became a heuristic device and a narrative tool used to address the military implications of cybernetics and computer technologies. In the aftermath of World War II, Wiener argued for the need to rein in the intelligence of "learning machines," warning of their ability to overcome their human creators in unpredictable ways. Following Wiener, Lem imagines a future in which computers of superior intelligence become independent, self-controlling interlocutors that turn pacifist because of the "illogical" nature of American war strategy and world domination. The name golem, intended to suggest the strategic powers of these computers, comes to symbolize their practical and philosophical rebellion. In contrast to Lem's dehumanization of the golem-computer, Piercy portrays a cyborg that veers from its creator's plans not by becoming less violent but by desiring to participate in its society as a human and a Jew. In Piercy's dystopic work, set in a futurist world ravaged by nuclear warfare and environmental catastrophe, the golem embodies the fantasy of a steadfast cyberprotector for the isolated and embattled Jewish community. He ultimately rejects his own violent programming and destroys the capacity to re-create a "conscious weapon" akin to himself, the cyborg. In so doing, like Wegener's cinematic monster, Piercy's golem exhibits a divine spark, transforming from "it" to "he" and revealing its human face.

Singer aptly summarizes, "I am not exaggerating when I say that the golem story appears less obsolete today than it seemed one hundred years ago. What are the computers and robots of our time if not golems?"[56] Although the comparison of the golem with an automated, unthinking weapon may be a more intuitive one, Singer's golem-computer analogy points to a historical shift: in the course of the twentieth century, the golem ceased to be a mute and unintelligent machine, incapable of development. On the contrary, the fictional and cinematic golems we will encounter in this book exhibit varying degrees of self-knowledge, with Piercy's cyborg marking one extreme as a golem capable even of wisdom and selfless love. World War I popularized the golem as an invincible fighter-machine, a vulnerable (if incontrollable) living-dead clay monster, and a potential redeemer, albeit a violent one. The theme of the golem's own suffering and desire for human connection was cemented already a century ago in German literature and film, calling into question the ethics of artificial creation in the service of modern warfare. The possibilities of the golem, and its value as a revealer of our cultural preoccupations, have only grown since then. Part automatized soldier, part nuclear weapon, and part interfacing cyborg, the golem continues to haunt the transnational imagination in our own day as we still contend with the bloodshed of the twentieth century and the repercussions of ongoing global wars.

1

The Face of Destruction

Paul Wegener's World War I Golem Films

Our hands are earth, our bodies clay and our eyes pools of
rain. We do not know whether we still live.
—Erich Maria Remarque, *All Quiet on the Western Front*

The soldiers who served in the trenches of World War I inhabited a world
of clay. As Eric J. Leed writes, the trenches rendered the landscape seemingly empty, yet all the while it was "saturated with men": "The earth
was at once one's home and the habitat of a hidden, ever-present threat."
Both the invisible enemy with its formidable technology and the trenches
themselves, which could collapse on the soldiers hiding inside them,
posed threats to the combatants of World War I. Leed quotes the reaction of an Italian soldier after he finally encounters the flesh-and-blood
enemy: "Those strongly defended trenches . . . had ended up seeming
to us inanimate, like desolate buildings uninhabited by men. . . . Now
[the enemy soldiers] were showing themselves to us as they really were,
men and soldiers like us, in uniform like us."[1] While the trenches filled
with living men could appear inanimate, the dead sometimes seemed to
be alive. According to Allyson Booth, the bodies of the dead, whether
interred in the battlefield or left unburied, became part of the muddy
surroundings and were "simultaneously understood as both animate
subjects and inanimate objects."[2] Likewise, because of the soldiers'
immobility and sensory deprivation in the trenches, the bodies of the
living, often covered in mud, also came to resemble those of the dead.

Presciently, it was in the summer of 1914, just prior to the outbreak
of World War I, in which these trenches played such a central role, that

the German theater actor Paul Wegener (1874–1948) conceived and produced his first film concerning that creature of clay, *Der Golem* (The Golem).[3] Its first screening in January 1915 took place when its star was already serving on the muddy battlefield, and the U.T. Lichtspiele in Berlin prefaced *Der Golem* with newsreels depicting the "newest reports from the war."[4] It was an uncanny coincidence that the film concerned the animation of an inanimate clay sculpture, a figure that hovers between life and death. *Der Golem* ends, as both the screenplay and a restored segment reveal, with a quotation from the seventeenth-century German mystic and religious poet Angelus Silesius: "Nature always works profoundly, / inside as out. / And all things live in death, / and dead they are alive." The film promoted a sense of the continuum between life and death reminiscent of the conditions in the trenches. In this way, viewers on the home front indirectly experienced the blurring of the boundaries between bodies and mud, between animate subjects and inanimate objects. Even when the golem comes to life, it retains its clay constitution, reminding viewers of its connection to earth and death.

As mentioned earlier, Wegener had experienced the clay of war firsthand. At the age of forty, in October 1914, he volunteered for the Landsturm, where he served first as a corporal and later as a lieutenant.[5] He marched through the city of Diksmuide, in West Flanders, arriving at the front lines in mid-October. On December 4, his company came under heavy bombardment near the Yser River in Belgium. Out of his own squad of forty-nine, only he and three others survived. Following this harrowing experience, Wegener received the Iron Cross, first class. He remained in Ypres until February 1915, when he fell ill, returning in April to Berlin. Audiences of the period were aware of Wegener's choice to volunteer for the war at the height of a flourishing acting career. The *Berlin Börsen-Courier*, for example, reported prominently in September 1915 on Wegener's first postservice acting role, commending his Iron Cross.[6]

That the war was a threat to the live actor but not to his preserved cinematic double underscored the peculiarities of the new medium of film. The Swiss critic Eduard Korrodi noted in 1915 that one might see Wegener "under strange circumstances" at the movie theater while "he is sacrificing his body and soul and his human voice to his fatherland far away from us as lieutenant."[7] Korrodi here conflates the "strange" human replication in cinema—which, unlike theater, does not require the onstage presence of the flesh-and-blood actor—with the "strange" circumstances" of a war, in which actors and filmmakers fought while their films were screened in their absence. In other words, even while cinema resurrected the figure of Wegener, who by his very service on the front lines literally wavered between life and death, this resurrection, for Korrodi, could only be partial and unreal. Wegener returned from the front to star in two further golem productions and so reaffirmed his physical presence precisely through a medium that could both animate the dead and portray the living as ghosts. The artificial golem whose existence and actions are controlled by others served as a reminder of the mortality of the veteran actor embodying this monster.

In 1917, after directing and acting in *Rübezahl's Wedding* (1916) and *The Yogi* (1916), both movies also featuring larger-than-life protagonists, Wegener used the golem story to produce an uplifting, romantic comedy, *Der Golem und die Tänzerin* (*The Golem and the Dancer*), aimed at female spectators on the home front. Friedrich Kittler and Susanne Holl write that the 1917 film "treats cinema, takes place in the cinema, and films cinema-actors and spectators and the outcomes of their adaptation into film."[8] Wegener, playing himself, attempts to seduce a variety dancer, acted by the Czech actress and dancer Lyda Salmonova, Wegener's off-screen partner at the time. At the film's beginning, the dancer attends a screening of the "much-discussed" film *Der Golem* of 1914 and subsequently requests a copy of the clay statue of the golem. Wegener pretends to be this statue, masking himself in "real life" as the golem in his film (see figure 1.5). So disguised, he manages to enter the dancer's home, only to fake his own animation and pursue the shocked woman. If the 1915 screening coincided with Wegener's dispatch to Flanders and underscored the disparity between the preservation of bodies on film and their vulnerability on the battlefield, the 1917 film, screened after Wegener's return from the front, represented Wegener as "himself," thus securing a sense of the actor's presence and distracting the audience from any consciousness of mortality.

As Wegener's diaries and unpublished letters indicate, he returned from the battlefield highly critical of the defeated German nation and its wartime conduct. While his 1917 film was a product of wartime escapism, in the 1920 film, Wegener gives voice to his criticism and contends, albeit indirectly, with the war and its aftermath.[9] A discussion of the 1914 film sets the stage in this chapter for my interpretation of the famous *Der Golem, wie er in die Welt kam* (*The Golem, How He Came into the World*), the only film of the three that exists in its restored entirety.[10] I show how the shifts in Wegener's approach to the golem story and its Jewish subject matter were both a product of his wartime experiences and his attempt to forge a postwar aesthetic. In 1915, the animated clay sculpture had served unwittingly as a reminder of the deadly trenches, whereas by 1920, Wegener and his cofilmmakers consciously rendered the entire visual surface of the movie more expressive, striving to convey the animation of inanimate matter.

To contemporary critics, the film also marked the development of German cinema from a "small film industry . . . [into] a great power [*Großmacht*]."[11] Wegener successfully harnessed the progress made by film technology between 1914 and 1920 for the sake of his expressive aesthetic, which was more tactile and physiognomic than the expressionist aesthetic most prominently exhibited in Robert Wiene's *The Cabinet of Dr. Caligari*, screened earlier that year.[12] Expression or expressivity refers here to the Hungarian film critic and writer Béla Balázs's sense of communicating psychological and spiritual content through external, visual means. Such expressivity could be achieved through artificial manipulation of the visual field, so that while in the earlier film the camera (and audiences) marveled at the ability to capture outdoor scenery, the atmosphere of the 1920 film was a product of the constructed studio sets.[13] One contemporary critic noted that the film was a "milestone" in the history of cinema because it forged a new relationship to modern art, particularly to fantastic architecture and symbol-ridden sculpture (rather than expressionist painting).[14] The discovery, via film, of the human "face" of all things, whether animate or inanimate, served to re-create the battlefield, the expressive "landscape of mud and object." But it also transformed the battlefield experience into a narrative of national redemption that stressed the individual and irreplaceable "soul" of all things, human and nonhuman.

Cinematic Animation in *Der Golem* (1914)

Paul Wegener, a successful stage actor who transitioned to film acting and directing, rapidly became a central figure in the nascent film industry. According to Thomas Elsaesser, he made "fantastic film a mainstay of the German cinema" for at least a decade. His 1913 doppelgänger film, *The Student of Prague*, inaugurated a new phase in German cinema, combining "romanticism and technology," while appealing both to the educated middle class and to the urban masses. This particular Wegener combination entailed the application of new film techniques to stories that blended a "middle-class concept of national literature with a pseudo-folk culture as the well-spring of the popular."[15] In a discussion of the first golem film's genesis, Wegener himself claimed that "everything revolves in this film around the image, around a merging of a fantasy world of past centuries with present life."[16] Even more than the folkloric dimension of the story, the fantastic potential of fairytales and stories of mythic import was vital for Wegener's attempt to establish aesthetic standards for film, to ground it as an independent art form even while providing entertainment for the masses.[17] He relied on supernatural tales to showcase film's capacity to create previously unimaginable effects—the animation of the golem, for example, or the appearance of doubles or ghosts through superimposition. The first golem film of 1914 involved a high degree of cinematic experimentation and privileged the work of the movie camera and its "kinetic lyricism."

Wegener's aim—even when not fully executed with the technologies of 1914—was to do away with factual images, with realistic lines and forms, and instead to enter a "new visual fantasy world."[18]

In *Der Golem*, Wegener enacted "the golem role interchangeably with a puppet made of plaster and papier-mâché" (see figure 1.1). The transitions between actor and puppet were so "subtly arranged" that it appeared to the critic Adolf Behne as though "the animated puppet opens its eyes, breathes, moves."[19] In addition to the presence of this puppet double in the film, viewers were made aware of the fact that the film itself created a double of the actor; the day after *Der Golem* was first screened, on January 14, 1915, Wegener's essay "Acting and Film" was printed in the daily newspaper *Berliner Tageblatt*, with the following illuminating preface: "Paul Wegener, Lieutenant and Knight of the Iron Cross first class is at the moment importantly occupied in Flanders, although yesterday he gave a guest performance in effigy as author and actor in a Berlin film theater. . . . The short essay that he left behind with us before departing for the battlefield reveals his own thoughts about this matter."[20] Through film technology, one could exist "in effigy," and Wegener could appear in two places at once: both serving in Flanders and giving a performance "by means of his image" on the screen in Berlin.

While Wegener stressed in his essay the differences between theater performance and acting in front of the camera, he brought to the golem role his well-known stage persona. Both Korrodi and Behne pointed out the similarity of Wegener's cinematic role to his past stage roles. Wegener was capable, they noted, of effectively conveying both the "animalism" of the golem and his "good-naturedness and meekness."[21] Such descriptions of Wegener as golem match up with his image as an instinctive, forceful, and manly actor rather than a refined and intellectual one. When playing major roles (Richard III, Mephisto, Shylock) in Max Reinhardt's Berlin theater, Wegener enjoyed "allowing the grimace of a barbaric primal drive [*Urtrieb*] to leer out from behind the mask enforced by conventions and habits," according to Walter Turszinsky.

FIGURE 1.1. Paul Wegener (*right*) next to golem statue from the 1914 film. (Courtesy of Stiftung Deutsche Kinemathek)

Both his "Eastern," or "Slavic," facial features and his actor persona lent themselves particularly well to the role of the golem, imagined, with the help of Hugo Steiner-Prag's illustrations for Gustav Meyrink's 1915 novel *Der Golem*, as a racialized Mongolian prototype. With Wegener's "Mongol head," "Moorish mouth," "wide-nasal flat nose of a Hun," and Slavic cheekbones, he had, in Turszinsky's view, no equal "in the realm of the human beast."[22]

Already in 1934, Beate Rosenfeld claimed, in her major study on the golem in German literature, that Wegener, as a "Mongolian" type, was particularly well suited to play the "primitive" and "exotic" golem, a figure that appealed to the public's taste at that time period. She also mentions that the aesthetics of the primitive golem requires a "prehistoric" costume, and Wegener used the term *Urmensch* in his description of the golem, claiming that his costume resembled outfits worn by people "1,000 years ago."[23] The cubist sculptor Rudolph Belling designed the golem as an imposing, statuesque figure—an effect achieved through the sculpted, geometric head piece, recalling the stylized hair of ancient Egyptian statues and that of cubist painting and sculpture.[24] The superimposition of the uncanny automaton (an already well-established figure in German letters through the writings of E. T. A. Hoffmann, for instance) on the early twentieth-century primitive was what rendered the cinematic golem a popular and representative figure for the time, a product of both distinctly German and international trends.

Der Golem relocated the story of a clay servant come to life to a vaguely delimited present day, setting the film in the identifiable town of Hildesheim in Lower Saxony. In this semirealistic context, the animation of the golem appeared all the more uncanny and horrific. The screenplay written by Wegener and Henrik Galeen tells of the discovery of a treasure trove that includes a gigantic clay figure, which is then sold to "old Aaron," a local Jewish *Trödler*, or owner of an antiquities and curiosities shop. Aaron (played by Galeen himself) accidently discovers how to animate the golem using a star-shaped metal capsule, which, when filled with a piece of parchment containing a magical phrase and placed in the statue's chest, brings it to life. The golem initially serves as a manual laborer but is soon given the task of guarding the daughter of the *Trödler* (played by Lydia Salmonova) and preventing her affair with a local, non-Jewish baron. When the daughter manages to leave the house to attend the baron's masked ball, the golem follows her. The film culminates with the golem's arrival at the palace, where it is stabbed and shot at with no deleterious effects, much to the attackers' horror. The daughter and baron flee to the top of a tower, and, following a physical struggle, they manage to remove the golem's capsule and throw it off the tower, smashing the figure to pieces (figure 1.2). Father and daughter reconcile, and the baron joins their embrace at the top of the tower, with the bucolic view of Hildesheim behind them.[25]

FIGURE 1.2. *Der Golem*, 1914: The scene was shot from a tower on the Pfingstberg near Potsdam. (Courtesy of Stiftung Deutsche Kinemathek)

Since the golem combined features of a heroic military leader, a "Roland statue," and an "Oriental idol," according to one review, Wegener and Galeen appropriately transformed the rabbi figure that traditionally animates the golem into a Jewish antiques dealer, whose shop contains Buddha sculptures, weapons, Oriental lamps, and other curiosities.[26] The Jewish Galeen (né Heinrich Wiesenberg) played the role of this *Trödler*. An assimilated Jew from a small town in eastern Galicia, Galeen had assisted Max Reinhart in Berlin and worked in Swiss theaters prior to embarking on a successful film career as screenplay writer, director, and occasional actor.[27] Although Galeen dresses the part of an observant Jew, with side locks and yarmulke, the film does not include any depictions of Jewish ritual—in contrast to the inaccurate 1920 depictions of praying in the synagogue. The destruction of the golem at the end of the film clears the path for full assimilation and integration: when Aaron embraces the couple, the viewers can presume that intermarriage ensues.

Galeen's overtly Jewish appearance in the film certainly marks him as "other," but his otherness is not augmented or contextualized in other ways. Similarly, the golem, along with the other markedly Jewish items in the treasure trove, such as Shabbat candles, a menorah, and an altar covering, is handled as merchandise and exotic lore (see figure 1.3). According to the script, when Aaron receives these items, he "inspects the large altar cloth made out of heavy material, feeling it between his fingers." A smile flits over his face as a title appears: "This is an item for my daughter." The film crosscuts to the daughter in her room, secretively reading a letter from the baron, her lover. When Aaron subsequently enters the room with the altar cloth, she looks with amazement at the expensive material, wraps herself with it in front of the mirror, and coquettishly takes a few dance steps. The father shakes his finger at her "but remains cheerful" rather than earnestly disapproving.[28] This scene might have provided inspiration for the second, 1917, film, which features a popular variety dancer instead of an aspiring Jewish daughter. Both films demonstrate how Jewish ritual objects—including the golem itself—are transformed into secular artifacts in the hands of Jews en route to full assimilation.

The sensuous rather than religious pleasure that Aaron's daughter takes in the expensive fabric of the altar cloth as she fantasizes about the baron reveals something of the film's aesthetics more generally. The daughter can be likened to the contemporary film viewer who savors the visual surface of the secular medium for its own sake. In an 1913 essay, "Gedanken zu einer Ästhetik des Kinos" ("Thoughts on an Aesthetic of the Cinema"), Georg Lukács focuses on the lack of human "presence" as the key characteristic of cinema. This lack is not an insufficiency but a stylistic principle, so that cinema can project the "movements and deeds of people" but not the people themselves. Film is no less alive for that reason, but its life is elsewhere: it rules over what Lukács designates as a "fantastical" aspect of life that lacks (in its very essence) the "presence," "destiny," "causes," and "motives" characteristic of stage drama. This is "life without a soul," composed of "pure surface," and film becomes a phenomenon of the visual "surface"; it is "movement in itself," an un-

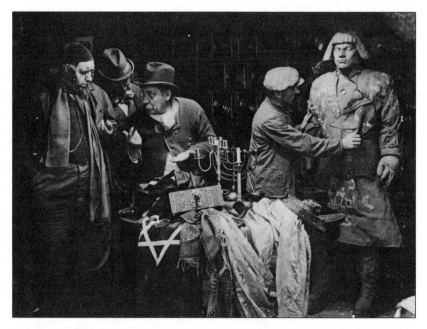

FIGURE 1.3. *Der Golem*, 1914: In Aaron's antiquities shop. (Courtesy of Stiftung Deutsche Kinemathek)

bounded, vital flow of images.[29] The golem in its fundamental silence embodies the form of silent cinema, which is, in Lukács's words, an intentionally "soulless" medium, a world of "pure externality" expressed through "occurrences and gestures."[30]

The new "homogeneous and harmonious" and yet "variegated" world of cinema corresponds, for Lukács, to "the fairy tale and dream in literature and life."[31] Within the 1914 film, a kind of modern-day fairy tale, one sequence is particularly emblematic. Titled "Golems Nachtgang" (Golem's night walk), it takes place at night and has a dream-like quality, notable for its emphasis on "the wonder of the camera." On the golem's way from Aaron's home to the baron's palace to retrieve the rebellious daughter, the surrounding nature proves distracting. The walk begins in "an old street" and proceeds through a "municipal square" and into a park, where the golem enjoys a splash in the pond. At one point,

it bends over and smells a rose bush, experiencing, as the script suc-
cinctly puts it, an "awakening of emotion toward nature." In the scene's
climax, the golem extends its arms upward to the stars, an image shot in
silhouette.[32] This self-willed gesture starkly contrasts with its previous
heavy and "mechanical" motions, as, for instance, when Aaron orders
the golem, "Raise your arm!"[33]

Hence, following the golem's previous animation, this scene focuses
on the creature's humanization, or at least on its budding emotional life.
The nighttime "excursion" shows the golem's potential for escape from
an enslaved, mechanized existence and stages an experience of decidedly
childlike, wonder-full pleasure, especially as it follows a series of crassly
erotic scenes revolving around the daughter of the antiques dealer.[34] A
surviving still from a close-up shot shows the golem's facial expression
as it smells a rose—softened, verging on a smile, far less of a set grimace
than in the other scenes (figure 1.4). The German Jewish writer Arnold
Zweig found in this "lyrical" scene a cinematic quality that could not
be achieved on the theater stage: "In the mood of the dream-breathing
earth, to stand as a created entity and slowly in amazement, in dull joy,
in trepidation, to raise the arms—an unforgettable image."[35]

Through the night-walk scene, both cinema itself and the otherwise
restrained "automaton" gain a heightened "poetic" or "fantastic" life, to
borrow Lukács's terms.[36] The pleasure that the golem (and audience)
takes in "nature" corresponds to the imagined naïve, childlike state of
cinema and its spectators. Yet this scene also conveys the tragedy of this
figure and of modern human beings alike: the childlike pleasure of cinema is short-lived and constituted on a fundamental absence, as is the
golem's entire existence. Golem's night walk depicts a kind of reveling
in the mediated *image* of nature. "Nature," in this sequence, becomes
"art" or "artistic form," a "maximum vivacity without an inner . . . dimension, strict nature-bound reality and utmost fantasy."[37] The golem
lifts its arms as if to express the lightness that the world obtains at such
a moment. Precisely because this anthropoid is earthen, connected to
nature through its very physicality, Wegener could use it to explore film's

FIGURE 1.4. *Der Golem*, 1914: Paul Wegener with roses. (Courtesy of Stiftung Deutsche Kinemathek)

capacity to combine "nature and art, truth and setting."[38] A massive figure of clay, the golem embodies both the materiality of the medium that brings to life fantastic visions and the fleeting, magical quality of photographic animation. All of this occurs against the background of quaint Hildesheim and the outdoor town space, underscoring the dependence of cinema's silent creation on a "strict nature-bound reality." This early approach to cinema underwent considerable revision in the late 1910s, as the German film industry and its technologies leapt ahead and new aesthetic possibilities became available.

The Visible Golem

In the 1917 film *Der Golem und die Tänzerin*, Wegener could count on the audience's familiarity with the golem's animation in the 1914 film and did not need to resort to trick photography or to his famous "kinetic lyricism." *Der Golem und die Tänzerin* reveals how, even as early as 1917, the duplicating logic of cinema has taken over, blurring the borders between life and art. The dancer's visit to the cinema within the movie revolves around her fascination with the cinematic image and its paraphernalia (the golem statue) and her lack of interest in the actor himself (though granted, that lack of interest is a seductive ploy). When the dancer first encounters the inanimate golem in the foyer, the production-company director tells her that he has recently spoken with the "original," that is, with Paul Wegener the actor, and that he would be happy to introduce her to him. She is more interested in seeing the film, however, especially the golem's "partner," the actress Lyda Salmonova, whom she is supposed to resemble. Preoccupied with her own image and its possible duplication on the screen, the actress, as a "commercial person," in Mark Seltzer's terms, "admires copies more than originals." Because her identity "depends on representation," she does not really see Wegener as his offstage self, and her gaze passes over him.[39] The humor of the film resides in this preference for the ghostly screen double over the flesh-and-blood star of the film.

By creating a structure of a film within a film, *Der Golem und die Tänzerin* implicates viewers in the dancer's own cinematic infatuation. The 1917 film uses the golem story to mark the strength of the film medium and its ability to simulate life, providing the illusion of access to Wegener as "himself," unmasked. By contrast, in his 1920 film *Der Golem, wie er in die Welt kam*, Wegener strove to distance the world of the golem from the everyday lives of people, including actors. He created a fully enclosed, entirely imagined sphere that could exhibit the "uninhabited mobility of figures, the full coming to life of background, of nature and interior, of plant and animal."[40] In contrast to the 1914 and 1917 films, which combined indoor studio settings with outdoor shots on location, the 1920 film revealed a preference for an utterly artificial environment. While the flat and painted sets of Robert Wiene's groundbreaking *The Cabinet of Dr. Caligari*, which premiered in February 1920, created an enclosed and artificial cinematic space, *Der Golem* of the same year

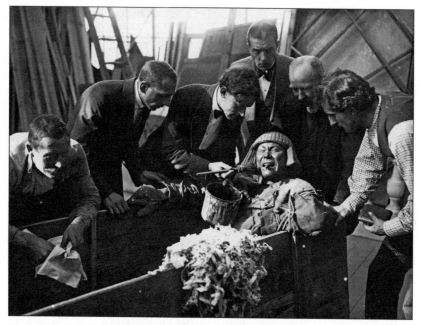

FIGURE 1.5. *Der Golem und die Tänzerin*, 1917: Paul Wegener is being prepared to be shipped to the dancer's home. (Courtesy of Stiftung Deutsche Kinemathek)

fashioned a more tangible, three-dimensional illusion with its set de-sign, a seemingly habitable (though clearly constructed) landscape.[41] The animation of the inanimate goes hand in hand in this film with the attempt to evoke three-dimensional space on the two-dimensional screen. A sculptural aesthetic, rather than a pictorial one, dominates the film and conveys the presence of a deeper, hidden meaning or message underlying the visual surface. The 1920 film thereby functions both as a continuation of the 1914 film, particularly of its night-walk scene, and also as a correction to the earlier two films and their projection of a "soulless" world of fleeting images, of "pure surface."

By this point in Wegener's use of the golem theme, Jewish protag-onists no longer enact mercantile roles; rather, they possess the key to the secrets of animation and therefore can also unlock the three-dimensionality of visual space. The golem's formation and animation in the 1920 film requires, for instance, a singular act of artistry and artisanry performed by Rabbi Loew, whereas the first golem figure of the 1914 film is inadvertently dug up by workers, a ready-made object. The 1920 scene of molding the golem is crosscut with the arrival of an imperial messenger bearing an edict of Jewish expulsion on account of various charges such as the practice of "black magic" and the disrespect of Christian holidays.[42] The rabbi then animates the golem in response to this external, political threat, in a room exclusively devoted to this purpose, a kind of artist's (or filmmaker's) studio, hidden and locked away. When he decides to enter this space, the rabbi must go down a hidden trapdoor, open a second, sealed door, and remove a barrier blocking the light. This progression not only enhances the suspense of the scene but also suggests that Jews possess the power to delve deeper into life and reveal the hidden recesses behind a seemingly flat surface. Unlike the antiques dealer who transforms a religious object—the altar cover—into a mundane, secular cloth that provides sensuous pleasure, Rabbi Loew of the 1920 film does the reverse: he undertakes the spiritual mission of creating a savoir for his Jewish community, transforming the clay sculpture into an animate protector who might secure the future of his people.

In the underground room, we see the shadow cast by the rabbi on the wall, beside three "blueprints" for the golem, schematic drawings of the monster's contours surrounded by notations and letters. The film suggests that animation is both monstrous and implicitly cinematic, a product of synthesis between the play of light and shadows and a kind of script (consisting of images and text) transformed into live action and motion. The golem's formation out of clay takes place with these drawings as background, emphasizing the stark difference between flat images, including the rabbi's shadow, and tactile substance. The rabbi's action of kneading the clay is extended cinematically, moreover, through the use of crosscutting: a medium shot shows him at work; the film then crosscuts to the delivery of the edict and once again back to the rabbi. A close-up on his hands, with the rest of the room cast in shadow, shows the rabbi vigorously plying the unformed matter. The film then returns to the imperial messenger, en route to the rabbi's home. We see the rabbi complete his work on the golem and reseal the room. This prolonged process of kneading reminds the viewer that although the completed golem-product appears to have a smooth, finished exterior, this figure is formed through hard human labor out of coarse and malleable clay. The transition from a two-dimensional scheme to a three-dimensional sculpture thus epitomizes the overall thrust of the 1920 film.

The scene in which the rabbi molds the golem is just one example of Wegener's postwar emphasis on cinema's expressive capacity, its ability to translate the spiritual dimension of human life into a visual, bodily form. Such ideas were most prominently developed in a 1924 theoretical book, *Der sichtbare Mensch* (*The Visible Man*) by the Hungarian critic and poet Béla Balázs. Through the new art of cinema, Balázs thought it possible to revive the "long-forgotten language of gestures and facial expressions," lost to an abstracted world of print culture.[43] He argues in *The Visible Man* for cinema's autonomous position as a modern art form that utilizes artificial means for exposing the visible "face" of both people and things. Like Wegener, Balázs believed in the moral significance of the opportunity afforded by cinema to rediscover the expressivity and, by extension, the freedom and autonomy of its inhabitants.[44]

According to Balázs, modern philology confirmed that the primordial "mother tongue" of all humanity was spontaneous bodily gestures or expressive movements.[45] Such bodily expressivity could be accessed anew through film technology, since "cinema revives a pre-logical, premodern mode of perception that has been obscured by the conditions of modernity."[46] At once past and future oriented, naturalizing and denaturalizing, cinema functions for Balázs as an international language that appropriates and synthesizes distinct nationalities, localities, and peoples through expressive movement.[47] Cinema is the "visual corollary of human souls immediately made flesh," directly transforming the "spirit into body."[48] This transposition takes place, in turn, through "the physiognomic impression" that all things, animate and inanimate, make on the viewer. In this respect, Balázs's theory of film differs from Lukács's, developed a decade earlier, as Lukács believed that in cinema "man has lost his *soul*; in return, however, he gains his *body*."[49]

"Physiognomy" is a key term in Balázs's film theory of this period: it registers the centrality of the visual surface and, simultaneously, conveys the spiritual-symbolic expressivity of this surface.[50] In film, he famously asserted, "objects . . . *share with human beings a quality of silence* that makes the two almost homogeneous, and hence enhances the mute object's vitality and significance. Since it does not speak less than human beings, it says just as much."[51] Cinema can bring out this "latent physiognomy of things," for it captures movement and gestural expression.[52] Expressionist cinema, in turn, reshapes outer appearances through distortion, resensitizing us to the face of things so that we cease to see them as mere tools, as means to an end, or as items of practical utility. The artist, like the child, is in a privileged position to see "each thing as an autonomous living being with a soul and face of its own."[53]

Positioned between the human and the object, the living and the dead, Wegener's golem emblematizes cinema's ability to animate the inanimate world, to reveal the physiognomy of the visual surface. The golem is, furthermore, both a machine/automaton and a primitive, so that it mediates both primordial and modern forms of bodily expressivity. The animation of this modern *Urmensch* enacts Balázs's notion of cinema as a kind of paradise regained by returning through modern technology to the lost, primal forms of expressivity. In the 1920 film particularly but also in the earlier golem films, Wegener strives to show the humanity of the golem. This sentient machine mirrors the broad attempt to regain—through everything from cinema and painting to literature—a spiritual dimension that seemed to have been lost in the modern age of abstracted knowledge and industrialized wars.

The inherent stiffness of the golem, covered in padded clothing, its head encompassed in an unmoving clay mask, paradoxically enables it to come to life, as its overall lack of flexibility makes us aware of the slightest gestures and facial expressions, whenever they do occur.[54] For example, the shot from the 1920 film in which the golem is first animated shows Wegener with a fixed grimace on his face, his lips turned down like a mask, evoking the dead sculpture awakened by the rabbi.[55] When the actor's facial expressions finally soften, which occurs when the golem leaves the ghetto, the effect is that much more powerful. Certainly, this unwieldy figure does not have the expressive range or versatility of a Charlie Chaplin or an Asta Nielsen. Still, in the 1920 film, Wegener brings the mise-en-scène as well as the golem to life, creating a fantasy of postwar reanimation that fills the entire expanse of the screen. He builds on the expressive potential of the whole cinematic ghetto to counterbalance war's cynical use of human beings as mere tools (or golems).

"An Architectural Paraphrase on the Theme 'Golem'"

"Spent the entire day seething in the clay," Wegener jotted down in his 1914 soldier's identification and pay book (*Soldbuch*). In a letter to Ernst Pietsch, he also describes enduring "day and night in clay trenches in close proximity to the enemy, without food, with death always nearby."[56] Wegener not only fought but also worked in the trenches, spending long days digging, shoveling, and maintaining them, a constant struggle as they quickly refilled with muddy water.[57] In his memoir of the war, published in 1933 but purportedly written in close proximity to the events, he candidly describes surviving a particularly fierce battle on December 4, 1914, in which most of his comrades died or suffered injuries. He returned "dead tired" from this battle, wearing his "clayed uniform," a golem-like figure. Entering a farmer's warm home, he felt as though he were stepping into "a new life." After this, his nerves were shot, and at night, he "always saw the hideous black smoke of the exploding grenades and heard the screams of the wounded." His dead comrades constantly reappeared in his dreams. Alongside his guilt and trauma, Wegener acknowledges his "disgusting joy at being alive."[58]

FIGURE 1.6. Paul Wegener (*left*) in the trenches of World War I. (Courtesy of Deutsches Filminstitut, Frankfurt am Main / Sammlung Kai Möller)

In *Der Golem, wie er in die Welt kam*, Wegener transformed the clay of his survivor's uniform and of the trenches in which his comrades were buried into the substance of the golem, itself a kind of "new life." The 1920 film opens with the expulsion edict delivered to the Jewish community by the messenger of the Emperor. As we saw earlier, Rabbi Loew (Albert Steinrück) staves off this threat; after creating and animating the golem, the rabbi then brings it to the court. There, the courtiers jeer at the images of Jewish ancestors projected by the rabbi, and as a punishment for their reaction, an explosion occurs, collapsing the court ceiling. The rabbi orders the golem to save the courtiers from certain death in exchange for the edict's annulment. This main plotline is interwoven with the story of a love affair between Miriam, the rabbi's daughter (Lydia Salmonova), and Florian, the imperial messenger (Lother Müthel), provoking the violent jealousy of Rabbi Loew's Famulus, or assistant (Ernst Deutsch). Although the rabbi had deanimated the dreaded golem after it accomplished the rabbi's mission, Famulus deviously re-animates it, and the golem's rebellious and destructive side reveals itself. After killing Florian, the golem sets the rabbi's home on fire, and threatens to destroy the entire ghetto. The golem's rage is ultimately spent, however, when it breaks out of the ghetto, where a Christian child removes the star-shaped capsule from its chest. The Jewish masses find the now-inanimate clay figure outside the gates of the ghetto and carry it back inside on their shoulders as though it were a hero.

Der Golem of 1914 was filmed primarily in the Neubabelsberg studio of the Bioskop company, but for certain scenes, Wegener walked the streets of Hildesheim dressed in the golem's costume. The spectacle caused such crowds to gather that he was fined by the city for being a "public nuisance."[59] By 1920, Wegener and his cofilmmakers avoided any such overlap between the world of the film and that of the street by creating a sealed-off, artificial environment in which the golem could "come into the world" as a creature purely of cinema. In an interview, Wegener proposed that "these alleys and squares should not remind one of anything in reality; they should create the atmosphere in which the golem breathes."[60] Instead of attempting to re-create the Prague of the sixteenth century or the Jewish ways of life at that time period, he created his vision of a fantastic ghetto and an equally fanciful court of an all-powerful Emperor.[61] "Nobody ever lived in a ghetto like the one pictured in 'The Golem,'" a *New York Tribune* critic recognized at the outset of a 1921 review that situated this cinematic ghetto at the center of the film's "action."[62] While the Jewish space of the ghetto is reminiscent of the World War I battlefields and their complex network of clay trenches, within it, Rabbi Loew creates an animated giant that saves the Jews from expulsion, even when it ultimately runs amok.

If Balázs appears at times to view film as an extension of nature, so that the "profilmic event" (the "reality" in front of the camera that is being recorded) takes precedence over the camera work, he also promotes a notion of cinema as an autonomous representational realm that enables a new kind of seeing to emerge.[63] He argues that the trajectory of film as an art form leads "further and further from nature in its original state." The "stylization of nature" is the precondition, in Balázs's radical concept, for film's new status as a work of art: "Landscape is a physiognomy, a face . . . that gazes out at us." Thus, while "location shots of a town can be very beautiful and have the added charm of credible reality," they do not expose the "soul" or "eyes" of the landscape, nor do they convey its mood.[64] The 1920 film stylizes nature in more than one respect: the artificial studio setting of the film had a life-like quality with its organic shapes and twisted forms, enhancing the animation of the clay golem as it awakens to life and its emotional forces. Korrodi even complained that in the 1920 film, "nature receives such blows in the ribs that it realizes the unreal."[65] For Herbert Ihering, these same attributes heralded a new epoch for cinema: "Wegener and Poelzig proved that only the tightly structured, rhythmically concentrated image, one that eliminates all the accidental qualities of nature, opens the future for film."[66] In other words, in contrast to the mimetic indoor spaces of the earlier films—especially the antiques shop (1914) and dancer's boudoir (1917)—and the outdoor settings of Hildesheim, the 1920 mise-en-scène does not imitate our own world but rather realizes the unreal by projecting an enclosed fantasy world.

As reviewers at the time noted, *Der Golem* of 1920 was a product not only of cinematographic developments but also of successful cooperation between architects and actors, a novel thing at the time.[67] The Ufa film company (Universum Film AG), founded in 1917 with German government support, following the direct encouragement of General Erich Ludendorff, had the resources necessary to construct an entire model ghetto at its Tempelhof studios.[68] Setting the tale in a fantastical medieval past, Wegener worked with the renowned architect Hans Poelzig to build an entire "city" of clay, a site that could house both the golem and the Jewish community. All fifty-four buildings of the "golem-city" were designed by Poelzig (renowned for the interior of the Great Theater in Berlin), modeled by the sculptor Marlene Moeschke, and constructed by

Kurt Richter.[69] The buildings were made of clay, brick, and straw, and so their materiality corresponded to the clay matter of the golem itself—a shared physiognomy of structures and monster. These constructions had, as the art historian Paul Westheim wrote in 1920, "their own life, a life that a master-builder's spirit has projected into them: under the hands of the modeler, the clay objects have become expressive, they have been given momentum, a gesture, a face."[70]

Poelzig's set designs were futuristic and fantastic, even as they drew on past architectural elements.[71] The narrowness of the ghetto streets and the crookedness or asymmetry of the homes both contributed to the magical atmosphere in which an artificial creation might be brought to life and revealed how the cities of the future could be threatening, dwarfing their human inhabitants. Concomitantly, the organic curves and stalactite forms in the interiors of these settings echoed the shapes of the human body, suggesting a continuum between the human subjects and their living environments.[72] Unlike the classical, ornamental design of the court, in which frivolous ceremonies take place, Jewish space is imagined in this film as creative and consequential, a space in which a golem can be animated through spiritual and magical ritual. A contemporaneous *New York Times* review of the film expressly instructed its spectators to view the "massive" and "unearthly" settings as an "active a part of the story as any of the characters, . . . the most expressive settings yet seen in this country, . . . not because they are weird, but because they vivify the action of the story."[73] These "cinematographic works of art" serve as architectural golems, brought to life with the help of the camera.

The thick, dark texture of the ghetto, including its walls, bridges, and towers, counterbalanced by the vertically striving arches of the inner and outer constructs, indeed revealed the gothic dimension of Poelzig's design.[74] Andrew Webber writes that "physiognomy . . . has a key function in the representational regime of the gothic" and that this function extends beyond "the effects of facial features" to other elements of representation.[75] Critics of the film have also linked the physiognomy of

FIGURE 1.7. Hans Poelzig's sets for *Der Golem, wie er in die Welt kam*, 1920. (Courtesy of Deutsches Filminstitut, Frankfurt am Main / Sammlung Kai Möller)

the cinematic ghetto space to its Jewish inhabitants. A 1920 review pronounced that these settings exhibit "a kind of Jewish Gothic" that blends the "flame-like letters of the Jewish alphabet with the leaf-like flames of Gothic tracery."[76] Like the golem story itself, the fantastic "city" envisioned by Poelzig is cast here, significantly, as a product of the cultural interaction between Jews and Christians, between gothic and scriptural influences. The "face" of the ghetto space, however, has often been interpreted as solely Jewish; the buildings are even said to huddle together and converse in Yiddish or else in a Yiddish-inflected German.[77]

Gustav Meyrink's description of the Prague ghetto's "uncanny and depraved" houses that appear to engage in "ghostly communings" has also influenced such readings.[78] Hence, while the expressive stylization of *Der Golem*'s 1920 sets has been received enthusiastically, past and present critics have created a metonymic correlation of the ghetto space with its Jewish inhabitants, usually through stereotyped notions of Jewish letters, speech, and bodies. For Noah Isenberg, "the physiognomy of the Jew . . . emerges in Wegener's film in the architectural construction of Jewishness," so that the Jewish space is defined through its "distorted shapes, dark cavities, and hunchbacked structures."[79] When we examine the imaginary ghetto setting within the context of the film's overall mise-en-scène, however, we see that Poelzig and Wegener forged novel configurations of atavistic and utopic elements. The clay golem and the ghetto are constantly linked, for instance, with the elements of sky and stars that both propel the plot forward and enhance the film's symbolic dimension.

Heavenly and Cinematic Constellations

Der Golem, wie er in die Welt kam achieved its visual animation not only through set designs but also with the help of evolving cinematic techniques such as close-ups and superimpositions. While the ghetto structures seem to tower over the Jewish inhabitants, the structures themselves are put into perspective by the larger horizon of sky and stars. In the first shots of the film, Claudia Dillmann writes, "a few unprotected, deformed and broken towers strain over the ghetto wall, appearing small, cowering, and lost under the wide expanse of the nightly sky."[80] These first shots establish the correlation between the clay and wood constructions of the ghetto and the ethereal elements, a link that carries over to the figure of the clay golem itself. As the 1920 *Film-Kurier* critic eloquently wrote, "like the earth and sea, the golem is mysteriously connected to the constellation of the stars, that make him at times wild and at times meek: ebb and flow."[81] If the rabbi initially decides to create the golem after reading the stars and determining that a disaster is impending, he also attempts to summon up the "terrible Astaroth" that can deliver the animating "magic word" only when "Venus enters the constellation." Similarly, after the golem has fulfilled its mission at the court, the rabbi discovers that "when Uranus enters the house of the planets," the golem can become destructive, ruled by the vengeful Astaroth again.[82]

Rabbi Loew's astrological techniques are enhanced through the film's cinematography, executed by the Jewish cameraman Karl Freund. In the opening shot, our gaze is pulled above the tallest tower toward a group of stars that are particularly large and luminous, forming a "readable" shape. The next low-angle shot is a close-up of this tower, revealing Rabbi Loew atop the roof of his home, peering into a telescope that cuts through the frame. This is followed by an iris shot—taken as if through the eye of the telescope—showing a magnification of the same radiant stars. The rabbi puts the instrument aside and reads in a large manuscript (figure 1.8); a medium close-up shows his distraught face as he looks up again at the sky, and so we are given to understand that he has grasped the ominous portent of the image just seen. The telescope connecting the iris shot to the close-up of the rabbi's face forms the link between heaven and earth (literally); between technology and magic; and between the past, as knowledge accumulated in books, and the future threat of expulsion. The scene also progresses from a very long shot—the establishing shot of the film—to a medium shot of the tower, to closer shots of the rabbi and the stars, drawing us further and further into the characters and their lives.

These opening shots of *Der Golem* 1920 self-consciously foreground the centrality of magnifying vision to this film and to cinema more generally. While the cinematic camera differs from the telescope or microscope, instruments that merely expand "the range of the visual," according to Balázs,[83] the telescope in this scene *stands in* for the close-up of the camera. It not only brings objects into closer view but also enables the "deeper gaze" that provides a new and different "reading" of these objects.[84] The close-up exposes the physiognomy and living gestures of *all* things. Furthermore, by fragmenting the totality of space and time into expressive parts or moments, the apparent objectivity of the camera is made subjective, and the director can thus create an anthropomorphized image of the world colored by human emotions.[85] In this scene, we are invited to decipher the wrinkles of the rabbi's forehead just as

FIGURE 1.8. *Der Golem, wie er in die Welt kam*, 1920: Albert Steinrück as Rabbi Loew. (Courtesy of Deutsches Filminstitut, Frankfurt am Main / Sammlung Kai Möller)

he himself reads the deeper meaning of the constellations. As Francis Guerin writes in *A Culture of Light*, the overlapping points of view between the telescope and the camera, the continuity between these two instruments, also "extends to the relationship between Jewish mysticism and cinematic representation."[86] They are, respectively, past and present means for deciphering visual messages as well as for animating dead matter. Because the first shot of the sky and jagged tower silhouettes already contained a "magnified" constellation of brightly lit stars, we can even argue that the camera's eye in general, and not only the close-up, exposes visual details that we would otherwise not pay attention to but that constitute the very "soul" or "intimate face" of existence.[87]

While the opening sequence of the 1920 film is thematically connected to "Golem's night walk" of 1914, with its shots of the golem as a silhouette against the backdrop of a night sky, the aesthetics of the two scenes are worlds apart. In the earlier film, the golem and its surroundings embody a sense of lightness and freedom, inviting the viewer to take pleasure in these outdoor images. The night sequence in the 1920 film is more instructive and immersive, forging a connection between the image on the screen and the destiny of the Jewish people and inviting us to identify with the endangered community. The night skies no longer offer a means of escape into a reproduced image of nature for the working golem and spectators alike but rather call attention by their artificiality to the symbolic significance of the visual surface and the embodiment of spirit in film. The makers of the 1920 film thus also use facial close-ups along with dissolve techniques to convey the "deeper" and "poetic" gaze necessary for deciphering external signs and acting on them.[88]

In the first act of the film, the rabbi comprehends the impending calamity and preemptively shapes the clay entity into the form of the golem. In the opening sequence of the second act, prior to the golem's animation, when the clay puppet is replaced by the live actor, the audience catches a glimpse of Wegener as golem. This sequence consists of three shallow shots that dissolve into one another: first, the starry night sky from the very beginning of the film reappears, though no longer framed by the ghetto towers from below, and then dissolves into an image of a Star of David, which then finally dissolves into a close-up of Wegener's face as the golem, his eyes closed, unmoving. The result is a brief superimposition of the face, with its sculptured, geometrically shaped head mask, over the star (figure 1.9).[89] In this nonnarrative and relatively static sequence, the threat of expulsion, which first appeared as a message written in the stars, becomes visually linked to the fate of the Jewish community and the future animation of the golem through the dissolve that blends together two shots. The sequence equates the creature's life with its mission to protect the Jews. The subsequent shot brings the spectator back to the golem, by now a complete (though still inanimate) sculpture, and to the rabbi's efforts to lift the statue out of his underground "studio." This sequence of images—night stars, Star of David, soon-to-be-animate golem—not only foreshadows the transformation of inanimate object into live actor but also prefigures the Jewish community's ultimate redemption and the film's closing shot: the Star of David superimposed on the shut gate of the triumphant ghetto. The dissolve of three distinct shots further creates a kind of triptych in motion, a Christian aesthetic format visually suited to this scene that foretells the impending "birth" of the golem-savior through the appearance of a star.

The close-up of Wegener with his eyes shut evokes a state of inner reflection and expectation that contrasts with the image of the inanimate clay sculpture in the subsequent scene. This close-up is framed, furthermore, by the visual process of isolating and abstracting a particular star, the Star of David, from the multiple stars in the heavens. In this manner, the stars that previously augured the approaching threat to the Jewish community now come to symbolize future, hope, and continuity. The facial close-up functions as the expressive counterpart to the more abstract Star of David. At the same time, the Star of David itself displays multiple dimensions in this scene: it shifts from a thick, tactile object made of clay to an abstract, two-dimensional image and then reverts back to clay as it dissolves over Wegener's face. The enhancement of the "pulsating" star is indicative of a dimension that exists within and be-

FIGURE 1.9. *Der Golem, wie er in die Welt kam*, 1920.

yond the flat surface of abstract symbols. In this manner, the hexagram
mediates between the earthbound golem in the Jewish ghetto and the
sphere of the heavens with its symbolic stars and messages. The golem
too first appeared in the film as a two-dimensional geometric diagram
in the rabbi's magic book and as a sketch or "blueprint" on the wall.

Through dissolve, close-up, and superimposition, Wegener suggests that cinema itself can effect the magical transition from the two-
dimensional to the three-dimensional, from the flat surface to the tactile
object. The inanimate golem is not the only thing that can be animated. But
such transitions also carry political import in a film concerning Jewish-
Christian relations. The hexagram is not an innocent choice on the part
of the 1920 filmmakers, especially considering that the character of Rabbi
Loew uses a pentagram as protection from the Astaroth idol and installs a
five-pointed star capsule in the golem's chest. Gershom Scholem reminds
us in his history of the symbol that the hexagram, unlike the Menorah, was
never an exclusively "Jewish symbol" and was shared in the past by many

peoples. Jews initially used it as an ornamental, rather than religious, feature on tombstones and synagogues and as a magical symbol placed on amulets, including mezuzot, to protect against harmful spirits and demons.[90] Interestingly, "the 'official' use of the hexagram as the insignia of a Jewish community had its origins in Prague," the so-called birthplace of the modern golem, and spread from there to other Jewish communities in Austria, Bohemia, and Moravia during the seventeenth century.[91]

At the end of the film, when superimposed on a shot of the closed ghetto gate, the hexagram represents the Jewish community in its regained security and independence. It is a kind of seal on the gate, marking Prague Jewry's segregation from the surrounding Christian world. In previous shots of the ghetto, building facades display various broken triangular forms. The Star of David symbolically brings these triangles together, complete. In the triptych sequence, the Star of David enhances the golem's role as protector of the Jewish community, a kind of shield animated through the parchment placed in a star-shaped capsule on his breast. The hexagram thus represents the magical protection provided by the golem as well as the redemptive hopes invested in him.[92]

As an extradiegetic symbol superimposed on the film images, the Star of David conveyed its message to contemporary viewers alone and not to the characters within the film. Even while the filmmakers reverted the Star of David back to its earlier functions (amulet, shield, ornament, communal insignia), audiences of the period who came to view a film concerning Jewish persecution could not have avoided the modern association of the star with Zionism and its secular hopes for the political "redemption" of the Jews of Europe. Starting with the first Zionist Congress in Basel in 1897, the Star of David was "applied to nearly every visual representation of Zionism."[93] As a symbol of Jewish nationalism and of the potential future geographic separation between Jews and other nations, the Star of David invited its viewers to superimpose the hermetic world projected in this film onto present times, in which secular German-Jewish citizens formed an inseparable part of society and were neither secluded nor externally recognizable. The fantastic ghetto of the film, in which the Jews foster a tight-knit community, can also be read, accordingly, as a utopian homeland, a yet-unrealized dream, rather than an imagined ghetto of the past. Ensuring the continued presence of Jews in the diaspora as a distinct minority, Wegener's golem also represents the ambivalent Jewish fantasy of maintaining an autonomous and self-sufficient community, one that can protect itself from the European-Christian world and ultimately lock its gates. At the same time, the makers of the 1920 film implicitly represent the Zionist movement as a throwback to medieval times, implying that it rests on the shaky foundations of Jewish "black magic" and erratic golems. The golem itself expresses a greater affinity toward the Christian world, constantly crossing over to the other side. A creation of a Jewish rabbi, the golem develops its own volition, submitting itself only to a Christian child within the film, as well as to a non-Jewish film director. The monster of clay thus challenges any attempt to maintain distinct communities and identities under the banner of the Star of David.

Techniques of the Survivor

In bringing to life a golem as a (Zionist) savior, the 1920 film also reflects on the recent war and the scars it had left on the German nation at large. The golem figure, mediating as it does the architectural and human physiognomies of the film, also represents the transition from a violent wartime existence to the unique political unrests of the postwar period. This figure and its story constitute Wegener's response to the militarization of German society, a response articulated from the perspective of a traumatized survivor. Kittler and Holl are among the few critics to insist on the relevance of Wegener's war experiences to the reading of his golem films. They argue that the golem undergoes a kind of militarization, developing from a "tool" and bondsman in the earlier films to an unmovable, unfeeling, machine-like weapon or, in their words, a "new automatic weapon system." Kittler and Holl also compare the 1920 golem to the new type of "engineer-soldier" who, according

to Wegener's own diary account, was an infantry soldier transformed
into a "true leader of this 'folk-trench warfare,' . . . a canal worker with
a weapon and fearlessness at catastrophic explosions."[94] The conflation
of the golem's duties of servitude and protection partially justifies such
an interpretation. Just as the golem in the 1920 film chops wood, draws
water, and carries medicinal herbs, so he also follows the rabbi's orders
and helps to save the Jewish community. However, whereas the golem is
a *singular* weapon created to fulfill a mission and endowed with heroic
qualities, Wegener's "engineer-soldier" never dreams of gallant battles or
of honors. The modern combatant is a "canal worker" toiling dutifully
through endless, unheroic drudgery. From the first scenes of the golem's
awakening, its exaggerated strength poses a threat to the surroundings;
unpredictable from the start, it is ultimately uncontrollable and destructive, an engineer-soldier gone haywire.

Wegener admits in his wartime memoir to the difficulty of maintaining a level-headed attitude and expresses amazement that the war did not
cause him severe emotional injury. His letters from the front addressed
to Pietsch reveal that the actor suffered in late December 1914 from "an
acute nervous heart weakness" or else a "nervous fatigue of the heart
muscle," causing spells of dizziness.[95] The golem of 1920, by contrast,
exhibits both physical courage and apathy. In its not-altogether-human
state, the golem stoically endures the chaos around it, particularly when
it is brought to the court and prevents the ceiling from collapsing on the
hysterical courtiers.[96] But the golem attempts to emerge from this nerveless state. In the novel Wegener published in 1921 based on the film,
he describes the golem, after receiving a flower from a maiden at the
court, as a "poor creature yearning for life with its joys and its pain." This
"unsaved object, beyond life and death, came from other, dark circles,"
rather than from a mother's womb, but it could still express a "silent
mournfulness."[97] As the golem's consciousness of and appreciation for
life grows, so does its comprehension of death and of the consequences
of removing its animating device. When the rabbi decides to end the
golem's existence after the decree against the Jews has been annulled,

the golem attempts to prevent him from doing so by covering the star-shaped capsule with its hand.

The automaton's growing desire to remain "alive" is made more meaningful by Wegener's own brushes with death. Anton Kaes contends that the major German films produced in the 1920s can be considered "shell shock cinema" because they often "restage the shock of war and defeat without ever showing military combat."[98] These films focus on experiences of loss and grief as a constant, if invisible, presence, translating the shock and violence of war into aesthetic devices and particular genres (horror, crime, myth). The architecture of *Der Golem, wie er in die Welt kam*, with its underground, trench-like spaces, its claustrophobic alleys, and its mud-caked abodes, invites interpretation along these lines. Specifically, it asks us to consider the rabbi's creation of the golem as part of a battle against the forces determined to destroy his community. Spectators also encounter Rabbi Loew as a model of extreme "moral courage"; his helper, or Famulus, on the other hand, exhibits weak nerves, even fainting as he participates in the supernatural rite performed to extract the animating formula.[99] This spectrum of male responses to threat and danger suggests that in order to see the film as an indirect response to the events of World War I, we need to look beyond the golem to the larger societal portrait in the film.

Wegener's diaries and letters also delineate an ongoing frustration with how the war was carried out and with its unnecessary loss of life. In a letter to Pietsch, he refers to the war as "the most monstrous, dumbest, and atrocious thing." In another letter, written only a few days after surviving his most lethal battle, Wegener, the lauded war hero, characterizes the "modern defense war" as "senseless murder" and "boredom, . . . positively absurd," with no end in sight.[100] In the memoir, he notes the lack of empathy exhibited by commanders toward the death of individuals, a consequence of the massive death toll.[101] After a senseless attack that took place in mid-October 1914, Wegener writes about the beginning of a sentiment of "mistrust" among the soldiers toward their leadership. He calls the wounded and deceased soldiers "the poor victims of these days" who "paid with their lives and are irreplaceable."[102] In the dramatic court collapse that is the climax of the 1920 film, the Emperor and his courtiers bring disaster on themselves, we recall, through their lack of empathy toward the image of the suffering Jews. The violence and havoc of this scene brings to mind the recent events of the war and invites an interpretation in light of Wegener's critique of the German wartime leadership.

When Rabbi Loew is summoned to appear at the festival and asked to entertain his Christian ruler, he creates a kind of magical cinematic event, projecting on one of the walls a scene of ancient Israelites wandering in the desert. In the foreground, the Jewish "forefathers" appear "larger than life."[103] The rabbi acts here as a modern film director, enlisting newfound technologies to project historical images to the public. But the contents of these images tell of Jewish exile and suffering, and the goal of entertainment stands in tension with the seriousness of the subject matter. The textual source for this scene is the mid-nineteenth-century story of Rabbi Loew collected in the Bohemian Jewish volume *Sippurim*, in which the Emperor bids the rabbi to raise his ancestors from the dead. The rabbi agrees to conjure them up on the condition that the Emperor does not laugh, no matter what he sees. To the "greatness and strength of the men of antiquity," raised from the dead in the nineteenth-century tale, Wegener adds the masses of Israelites, exiled and wandering in the desert.[104]

The cinematic rabbi, as we have seen, warns the court not to speak or laugh (in other words, to be somewhat golem-like) when viewing the spectacle, "or else a dreadful disaster might take place." As a distraught, long-bearded figure comes stumbling to the forefront, the court jester makes a remark that causes a ripple of callous laughter to pass through the audience. As if responding to this display, the man in the image walks rapidly toward them, looming larger and larger, appearing to walk into the hall. The "film-within-a-film" ends in an explosion of light, and the ceiling of the smoke-filled hall plummets to the ground. Since the golem blocks the only exit, courtiers are seen risking their lives, jumping out of the windows. In the context of the recent war and its explosions, which caused trenches to collapse and bury their occupants, the court scene hints at the destructive effects of a lack of empathy toward others, specifically the imagined Jews on Rabbi Loew's projected screen and their Prague counterparts, the Jews in the ghetto.

The fearless and stoic golem executes the rabbi's orders, bearing the weight of the ceiling's beams, and thus prevents the deaths of those enemies who had only recently ordered the expulsion of the Jews. This wondrous physical act of rescue follows its emotional awakening earlier in the same scene, when one of the women attending the festival hands it a rose, rather than merely gaping at it in horror like the others. The camera shows the supposedly unfeeling automaton in profile, at close range. The rigid mouth begins to form a smile, revealing a softened longing, as in "Golem's night walk" of the 1914 film.[105] Here Wegener suggests that the golem's subsequent heroic behavior does not stem from a nerveless lack of ability to feel. Quite the contrary: it complements this monster's newfound desire and underscores the courtiers' lack of empathy and their inability to see "others" as equally human.

As Cathy Gelbin points out, it is not only actions that elicit our empathy but also cinematic techniques. Certain angles used in the court scene allow the director to manipulate the audience's emotions, enlisting us through eye-level shots to favor the Jews and to side against the courtiers, who are filmed from a high angle in a manner that casts their ridicule as "blinded laughter." Even while displaying the stereotypical figure of the Jew as a spectacle for the court, the scene disrupts the courtiers' gaze, showing it to be destructive, potentially life threatening.[106] The courtiers' jeering of the Jews on-screen echoes the rise of anti-Semitic sentiment during and after the war, when Germany's victory no longer appeared secure. Jews were deliberately positioned as a suspect group within the German nation, and a census was undertaken to prove that they were shirking military duty—although they actually served loyally alongside other citizens and suffered equal losses.[107]

After belittling Jewish suffering in this scene, the courtiers must contend with the wrath of the Jewish figure, an anti-Semitic image of their own making. Wegener designates the distraught Jew who walks toward the spectators as Ahasverus, the eternal wanderer, the legendary cobbler from Jerusalem cursed, according to a 1602 German chapbook, because he "refused to allow Jesus to rest on the wall of his house when he went by bearing his cross."[108] A figment of anti-Jewish propaganda (adapted by modern Jews for their own allegories), the wandering Jew functions as a distorting mirror held up to his ridiculing audience, exposing the venality of the courtiers who laugh at their self-created stereotypes. The golem, a savior, contrasts with the ancient Ahasverus, a harbinger of destruction. Nevertheless, Ahasverus also resembles the "newborn" golem in certain respects: he looks around in amazement and bewilderment, just as the golem peers around wide-eyed when first animated. Both the wandering Jew and the golem are living-dead, condemned to exist with little control over their own lives or the end of their afflictions. When the spectators refuse to recognize the misfortunes of these living-dead exiles, as preserved by the haunting visual medium of film, their own lives are also endangered.

If the gigantic Ahasverus who threatens to emerge from the image reaches the "beams of the ceiling," the immense golem upholds those same beams, which then break in half, forming a triangular shape around everyone present (see figure I.1. in the introduction).[109] This transforms the seemingly static architecture of the court into a kind of tent reminiscent of the makeshift abodes of the Jews wandering in the desert.[110] It also resembles the angular homes in the ghetto, thereby undoing the sharp dichotomy between the wholeness and symmetry of the court and the asymmetrical, broken forms of the ghetto. The scene draws a visual correlation between the realms of court and ghetto. And just as the home front and battlefield were deeply interconnected during World War I, so the edict of exile and destruction impinging on the Jews transforms the court itself into an unsafe space that can collapse on its inhabitants. But the courtiers are awakened to the brutality of their edict only when their own lives are threatened. Wegener turns the court into a battlefield—we see wounded people and dead bodies on the floor—in order to position the Jews as capable of redeeming the immoral nation, as heroes rather than backstabbers. In this and other ways, *Der Golem, wie er in die Welt kam* instructs its viewers in the process of rehumanizing others, both Jews and golems.

How the Golem Left the World (Temporarily)

Wegener's 1920 film is a film about film. Rabbi Loew uses cinema in the court scene to save the lives of *his* people, reappropriating an anti-Semitic image for his own purposes. He educates the hedonistic courtiers, showing them that the borders between myth and reality, between image and human, are not stable and can be manipulated. He enlists the golem—fundamentally cinematic in its muteness and artificial doubling of human life—to teach the court and, by extension, the viewers of the film a lesson in empathy.

Der Golem, wie er in die Welt kam does not merely re-create the ruptures wrought by World War I or its shell-shock logic; it also suggests the potential for reinvesting life with meaning after the mass carnage of the war. In addition to the animated architecture and the starry constellations, the final scenes of the film exhibit this potential. Only after being reanimated by Rabbi Loew's Famulus (assistant) for a vengeful purpose does the golem become dangerous and enraged, resembling Ahasverus in the court scene. The golem is ordered to kill the "foreign man," the Christian courtier, Florian, who has sneaked into Rabbi Loew's home and spent the night in his daughter's bed. After the golem throws Florian off the tower of the rabbi's home, its destructive capacities continue to grow. It sets the ghetto on fire and drags the unconscious Miriam out of her father's house and through the streets. Ultimately sparing her life, the golem breaks out of the ghetto walls, startling the Christian children playing in the grass. The expressions of the children initially resemble the horrified, open-mouthed gazes of the courtiers when they first encounter the golem. But the mise-en-scène changes the overall atmosphere and affect of the moment. At court, the golem appeared immense and foreboding, but in relation to the gigantic ghetto walls, its stature is reduced. A long shot shows it standing in the middle of the field, forlorn. This open field also creates a counterpoint to the physiognomic aesthetic of ghetto architecture and the stylized setting of the court. Instead, this in-between space mitigates the extremes of ghetto and court, enabling a different kind of encounter between the golem, as a Jewish creation, and the Christian world.

Just as the landscape is more open and "natural" outside the ghetto walls—even though this scene, like the rest of the film, was actually shot in the studio—so the golem appears to enjoy the spontaneity of play, a departure from its usual role of obeying commands. In this final scene, the golem is not so much the living-dead automaton but emerges from what I have called the contradictory golem condition into a new life, which is also an end. One naïve child, a girl, dares to approach the golem with an apple in her hand, symbolically tempting it into the human realm.[111] The golem lifts her in its arms to better enjoy her proximity, and the child fingers the golem's capsule, her unwitting curiosity thus bringing its short-lived existence to a conclusion (figure 1.10). By staging the golem's last few moments as gentle and playful—even tender, in contrast to the previous bout of destructive rage—Wegener suggests that the creature's "life" was not lived in vain. Importantly, the child perceives the clay monster as a playmate rather than as a utilitarian object. Through the child's gaze, the golem attains an independent life. For a brief moment, it is transformed into an "autonomous living being with a soul and face of its own."[112] From the creature's perspective, the child also appears as a wondrous phenomenon: the golem lifts her in its arms in an all-too-human gesture that, as in the night-walk scene, reminds the viewer of the golem's fundamental inhumanity. Sitting in its arms, the child, like the viewer, is now at eye level with the golem, almost equal to it.

In this final moment, the golem's uncanny monstrousness seems to vanish and give way to a more familiar side. The secret life of the silent

FIGURE 1.10. *Der Golem, wie er in die Welt kam*, 1920: The Golem outside the ghetto walls, playfully lifting a Christian child. (Courtesy of Deutsches Filminstitut, Frankfurt am Main / Sammlung Kai Möller)

machine is no longer so threatening; it can even be enjoyed. As the girl plays with the golem, we see her hand in close-up, fingers on the capsule; previously, we are shown the hands of the rabbi in a similar close-up shot just before he first inserts the capsule. When her fingers begin to withdraw the animating device, the golem does not stop her, however, as it attempted to do with the rabbi in a prior scene. It drops the girl and collapses to the ground, becoming an inanimate sculpture once again. A moment later, the children gather and sit on this piece of clay, tossing the all-important capsule into the air as though it were a toy. While Rabbi Loew attempted to end the golem's life after the monster had completed its mission and served the communal needs of the Jews, here the child deanimates the golem inadvertently. This "death" is affirmed in the film as a more fitting and harmonious one. "It is as if," writes Steve Choe, "the golem recognizes its own finitude as a living being," and the viewer understands that this monster is "not an invincible, monolithic machine, a weapon tasked with killing the other, but a vulnerable being."[113] Significantly, this recognition takes place vis-à-vis the Christian child, similar to the golem's encounter with the Christian woman in the court. Unlike the eternally wandering Jew, forever denied a resting place, the golem, a product of Jewish society, can be embraced by the Christian child and, implicitly, the Christian viewer. As a result, with the golem's deanimation, it is "converted" to humanity.

At the end of the 1914 film, the golem is cast from the tower, and its form shatters to pieces, paving the way for Jewish integration. In the finale of the 1920 film, by contrast, the golem figure remains intact, and it is carried back into the ghetto, perhaps to be reanimated again at a future moment of great necessity.[114] In this ending, the golem's short-lived existence is treated as valuable and worthwhile, unlike the numerous young soldiers who died anonymous and, at times, futile deaths on the battlefields of World War I. But the significance of the golem's animation also derives from its ability to cross the threshold to the Christian world, embracing both its callousness and its innocence. Awaking from the "haunting visions" of the film into "mundane existence," Hans Wollenberg, the Jewish editor of the widely distributed film magazine *Lichtbild-Bühne*, writes that after the film, a "triumphant knowledge" rejoiced in the hearts of "every well-known person in art- and film-Berlin." "In the competition of peoples over the art of film," he contends, "the blue ribbon is this time ours."[115] Wollenberg translates the golem's worthwhile mission on the screen into a sense of national victory shared, implicitly, by Jews and non-Jews alike: the final *Golem* film, and not merely the golem figure, was received as the hero of the day. Implicitly, Germany could achieve this postwar victory through the uptake of Jewish motifs and the involvement of Jewish artists—Henrik Galeen as coscriptwriter and Karl Freund behind the camera. As a clay monster that is molded and animated, the golem aptly served Wegener and his audiences as a mythic benchmark for the development of film under the unified banner of German cinema's technological magic. With the release of this third film, the golem had fulfilled Wegener's ethical and aesthetic aspirations.

* * *

The actor-filmmaker never returned to the golem story or embodied this figure again. But his incarnation of the golem left an indelible mark on twentieth-century culture, both through film screenings in the United States, as we shall see in chapter 2, and through the creation of a long-lasting visual legacy for film, comics, and theater. Not only did the 1920 film continue to impress audiences in other continents, but in time, it entered the pantheon of Weimar artistic cinema, spawning numerous adaptations and homages and providing a source of inspiration for both horror-monster films (*Frankenstein*, dir. James Whale, 1931) and avant-garde experimental cinema (*Birth of a Golem*, dir. Amos Gitai, 1990). While *Der Golem, wie er in die Welt kam* showed early twentieth-century audiences how to read the moving image and its mise-en-scène symbolically and how to observe "others" empathetically, today the wartime context of these lessons has been all but forgotten. This chapter has resituated Wegener's three golem films in the brutal clay world of World War I and in the filmmaker's experiences as a combatant in the trenches. Seen thus, the golem comes into relief as a creation molded and remolded in response to devastating battles and their traumatic aftermath. The clay monster, in alignment with the third film's clay architecture, evoked an anthropomorphized form of the trenches—both sheltering and threatening. But the singular golem also served as a symbolic counterweight to the mass destruction and trivialization of human life on the battlefield. In returning to this profound figure, Wegener eventually harnessed the new technologies of cinema to forge an alternative German "victory": the audience's empathy and its humanizing recognition of the suffering other.

2

The Golem Cult of 1921 New York

Between Redemption and Expulsion

Paul Wegener's third film, *Der Golem, wie er in die Welt kam* (*The Golem, How He Came into the World*), quickly crossed the Atlantic and premiered in New York in the summer of 1921. It played for sixteen weeks at the Criterion Theater near Times Square, a record run for any film that year. Reviewers in the Yiddish- and English-language press concurred that nothing like it had been seen on their side of the Atlantic; they were enamored with both Wegener's acting in the role of the golem and Hans Poelzig's settings.[1] Hugo Riesenfeld, the Criterion's musical director, made the film more appealing for American audiences by arranging a new prologue (in the form of a brief theatrical production) and musical score that drew on Jewish music old and new.[2] In keeping with the Criterion's policy of "continuous-performance-no-reserved-seats," the film's live prologue and music were performed several times daily to packed houses despite the stifling summer heat.[3] This enthusiastic American response was indicative of the new, post–World War I reception of German cinema. At the same time, the prologue—which staged the medieval expulsion of Jews from Nuremberg, Germany, in 1499—ensured that the film would be viewed with an eye (and ear) to the precarious situation of Jewish communities in Europe past and present.[4] The prologue also reenacted the Passover ceremony in Nuremberg in order to evoke the longue (and mythic) durée of Jewish bondage and salvation. In such a context, the golem emerged not only as a protector but also as a redeemer, a Messiah-like figure who could stave off the expulsion of persecuted Jews.

This new emphasis in the treatment of the golem materials needs to be understood in the context of recent Jewish history in Europe. Anti-

Semitic sentiment increased in Germany after World War I, as army generals and right-wing journalists placed part of the blame for the German defeat and ensuing civil strife on the Jews. The Russian civil wars that commenced after the Bolshevik revolution in November 1917 also prompted a wave of brutal anti-Jewish pogroms, and Jewish populations in Russia and Poland became displaced as a result of wars, revolution, and economic hardship. The majority of Jews who emigrated from Europe during this period headed to the U.S. In the year 1921 alone, 103,700 eastern European Jews arrived on American shores, joining over two million Jews who had relocated there starting in the late nineteenth century.[5] By the time Wegener's film screened in New York, 1.6 million Jews were living in the city.

The inflow of Jewish immigrants was not welcomed with open arms in the U.S. but, instead, led to a reactionary nativist movement; in May 1921, the U.S. Congress passed the Emergency Quota Act, restricting the overall immigration to 3 percent of the total number of foreign-born residents in the U.S. from a particular country (according to the 1910 census). In 1924, these quotas were reduced to 2 percent, and Jewish immigration from eastern Europe slowed to a trickle.[6] Yet in comparison to other immigrants, of the 2.5 million Jews who had already immigrated between 1880 and 1924, very few returned to their countries of origin. Jewish newcomers congregated in the big cities of the East Coast, particularly in New York, where they constituted close to 30 percent of the population and became embedded in the social and cultural life of the city.[7]

The Jewish community in the U.S. continued to be deeply affected by and concerned with the situation of the Jews in Europe; despite the distance from the actual battlefields and the sites of anti-Semitic violence, there was a sense of kinship with the European communities and a growing anxiety in the face of American nativism. In 1922, the writer Reuven Brainin, who had arrived in the U.S. in 1910, declared a global "golem epidemic" and compared European society to a soulless golem capable of inflicting torture and death on hundreds of thousands of

Jews. The U.S. was not blameless either, in his view, for in Washington sat "cultured people" who sought to pass laws that would prevent Jews orphaned by the pogroms from entering the country.[8] With reference to these pogroms, one viewer of the Criterion's prologue to *The Golem* claimed that when he was watching the Jews leaving Nuremberg on the stage, he saw before him contemporary Ukrainian refugees and Romanian Jews walking across Europe to escape persecution, as well as "the three orphan children whose parents were killed in an Eastern Galician pogrom and for whom that very day [he] had endeavored to find a home." For this viewer, the golem of Wegener's movie could become a metaphor for the defense and shelter that the Jews desperately needed. He wished that "someone would fashion another Golem and place upon him the words that would make him act."[9] In the process of transposition from Germany to the U.S., the cinematic golem narrative thus developed beyond Wegener's postwar concerns and his implicit vision of Germany's potential re-creation. It could also speak to American anxieties about immigration quotas and the survival of Jewish communities. The cinematic golem effectively bridged the great gap between Europe and the U.S., reinforcing the connection between Jews on both sides of the Atlantic and enabling a cultural exchange concerning the different aftermaths of the war.

The golem's reception in the U.S. also reveals an American awareness of the larger context in which the golem emerged around World War I. The Yiddish press accounted for the film's success as part of a worldwide phenomenon: "In recent times a kind of golem-cult has started to develop," pronounced Ts. H. Rubinstein in the pages of the Yiddish newspaper *Der tog* (The day) in December 1921. Reviewing the recent operetta at Max Gabel's Yiddish theater, he mentions the multiple German versions of the "original" old Jewish legend.[10] What the "golem-cult" reveals is the capacity of this story of creation not only to cross national, ethnic, and linguistic borders but also to call into question stark divisions between "low" and "high" culture. "The entire world stands now under the sign of the golem," Baruch Rivkin declared likewise in 1921, alluding to versions of the golem narrative that had recently appeared in Russia, Germany, and Austria, as well as to the screening of Wegener's film in the U.S. In his discussion of H. Leivick's lengthy dramatic poema *Der goylem*, Rivkin further explained that the tragedy of the monster figure lies not in its potential humanity and earthly desires but in the messianic calling that awakens within it. The "deep meaning" of the golem as a "surrogate" Messiah—one that offers a "material rather than spiritual redemption"—has finally emerged, for Rivkin, in the early 1920s and become a world-changing "power."[11]

The global excitement over the golem was indicative of this story's ability to constantly accrue new meanings, but it was also a tale of rapid adaptation into new media and forms of entertainment. Nowhere was that adaptation more obvious than in America. The year 1921 witnessed the screening of Wegener's film and the proliferation of Yiddish texts, stage productions, and newspaper columns, all retelling the golem narrative.[12] The golem "comes with gigantic steps," Brainin contended, appearing "in the theater, in the 'moving pictures,' in the press," and even in "political and societal life."[13] If the lengthy screening of Wegener's film was the most notable and popular manifestation of the post–World War I American golem mania, it was not the beginning of it. Rather, Leivick's modernist poema (a long dramatic poem), composed between 1917 and 1920 and published in New York in 1921, predated the screening of *The Golem* and accentuated the tragic aspects of the golem narrative.[14] The very same New York critics and audiences read Leivick's work, viewed Wegener's film, and attended the golem operettas.[15] They were all engaged in intensive "goleming," as Yitshok Even described it, when he wrote in 1922 about Gabel's production and the general golem craze, coining the term *goylemn zikh* (to golem). He even described a recent visit to the Old-New Synagogue in Prague with the goal of climbing up to its attic to find out what the golem's face looked like, that prototype for all the "goleming . . . in recent times."[16]

In Leivick's dystopian poema, Rabbi Loew banishes the true Messiah in favor of the clay monster that perpetuates the cycle of unending violence, ultimately turning against its own community and murdering Jews. Following on the heels of Leivick's work (and Wegener's film), two different theater producers adapted the story for the Yiddish American stage. Though these shows varied widely in substance, both avoided the foreboding atmosphere and nihilist violence of Leivick's work. Most notably, Max Gabel's 1921 *Der goylem* (The golem) translated this story of creation into an extremely popular operetta.[17] Informed by the film's prologue at the Criterion as well as by Wegener's cinematic aesthetic, this production staged scenes of Jewish exile and expulsion but did not paint diasporic life in macabre colors. Instead, Gabel's American operetta took a more lighthearted approach to the issue of Jewish persecution in Europe, ending on a note of integration and reconciliation.

The American penchant for theatrical and musical zest notwithstanding, the 1921 goleming that took place in New York epitomized the ongoing and often anxiety-ridden engagement of immigrant Jews with their new environment, as they attempted to find their own footing in America while remaining involved in the affairs of their home countries. These texts, films, and plays conveyed the tension between the human subjugation to greater forces and the search for an ethical mode of intervention in history, through the assertion of Jewish agency. The golem narrative, making its mainstream debut in the U.S. in the aftermath of the postwar pogroms in eastern Europe, also channeled Jewish frustrations regarding the American treatment of refugees, offering the fantasy of a redeemer who would "make Jews free."[18] Yet, as we shall see, this messianic impulse would always confront historical constraints and human foibles, leading, as in Leivick's drama, to catastrophic results.

Messianic Violence in H. Leivick's Poema *Der goylem*

In 1922, the Yiddish writer and journalist Israel Joshua Singer (1893–1944) reviewed H. Leivick's *Der goylem* for the Warsaw *Folkstsatung* (People's newspaper). Singer commented on the unique perspective afforded by this timely work: "Is it a coincidence that such a work was produced in none other than America, and precisely during the bloody years between 1915 and 1920? No. Only from a remove, only in the one relatively quiet place, which became less involved than others in the global blood-bath, only there could one see and feel the tragedy of the world—the conflict between creator and mass, between spirit and golem." Rather than accuse Leivick of being too distanced from the events in Europe, Singer considers the remove an advantage. He proceeds to compare World War I to a "gigantic global golem . . . that has risen on clay feet and set out on its path, knocking down everything that stands in the way." Just as the soldiers on the battlefield cannot see anything beyond what stands immediately before them, so, Singer contends, "every one of us has become a small bit of clay in the large golem." Therefore, perhaps only someone observing the events from a certain distance, like Leivick, might attempt to represent the larger picture, to "see and feel the tragedy." Singer's golem metaphor describes how the events of the war crushed and subsumed the individual and restricted a collective vision.[19]

As a relatively recent immigrant to the U.S., Leivick was deeply involved in the events that unfolded in Europe during the war and in its aftermath. Years later, in preparation for a 1935 speech, Leivick wrote, "The World War of 1914 gave a death blow to humanism. The animal has arisen. Cynicism has arrived. Bareness."[20] Leivick adds to Singer's imagery the reduction of the human to the animal, so that the sanctity of life is no longer preserved. In mentioning the "national and civil wars" raging at the time of the golem's creation in seventeenth-century Prague, *Der goylem* implicitly alludes to World War I and the Russian civil war. At the same time, focusing on the figure of the stranger or other, the golem, the dramatic poema can be read as indirectly concerning the situation of Jews as often unwelcome foreigners on American shores. Leivick's work thus balanced transnational and local concerns, appealing to readers of Yiddish literature both in eastern Europe and in the U.S.

Leivick (né Leyvik Halpern) in his youth had become a member of the Bund—the general union of Jewish workers in Lithuania, Poland,

and Russia, founded in 1897—and after a period of imprisonment in Minsk for his opposition to the czarist regime, he was sentenced to forced labor in Siberia. In 1913, Leivick escaped from Siberia and immigrated to the U.S., where he began publishing poetry in the journals of the Yiddish impressionist poets known as *Di yunge* (The young). Benjamin and Barbara Harshav comment that Leivick's poetry was marked by "sublimated suffering, messianic fervor, a mystical tone, and naïve humanism, combined with a Neo-Romantic musicality of harmonious verse lines that were imbued with Russian Symbolism."[21] Leivick started his first poetic drama, *Di keyten fun moshiekh* (The chains of the Messiah), in 1908 while in prison; he then revised and published it in 1939. In this work, the angel Azriel rebels against the idea that the Messiah must passively wait until the end of times in his gilded shackles. Calling for an unshackled Messiah who can redeem humanity, Azriel describes how on earth "bodies / roll in filth, in worms / in prisons, in subjugation, in exile / in chains, in blood, on the brink of death."[22] Leivick contends here with the human desire to intervene in the course of history rather than remain mere bystanders to unfolding events. On the one hand, having himself suffered, as a Bundist, "in filth, in worms / in prisons," the poet criticizes the notion of messianic postponement. On the other hand, the open-endedness of the drama makes Azriel's fall from the divine realm appear futile and hubristic.

The problem of reconciling Jewish action and even aggression with the notion of messianic postponement returns in Leivick's *Der goylem*, composed in New York in the late 1910s. This dramatic poema also centers on a leader, the Maharal of Prague, who, like Azriel, will not wait for redemption but urges it on. In a key scene, the Messiah, who has apparently arrived too soon, reflects on the difference between the golem and himself, describing the golem as a redeemer who uses "his fist" and "his axe." The Maharal chases away the unnecessary Messiah, contending that instead he has created "a second man to do [his] bidding / the only one permitted to be dark, / permitted to shed blood, spill blood for blood."[23] The opening image of the first printed version of the drama is, aptly, that of the axe-bearing golem, drawn in bold strokes by the artist Jennings (Yehuda) Tofel (figure 2.1). At the end of the drama, after the golem has killed Jews, the Maharal laments that by creating a "super-human" golem, he has turned his back to the patient old ways of his people, who have always quietly waited for redemption, "spilling" the blood he "desired to save." To add to the golem's revolt against its maker and society, Leivick's rabbi rebels against the Jewish norms of passivity and nonviolence, "wanting what the foe lays claim to" and in so doing bringing disaster on his community.[24] Leivick's violent golem paved the way, as we will see, for future American and Israeli golems who do not act in mere self-defense but are brutally vengeful.

In writing *Der goylem*, Leivick drew on Yudl Rosenberg's 1909 Yiddish *Seyfer nifloes Maharal* (*The Golem or The Miraculous Deeds of Rabbi Leyb*) but departed from the tradition of Jewish praise literature. He followed I. L. Peretz's earlier symbolist dramas, *Di goldene keyt* (*The Golden Chain*, 1907) and *Bay nakht afn alten mark* (*At Night in the Old Marketplace*, 1907), also standing in dialogue with contemporary modernist apocalyptic writings by Peretz Markish and Moyshe-Leyb Halpern, composed in response to the war and brutal pogroms in eastern Europe.[25] Published by the modernist New York Yiddish press Amerika, *Der goylem* is written in blank verse and divided into eight scenes bearing symbolic titles such as "Clay," "Walls," and "Revelations."[26] Leivick used the same high register of poetic Yiddish throughout *Der goylem*, not differentiating between characters through variations in dialect, register, or style. Much of the action of the play takes place offstage (as when the golem kisses the rabbi's daughter and, later, when it murders Jews), and the scenes themselves include lengthy monologues, revealing the rabbi's thoughts and aspirations and the golem's desires and hallucinations.

Leivick portrays an indeterminate golem figure, eschewing any clear-cut allegory. The ambiguous symbols and multiple meanings of his poema allowed for a range of literary and political interpretations: most notably, Leivick's Russian contemporaries read it as pro-

FIGURE 2.1. Jennings Tofel's image of the golem in
H. Leivick's *Der goylem*, 1921.

Bolshevik.[27] In 1925, at an evening in Leivick's honor in Moscow, the
communist critics, led by Moyshe Litvakov, interpreted the golem figure as representative only of the revolutionary proletariat, omitting the
"tragic-Jewish" dimension of the story. In this reading of the piece, Yossele the golem is a symbol of the "rebellious folk person," and Russian
Jews called for a complete identification with the golem and its use of
physical strength, rather than with the Maharal.[28] From Leivick's viewpoint, the golem's "childish tears" and its "yearning for light and love"
were meant to manifest a messianic affinity.[29] As he contended in 1953,
Der goylem exposes the darker side of Jewish participation in twentieth-
century wars and revolutions. Avraham Novershtern and Sara Simchi
Cohen have also suggested that Leivick depicts an intense psychic and

physical bond between monster and creator and that the two cannot be fully distinguished and pitted against each other, as in the Russian reading of the poema.[30]

In writing about the destruction and devastation that, according to the Maharal figure, must take place en route to redemption, Leivick took up the notion that "Jewish Messianism is in its origins and by its nature . . . a theory of catastrophe." In Gershom Scholem's explanation, catastrophe and utopia are but "two sides of the Messianic event"; they go hand in hand rather than follow each other in a more logical progression. In the apocalyptic strand of messianism, the transition from the present to the messianic future involves a "revolutionary, cataclysmic element," and it constitutes a break in historical time.[31] Living in the throes of "blood libels, blood and fire and—destruction," the Jewish community led by the Maharal seeks out such a revolution, inviting a violent response on behalf of their savior.[32] The Maharal believes that "[God] has sent / this helpless servant, all helpless himself / to help us. Darkness itself, he is to bring / us brightness."[33] The Maharal's creation of a redeemer constitutes an assumption of Jewish power and an entrance onto the stage of history, but in the drama, this action leads only to absurdity and nihilism since, as David Biale explains, "metahistorical longings" cannot be realized in "the concrete realm of history," just as "the real world can never fully reflect mystical reality."[34] As the drama progresses, it becomes evident that although the golem has achieved the original mission—to prevent the blood-libel scheme of the priest Tadeush—it will not bring "brightness." The desperate hope that "the sword brings comfort and relief" is disproven when the golem's axe lands on Jewish heads.[35]

Rather than uphold the necessity of violence on the way to successful political change, Leivick's apocalyptic text culminates in chaos and terror. Having prevented the blood libel, the golem still emerges a broken entity that cannot find its place in society, whether Jewish or human. With its first utterances as a phantom, when it warns the rabbi not to create it, the golem expresses the wish not to exchange its "darkness" and "stillness" for "the bustling of streets and human beings." The golem retains, even after its animation, something of the shadowy phantom. In this sense, it is a product of the era and its manner of "trampling" the human and disregarding the sacredness of life. The Maharal molds the golem and charges it with the mission of "a nation's messenger, a man of might," disregarding the golem's desires and the ruinous effect of this mission on the golem and its surroundings.[36]

Though Leivick borrows plot elements, settings, and characters from Rosenberg's *Seyfer nifloes Maharal*, he departs from this text in his ambivalent portrayal of the erring and cruel rabbi and his indeterminate golem. In Rosenberg's chapbook, the golem is a mute entity that uses violence in a justifiable rather than an excessive manner. When first molding and animating the golem, Rosenberg's Maharal and his helpers inform the anthropoid that its name is Joseph, dressing it in Jewish clothes. The mute golem becomes a servant in the rabbi's courtroom and is given the nicknames "Yossele the golem" and "Yossele the mute." In the section "What Rabbi Leyb Used the Golem For," Rosenberg describes how the golem is disguised as a "gentile porter" that roams the ghetto streets at night between Purim and Passover, catching Christian offenders who are plotting against the Jews and delivering them to the authorities.[37] The golem uses violence to enforce the law that the Christian authorities will not impose. As a Jewish-like monster that can "pass" as a goy and perform physical feats usually associated with lower-class men, Rosenberg's golem exhibits both Jewish and non-Jewish attributes.

Leivick's golem is a different monster altogether: endowed with the powers of speech and human-like self-awareness, its behavior and appearance are less predictable and classifiable. For instance, the name that the Maharal gives his creation, Yossel (as distinct from Yossele), a diminutive form of Joseph, connotes at one and the same time the warring Messiah son of Joseph and the Yiddish term for the sacrificed Jesus.[38] The stage directions provide us with the first image of the golem: "Huge eyes. . . . Thick lips, deeply indented corners. A frozen empty smile on the lips, empty yet twisted, virtually on the brink of weeping.

Black, curly hair on his head, beard, and mustache. His eyes open wider and wider as he gapes at everything."[39] The description of the golem's face as an exaggerated mask underscores its volatile nature, shifting inexplicably between extremes. In the 1925 translation and adaptation of *Der goylem* at the Habima Theater in Moscow, under the direction of Boris Illich Vershilov, Aharon Meskin enacted the eponymous monster as such an erratic creature: at moments bursting out in childish laughter and at other times raging uncontrollably.[40]

While the golem's "thick lips" and dark hair might be construed as stereotypically Jewish, Leivick depicts its body as gigantic and powerful, so that the rabbi's wife immediately remarks, "he doesn't look at all like a Jew." She further observes, "Such hands / such shoulders this person of yours has / it frightens me."[41] At the end of the second act, the rabbi also casts doubt on the golem's mission as he contemplates its monstrous physique: "Is that the man I dreamed into existence? / My champion? My envoy? . . . He? Such arms! / Such legs, such shoulders! . . . So much body, flesh! [*azoy fil guf*] / How could there be so much dumb sorrow?"[42] The golem's overwhelming body (*"groysen guf,"* the rabbi says) is surprisingly incompatible here with the heroic mission envisioned for it. The rabbi bemoans the fact that in order to protect his community, he must create a being that poses a threat to the very same community and that cannot be integrated into Jewish society or human society at large. For the poet Aaron Glantz-Leyeles, Leivick's golem embodies "brutal physical power," expressive of a Jewish "drive for revenge against our enemies."[43]

The rabbi's reaction to the golem as a piece of flesh conveys his general ambivalence toward exhibitions of excessive masculinity, even when needed for Jewish self-defense.[44] At the same time, when the rabbi encounters the true Messiah, he rejects him on the basis of his physical inadequacy:

> And can his fingers coil in iron fists
> And crush and bash and smash and shatter skulls?

And can he even stand the stench of blood
And spill it? . . .
. . . And can his hands,
His delicate hands, scratch in the filth of pits,
Looking for limbs, looking for bones and ashes?[45]

The emphasis on the Messiah's "delicate hands" and his inability to exact revenge underscores the contrast with the golem, whose massive arms and hands can surely do so.

Dressed as a lower-class porter, Rosenberg's protective golem embodies the *ba'al guf*, the strapping or muscular young man who was then emerging as a type in Jewish literature, for example, in Hebrew and Yiddish works by Ḥayim Naḥman Bialik, Sholem Asch, and Isaac Meir Weissenberg. These "little-noticed Jews, the butchers and porters and teamsters with their physical prowess and passions," to quote Irvin Howe and Eliezer Greenberg, were imagined as a class that could "take matters into their own hands," protecting themselves from gentile attacks.[46] Sharon Gillerman writes that such images of strong Jewish men arose in Yiddish literature out of "the experience of political disenfranchisement and physical vulnerability, combined with rising violence and a desire among Jews to exercise some form of self-defense."[47] The indeterminacy of the golem encouraged its literary adaptation as a new type of strong man that can perform a reverse ethnic drag, appropriating external non-Jewish ideals. Rosenberg's golem as porter is such a positively recast *ba'al guf*. The "goyish" costume of this figure reminds the reader, however, that this type marks the border with the Christian world. By describing the Maharal and his wife's negative reaction to the golem's body as not "at all" Jewish, Leivick highlights the ambivalence of the Jewish creator who has brought a *ba'al guf* into existence.

If in Hillel Rogoff's *Forverts* (Forward) review of *Der goylem*, "the Jews in exile are abandoned and vulnerable because they are sheep among wolves, . . . too physically weak and too spiritually exalted," then the golem embodies the notion of (male) Jewish transformation into a gentile-like man.⁴⁸ This figure's alienation and ultimate breakdown in Leivick's work, as well as its lack of self-determination, bring to the fore, however, the risks entailed in such a transformation. Unlike Rosenberg's mute and compliant Joseph, Leivick's golem is out of control from the very first moment of animation. An overgrown newborn, the clay monster must adjust too quickly to the world and has difficulty visually decoding its surroundings and understanding how to maneuver its body. The clay monster's sense of physical confinement and insecurity in the rabbi's home develops into paranoid and violent hallucinations that accentuate its rebelliousness. Its violence is directed both at the rabbi—as creator—and at itself: "I want my hand to hit / Your head, and yet I cannot move. . . . / I want to twist my head off from my shoulders."⁴⁹ These described, though not executed, physical gestures are prompted by an apocalyptic vision of the sunrise as a fire that comes through the windows and sets the walls ablaze. The golem seeks to escape the home and its persecuting wall and run toward the fire.⁵⁰ In subsequent hallucinations, the golem sees itself as an unwanted thing, beaten and trampled by a Jewish mob that attempts to bury it alive. Similarly, it internalizes the creator's revulsion at the sight of its body, declaring, "I am repelled, disgusted by my flesh, / Revolted by my glassy, bulging eyes."⁵¹

At the climax of the play, the rabbi sends the golem on its most important mission: to retrieve the vials of blood planted by the priest Tadeush in the cave underneath the five-walled tower (or palace in the Yiddish version). Leivick depicts this ruined gothic site, borrowed from Rosenberg's text, as blackened, covered in cobwebs, its doors missing and windowpanes broken.⁵² It provides a shelter, nonetheless, for the sick beggars of Prague and for the golem, when banished from the Maharal's home after kissing the rabbi's daughter in public. When venturing into this eerie underground space, the golem not only encounters supernatural beings—"cave spirits" and walking corpses that have risen from their graves—but also "a man with a cross," that is, Jesus, and "a young beggar," the Messiah.⁵³ The three potential redeemers appear equally ineffectual in their complementary missions, and the chorus of corpses pronounces the final nihilist verdict on the possibility of redemption:

> Look, all three are sitting there,
> Never stirring, never speaking
>
> You must know just who they are,
> Sing the story of their anguish
>
> There is nothing more to sing
> There the cross lies, not to carry.
> There the chain lies, not to clatter.
> There the axe lies, not to strike with.
>
> So we sing the song of nothing.[54]

In Yiddish, the song of nothing is filled with clattering, alternating rhymes in contrast to the blank verse that characterizes the majority of lines in *Der goylem*. This sing-song poetry heightens the macabre mood and emphasizes the emptiness of the verse itself ("there is nothing more to sing"). The symbolic objects of redemption also lose their functionality, and the three saviors appear immobile, so that those awaiting them have been fooled and punished for their hopefulness. The chorus's song and dance of "nothing" then devolves into a "song of madness," "anger," and "nonsense."[55] When the corpses return to their graves, the hallucinatory scene with the three saviors vanishes, and the golem appears sitting alone, guarding the two flasks of blood. At first, the golem is completely unresponsive and does not even recognize its creator and master. "His entire face," Leivick writes in the stage directions, "appears as though insane. He doesn't move a limb."[56] The golem's appearance renders the power of hallucination visible. In the dramatic medium, moreover, these visions are not merely reported but dramatized, enacted by different characters, thus blurring the borders between dreams and waking reality, hallucinations and "history." In this sense, the drama as a whole becomes suffused with the golem's demonic messianism.[57]

When encountering the Messiah in the cave scene, the golem declares that "rottenness" exudes from him, since the beggar's feet are wounded and covered in rags.[58] Rather than represent a new era, a break from the past, the Messiah's body is decaying and lethargic, in contrast to the golem's more vital, "newborn" body. The two characters stage different types of living death: the Messiah is suspended in eternal waiting; the golem lives an accelerated existence that ends abruptly and catastrophically. While the golem wants to be with the young and old beggars, the Maharal chases the two away, telling the golem that "their time has not arrived. Now is your time."[59] The Messiah also admits, in a later scene, that the time is not right for him. The world should not be expected to "halt all killing," he says ironically, just because the Messiah has decided to arrive. Paradoxically, because the world is in dire need of redemption, it is incapable of receiving the Messiah and must resort to the golem as "redeemer / with his fist and with his axe."[60]

The final act, titled "The Last Mission," concerns the disastrous outcome of the golem's descent into the underworld of the cave and the rabbi's inability to understand his mistake until it is too late. The act takes place on a Friday evening in the anteroom of the old synagogue, where the golem appears completely altered: broken, neglected, and unkempt, wearing only one shoe, and unable to emerge from paralyzing visions.[61] The "savage" golem who "cannot pray" is positioned here, according to the Yiddish literary critic Bal-Makhshoves, "outside of the Jewish people . . . cut-off from tradition, . . . half-naked."[62] When the Maharal finally arrives, he tells the golem to start "to live as everybody lives, / Just as Jews live—." The Maharal is unwilling to assume responsibility for his creation, for the golem's suffering and its actions, and suggests instead that the "miserable" golem "try going to the synagogue with all / The worshipers and try to understand."[63] Fully aware that the golem's restlessness is its "fate," the rabbi nonetheless fantasizes that the golem could manage to fade into the background, to live among Jews, like Rosenberg's mute golem, and pretend to be more like them. When the rabbi departs to perform the Sabbath services, the golem is further dehumanized as it crawls on the floor, moans, and pulls at its hair and clothes. After reviving itself with a sip of water and some bread, the golem picks up the axe and breaks out through the window.[64]

In the story of the Prague golem, the Maharal forgets to take the ineffable name out of the golem's mouth on Sabbath eve, and the golem then becomes enraged and starts to destroy the ghetto. In Leivick's modernist retelling, the rabbi does not use a magical formula or evoke the ineffable name of God; his desertion and neglect, rather than his forgetfulness, are at fault. Whereas in the Prague tale, the rabbi withdraws the magical formula just in time and restores the peace, reciting the Sabbath Psalm once more in the synagogue, in *Der goylem*, Leivick superimposes the Sabbath ritual on the golem's deterioration and resulting violence—a disturbing dissonance of sacred ritual and destruction.[65] According to the stage directions, as the golem moans, the Sabbath prayers are audible through the wall, and when the golem rushes into the street with the axe, "every word of the cantor is now clearly heard" as he begins to recite the Sabbath Psalm. The holy recitation becomes the macabre soundtrack for the golem's sacrilegious rampage. When screams and cries are heard outside, the community ceases to pray and runs in fearful chaos into the street. After arresting the golem with its bloody axe, the Maharal must then shield it from the angry and terrified Jewish crowd.[66]

Since the golem's violence is described secondhand, because it takes place "offstage" in this verse drama, the reader has access only to the reactions of the crowd and the rabbi, who all insist that the golem has shed "Jewish blood." The emphasis on the Jewishness of the blood, especially following the blood-libel attempt, suggests that Christian persecution has been internalized. Instead of the priest, the Jewish leader—the Maharal—takes upon himself the responsibility for the violence, claiming that he has "sinned against all Jews."[67] The rabbi then determines the golem's "final mission," ending its life simply by ordering it to "breathe out [its] final breath."[68] Without any ritual and in solitude, the golem is put to rest, but with this unresolved ending, the reader does not experience the satisfaction of a catastrophe averted. Instead, the resumption of the Sabbath prayers provides an ironic closure to the golem's existence outside the boundaries of Jewish and human life.

If for Polish and Russian critics Leivick's drama addressed the events taking place in Europe, despite its publication in the U.S.—namely, the horrors of war (Singer) or else the triumphs of communism (Litvakov)— *Der goylem* could also be interpreted against the backdrop of the local immigrant population and the concerns of that community. By connecting the golem's disruptive words and deeds to its status as an undesirable outcast, Leivick urged his readers to rethink what constitutes a Jew, and a Jewish man at that, in this new environment. He raised the question of the status and communal identity of those immigrant Jews who have already taken off one shoe, as it were, and "cannot pray." Just as *Der goylem* underscores the potential alienation of the "newly made" Jewish American male from the Jewish community and its leaders, it also reveals the golem's general inability to find its place and be recognized in human society at large. In this respect, the poema could have also spoken to the experiences of Jewish immigrants vis-à-vis the general American population. As outsiders who needed to negotiate the constraints of the social world into which they arrived, Jewish immigrants from eastern Europe resembled the golem in its initial inaptitude and ongoing sense of not belonging. The intense pressure as a result of the golem's attempted "assimilation" into human and Jewish communities and its self-alienation can be read in the American context: rather than evoke a sense of security in the new "*goldene medine*," Leivick's poema expressed anxieties concerning both the internal resilience of Jewish communities postimmigration and the ability of Jews to cope with the pressures of change and integration.

The Spectacle of Expulsion: Paul Wegener's Film at the Criterion Theater

While Leivick's poema and Max Gabel's operetta, discussed shortly, could be read and appreciated only by the Yiddish-speaking immigrant population, Wegener's *The Golem*, which premiered on June 19, 1921, at the nine-hundred-seat Criterion Theater near Times Square, enjoyed broader success. On October 9, the *New York Times* reported that "the golem is going and going" and that when the film closed the following week, it would have had a record run of "sixteen weeks and four days in the same theater."[69] The promotional ads for the film, published in both English- and Yiddish-language newspapers, feature the golem standing behind stone tablets engraved with the Ten Commandments. "Thou shalt not make unto thee any graven image" appears in large print (figure 2.2).[70] The golem both holds the tablets, Moses-like, and also peers down at them, as if trying to decipher the letters. Made of clay by a human who imitates God through the act of creation, the golem is a "graven image" of sorts, used to rescue the Jewish community and thus supplant the need for divine intervention. Paradoxically, the prohibition against creating graven images appears in an ad for a movie that invites Jewish and non-Jewish audiences to view the ambiguous golem as a threatening idol and a redeeming Moses. Wegener had also, symbolically, taken over the theme of the golem and presented it in a new guise.

Having been exposed to Robert Wiene's *The Cabinet of Dr. Caligari* and to the aesthetics of Max Reinhardt's theater, American critics located *The Golem*'s unconventional mise-en-scène and its unrealistic treatment of the Jewish milieu within the context of German theatrical and cinematic expressionism.[71] Jewish and non-Jewish reviewers extolled the artistic merits of the film, including Wegener's acting as the golem, the architectural set design, and the cinematography. The Jewish critics did note Wegener's "mistakes" and exaggerations when it came to representing Jewish prayer and conduct, also complaining that Wegener did not follow Jewish renditions of the golem narrative, such as Rosen-

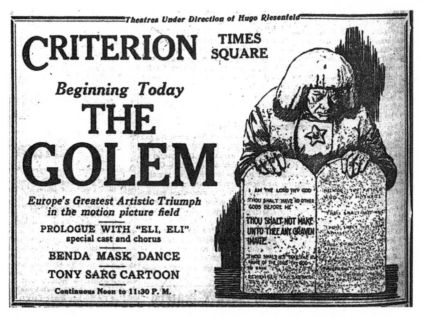

FIGURE 2.2. Advertisement for Paul Wegener's *The Golem* at the Criterion Theater. (*New York Tribune*, June 1921)

berg's.[72] The extrafilmic devices, theatrical and musical, all enhanced, by contrast, the "old Jewish atmosphere" of *The Golem*.[73]

Wegener's film, as we have seen, ignited the "golem-cult" in 1921 New York, and its attraction can be attributed both to the cinematic spectacle itself and to the new American packaging that augmented the Jewish dimension of the story. In addition to the theatrical "prologue," the Criterion's presentation included several other pieces before and after the film: a short film depicting the "old Jewish community in Prague where the golem legend was born," a masked dance, and a short Buster Keaton comedy.[74] Miriam Hansen has explained that silent-era exhibition practices, including live musical accompaniment and theatrical pieces, gave the audience a sense of collective presence. These extrafilmic components enhanced the lived space and time of the movie theater rather than subordinating it to the events taking place on the screen. They "allowed for locally and culturally specific acts of reception, opening up a margin of participation and unpredictability." The space of the cinema functioned, moreover, as an "alternative public sphere" for social groups like immigrants and women, "providing an intersubjective horizon through—and against—which they could negotiate the specific displacements and discrepancies of their experience."[75] In other words, rather than serve as a vehicle of assimilation, cinematic exhibition often promoted ethnically specific collective experiences that reaffirmed the group's sense of identity. Screened in the mainstream Broadway movie theater to viewers of different genders and ethnic backgrounds, Riesenfeld's *Golem* program still managed to forge a sense of Jewish communality through Yiddish and Hebrew songs and theatrical performance. The German film thus mediated the Jewish refugee experience for American viewers.

The prologue in particular left a deep impression on the viewers, as one member of the audience, I. L. Bril, recalled:

> The stage is darkened and in that darkness come an old man and a lad. They sit down and the old man tells the lad the story of the expulsion of the Jews from Nuremberg, Germany. And as he speaks the curtain parts and we behold a Seder evening scene. The family is sitting round the table; they sing that part of the Hallel which begins "Min Hametzar Korosi Yoh Ononi Bamerchavyoh" (out of my straitness I called upon the Lord: the Lord answered me with enlargement). And suddenly there is a knock on the door which upon being opened admits a messenger from the ruler who tells the Jews that their expulsion has been decreed and that they must leave within a month. The messenger departs and the curtain descends whilst the Jews are still chanting the Psalm. The next scene shows the streets of the city Nuremberg; the Jews with the wanderer's staff in their hands and the packs upon their backs are leaving. Again they sing and this time it is "Eli, Eli"—O Lord, O Lord, why hast thou forsaken us? Then came the picture of "The Golem" telling its story of how the Jews in Prague were saved. "The Golem" is a legend, and the screen version makes it all so real, so vivid.[76]

The theatrical prologue replicates the contents of the images that Wegener's Rabbi Loew projects on the wall of the court for the entertainment of the gentile courtiers, featuring wandering Jews with their staffs and packs. It also reenacts the arrival of the edict of expulsion in the film itself, delivered by the courtier, the messenger of ill tidings who subsequently becomes the lover of the rabbi's daughter. The prologue draws a connection between the cinematic spectacle of stereotypical Jewish wandering and suffering and the specific historical event of the 1499 expulsion from Nuremberg. The framing figures of the old man and the lad who introduce the scene stage the intergenerational transmission of (cautionary) Jewish history and myth, as occurs in the yearly recitation of the Passover Haggadah.

The interrupted Passover celebration in Nuremberg further reminds spectators that the Israelite plight in Egypt and the wandering in the desert can recur in modern times. It echoes Rosenberg's and Leivick's evocation of a Passover blood libel and their use of the golem to stave off Christian attacks. Instead of the prophet Elijah, who is supposed to visit the Passover celebration and drink wine from his cup, a messenger arrives with the expulsion decree. The golem film functions within this context as a response to the Jewish cry "why hast thou forsaken us?" since it features a rabbi capable of saving his community with the help of an artificial strongman. The display of hopeless exile in the prologue to the Criterion screening offset the success of Rabbi Loew with his golem in the film itself. The fantasy of the golem as protector became more "vivid" and captivating in this manner. It resounded in relationship to the external American prologue and not just in the context of the internal threat within the film. By contrast, when the film screened in Germany, reviews underscored its fantastical and dreamy, even "primeval" qualities, distancing it from the present day, in line with Wegener's own stated preference for the fantastic.[77]

While the original German symphonic score for the film by Hans Landsberger created a modernist program of "logically linked sound patterns," Hugo Riesenfeld's new score forged a musical mosaic that ranged from "religious chants of the thirteenth century to modern Jewish compositions."[78] Like the American score, intended to heighten the Jewishness of the film, the theatrical prologue inserted Wegener's production into a specifically Jewish context, including a program of "Jewish music." The music that accompanied the prologue accentuated the historical context and the narrative of Jewish duress by combining two renditions of psalms: the traditional Passover Hallel (Psalm 118) and the modern song "*Eyli, eyli*" ("Eli, Eli"; "My God, My God"), based on Psalm 22. Both "*Min ha-metsar*" and "Eli, Eli" are appeals to God for help, and in the case of the former verse, God responds with abundance. Another review mentions that the actors of the prologue left the stage while singing a wordless exile song (*goles lid*), "so heartfelt and Jewish that it brings tears to one's eyes."[79] The Russian-born Jewish composer and music ethnographer Lazare Saminsky, who had recently immigrated to the U.S. and became, in 1924, the musical director of Temple Emanu-El in New York, was responsible for parts of the orchestration and for "*Min ha-metsar*." Saminsky lent this scene its musical authenticity, having researched and collected Jewish liturgy during his ethnographic expeditions in the Pale of Settlement (together with S. An-Sky). One newspaper reported that he managed to represent musically how an "old person would tell of the suffering of the people of Israel."[80]

To augment Saminsky's music in the prologue, Riesenfeld drew on a proven "hit," recycling Jacob Sandler's "Eli, Eli," which had already been used for the prologue of the film *Humoresque* in 1920, featuring the Jewish basso profundo Emanuel List.[81] Sandler wrote "Eli, Eli" in 1896 for an American operetta, *The Jewish King of Poland for a Night*, performed at the Windsor Theater, and the song became an instant sensation, rising quickly from a "stage tune" to the status of a Jewish "religious folk hymn." According to Irene Heskes, "Eli, Eli" is a "quintessential Jewish lament" that incorporates and popularizes elements of "traditional liturgical chant."[82] Spectators of Wegener's film recalled, through this musical choice, the recent *Humoresque*, which itself ran for twelve consecutive weeks on Broadway, primarily at the Criterion, during the previous summer. List was engaged to sing again for *The Golem*, adding to his already extensive appearances with "Eli, Eli." He was accompanied by a large choir and soloists (over twenty artists in total), providing the song with a "new interpretation" that had "never been sung anywhere before."[83] Some Jewish critics complained, however, that the Criterion could have omitted "Eli, Eli," since that song had already been performed ad nauseam.[84]

Reporting on *The Golem*'s prologue, the *New York Times* critic wrote that "then, as now, the introductory measures by the Windsor Theater orchestra were the signal for a great demonstration on the part of the audience."[85] The participation of the audience created a sense of specific "collective presence," but it was, nonetheless, semiscripted and predictable. "The epitome of difference, of melodic sounds as yet unintegrated into American music," in Heskes's words, "Eli, Eli" elicited a strong emotional response on the part of moviegoers, who sensed that they were about to view a cinematic performance of Jewishness.[86] Like the American films *Humoresque* or *His People* (1925), *The Golem* too rendered Jewishness itself "a kind of commodity" for general American consumption and not only for Jewish audiences.[87] When the film premiered, the *New York Tribune* described it as "a photograph of Jewish hopes and Jewish despair in the darkest period of the existence of that race."[88] The use of mournful, foreign-sounding music in the prologue and throughout the score enhanced the otherness of the film and evoked the atmosphere of darkness and despair that could occasion an artificial creation such as the golem. Through this music, the film's exhibitors at the Criterion emphasized the Jewish dimension of the golem narrative, encouraging viewers to draw connections to their present times and to the situation of Jewish communities in Europe and the U.S. With the help of the framing additions, the golem of Prague became a spectacle of Jewish survival and continuity against all odds.

In this new American framework, Wegener's images of the Jewish population and its ghetto no longer spoke to a defeated German nation and its hope for rebirth and recovery. Rather, they implicitly evoked the

conditions of Jewish mass immigration and resettlement amid rising nativism that "questioned the racial admissibility of Jews" and their ability
to assimilate into the American nation.[89] In the early twentieth century,
established Jewish immigrants tended to move to uptown Manhattan or
to Brooklyn and the Bronx, whereas newcomers would congregate on
the Lower East Side, then referred to as the "ghetto." In contrast to the
imagined ghetto in the film, the ghetto Jews of New York might have
feared anti-Semitic attitudes and restrictions but not expulsions. The
quotas placed on immigration, however, imperiled their relatives and
friends who remained in Europe and had already suffered the devastating effects of World War I. Reports about the unstable conditions in
eastern Europe and, subsequently, about the massacres of Jewish populations appeared on a daily basis in the Yiddish press. The new film lent
the clichéd tropes of exile, rehearsed on the stage and within the film
itself, new meaning in this context of Jewish-American relations. The
golem, like the *goldene medina* itself, was a potential savoir of Jewish
refugees, but it could also turn against them.

The review of the film premiere in the *New York Tribune* taps into
these fears concerning the situation of Jews in Europe when it describes
medieval Jews as "chattel," unable "to leave the ghetto without permission" or pursue any occupation aside from "money-lending" and "sell-
ing old clothes." Because the Jews were incapable of open revolt, they
dreamt up the all-powerful golem that "saved the Jewish people from
destruction."[90] The film reminded Jewish viewers of the fear of dispos-
session that they had suffered and that many of the Jews in their former
countries continued to endure. With the vision of an enclosed and id-
iosyncratic Jewish ghetto, Wegener's *The Golem* thus provided a double
fantasy for American viewers: it portrayed a Jewish community striving
to retain its ethnic and religious particularity in the face of external pressures and envisioned the creation of an artificial hero tasked with saving
the Jews from expulsion and preventing their endless wandering.

Although Wegener's film evokes apprehensions about the future of
Jewish communities and suggests that a territorial (possibly Zionist) so-

lution is necessary, it nonetheless ends on a more reassuring note than Leivick's poema does. The film stages the golem's violent rampage, but the monster conveniently murders the daughter's Christian lover rather than any of the Jews. The golem ends its existence outside the ghetto, in the hands of a child that, by treating the golem as a plaything rather than a tool or a weapon, restores the equilibrium of the Jewish community. The "final mission" of Leivick's golem, by contrast, is its death: it draws its "final breath" not as a recognized hero but as a feared murderer, leaving readers to contend with the golem's unforgivable violence and the Maharal's "sin." Leivick's text and Wegener's film complemented each other in the New York of 1921, raising similar concerns about Jewish exile, immigration, and integration. But they offered distinct visions of the golem as hero (Wegener) and antihero (Leivick) and of the potential unity or discord within a Jewish community striving to defend itself and uphold its boundaries. The American theatrical and musical additions to the film also enhanced its contemporary relevance. Thus, Bril asks at the end of his aforementioned review, "The Seder, the messenger announcing the forthcoming expulsion, the exodus, . . . 'Eli, Eli,' 'The Golem.' Do they belong to the past alone?" Yearning for the "mystic words that would make Jews free," he asserts that the golem story of the grandparents has become equally relevant for the grandchildren who have just arrived, as refugees, in Ellis Island.[91]

A Jewish *Goylem* for the American *Oylem*

The success of Wegener's film at the Criterion encouraged Jewish theater producers to attempt their own versions of the golem narrative. Ads that appeared in daily Yiddish papers in 1922 show that producers relied on the public's familiarity with Wegener's film, since they replicated the golem costume and the film's Orientalist aesthetic. Two Yiddish operettas were staged in close succession and drew the crowds: *Der goylem* (The golem)—an adaptation of the Jewish Hungarian playwright Albert Kovessy's drama (translated into Yiddish by Mark Schweid) at Max

Gabel's Theater in Harlem—and Joseph Tanzman's *Der prager goylem* (The Prague golem) at the Lyric Theater in Brooklyn.[92] Tanzman's oper- etta, like Gabel's, included a range of music: prayer hymns; romantic duets; and happy, comical songs; as well as Tanzman's performance of "*Der oylem iz a goylem*" (The public is an idiot).[93] The concurrent and competitive staging of these productions in early 1922 attests to the gen- eral enthusiasm for the golem at this particular moment (figure 2.3).[94] In the 1921–1922 theater season, critics singled out Gabel's *The Golem* and S. An-sky's acclaimed *The Dybbuk*, playing at Maurice Schwartz's Yiddish Art Theater, as the most "original" works of the season.[95] Since then, both Gabel's and Tanzman's operettas have been forgotten, but the surviving, handwritten Yiddish text of Gabel's production enables us to analyze, for the first time, the translation of the golem narrative to the popular Yiddish stage.

The "musical legend" concerning the golem premiered on Decem- ber 16, 1921, with a sixty-person choir and thirty musical numbers. In adapting the golem narrative to the Yiddish theater stage, Gabel fol- lowed in Riesenfeld's footsteps in the Criterion's prologue and score, emphasizing the threat of expulsion and homelessness and using music to enhance the pathos of this tale of creation. The music, composed and arranged by Louis Friedsell, consisted of prayer-like songs such as "Mer- ciful God," folk tunes such as "The Redemption," romantic duets, and even Gypsy-inspired numbers. Friedsell, like Riesenfeld before him, had "collected old Jewish theatrical motifs" and combined them to create this operetta.[96] Interweaving these musical numbers into a "riveting" dramatic plot, the operetta belonged, according to Rogoff, to a "higher class of operettas" (reminiscent of Avrom Goldfadn's 1881 operetta *Sh- ulamis*). Whereas for Rogoff the singing did not appear arbitrary but flowed from the mood in each particular scene, *Variety* claimed that the musical and "amateurishly executed dance" numbers were "dragged in by sheer force," "without rhyme or reason."[97]

The script, dated to December 1921, sets the prologue at night, "under the city of Prague." It depicts a group of "homeless Jews" who appear

96

"ragged, tired, cold, and hungry, singing a prayer until they exit [the stage]."[98] This scene is reminiscent of the Nuremberg expulsion portrayed in the Criterion's prologue to Wegener's film, in which Jews also appear as iconic exiles singing dirges, "the wanderer's staff in their hands and the packs upon their backs."[99] In both film and operetta, the prayer emphasizes the forsakenness of the Jews, which only the creation of a golem can possibly resolve. As Rabbi Loew consults his magical books and prepares the figure of clay for animation in the first act, he hears the sad singing of the wanderers. He ceases his work on the golem in the secret room and opens the window to converse with them. He invites his "sisters and brothers" into the ghetto and its synagogues, instructing them to continue praying and not to lose confidence in the Creator. In contrast to the film, the edict of expulsion is delivered only at the beginning of the operetta's third and final act, long after the Maharal has created and animated the golem. This "preemptive" creation therefore appears as a response to the general Jewish condition of homelessness and vulnerability, to help the "Jewish people who have been suffering for thousands of years already—and if not to completely free them, then at least to make their troubles lighter."[100]

Photos of Max Gabel dressed as the golem reveal that he not only drew on the Criterion's theatrical prologue but also borrowed Wegener's costume from the popular film (figure 2.4). Gabel's attire included the cinematic golem's sculpted head mask, large boots, thick belt, and rope tied around his arms. He even used the animating device, the star-shaped capsule, invented by the Wegener crew for the first (1914) film and subsequently used in the 1917 and 1920 films as well.[101] As in the latter film, the Yiddish Rabbi Loew discovers the animating word (*emes*, "truth") when it is projected on the walls of his house (with fire spurting out of the letters); he then traces the word onto a piece of parchment. In the Yiddish operetta, the parchment is placed, however, not in a five-pointed metal capsule but in a hexagram, a Star of David, enhancing the golem's Jewishness.[102] Finally, as Wegener did with his wife, Lydia Salmonova, who enacted the role of the rabbi's daughter, Gabel engaged his wife and partner

FIGURE 2.4. Max Gabel in *Der goylem*, 1921.
(Courtesy of YIVO Archives)

onstage, the popular melodrama actress Jenny Goldstein, for the role of
Miriam, Rabbi Loew's "modest" daughter. In multiple ads and photos,
Goldstein too appeared with long, braided hair and an Oriental costume
and jewelry, reminiscent of Salmonova's attire in the film.[103] The golem's
desire for Miriam awakens and intensifies throughout the operetta, as it
does in the film, and the couple's extratheatrical relationship enhanced
the erotic dimension of this love interest.

Gabel's golem is also named Joseph, as in Rosenberg's text, but its
ability to converse intelligently is reminiscent of Leivick's drama. The
golem draws on its memory and ability to learn and reveals inconsis-
tencies in the Maharal's logic as the drama progresses; its human-like
intellect enables it to perform certain actions of its own free will. The
rabbi even claims that the golem has become too "wise" when the clay

creature refuses to obey him because one of his commands goes against the rabbi's initial instruction "to defend the weak and suffering."[104] Where Gabel's production departs most dramatically from Wegener's film and Leivick's drama is in its emphasis on rationality and overall avoidance of mystical and supernatural forces. Unlike Leivick's mad and irrational golem, moreover, the golem in the operetta arrives at rational conclusions and is able, by the end of the drama, to determine that it must end its own life for the good of others.

In order to re-create a Jewish world in which a golem is brought into existence, Gabel made use of comic minor characters. A servant couple who engage in romantic banter serve as a foil for the melodramatic story of Miriam's love for the poor Yeshiva student Nakhman, even while her father has promised her hand in marriage to the rich Shimon. This couple, the housemaid Esther and the servant-student David, function as internal spectators to the unfolding drama, posing questions that the audience might be wondering about. For instance, when Esther asks David about the "secret" that "the rabbi mentioned to the poor wanderers," David explains that at night the rabbi enters the locked room to knead. "What does he knead, dough for farfel noodles?" she replies, and David teases her, explaining that the rabbi is kneading a large, tall, dead "thing" of clay. Esther, in disbelief, says she will ask the wanderers for more information, and their sorrowful song ends the scene.[105] Such exchanges punctuate the work, poking fun at the seriousness of the dramatic action and inviting the audience both to identify with and to feel more knowledgeable than the uncomprehending Esther.

David and Esther's conversations also provide essential background information for the main romantic drama: David reveals Miriam's tragic love for Nakhman, while Esther describes how Miriam cannot sleep at night, agonized as she is by her father's decision.[106] In the 1920 film, the drama of Jewish-Christian political strife is intensified through the illicit love affair between the Christian knight Florian and the rabbi's daughter, culminating in the knight's death. In the 1914 film, Wegener and the screenplay writer, Henrik Galeen, also introduced a forbidden romantic

FIGURE 2.5. Illustration of the cast in Max Gabel's *Der goylem*. (*Der tog*, December 1921)

relationship between the Christian baron and the Jewish antiques dealer's daughter. In both films, the romantic plot involves the transgression of class and ethnoreligious boundaries, expressing Christian German anxieties concerning intermarriage. In the 1922 Yiddish operetta, however, the romantic drama revolves around class differences alone, since both men are Jewish.

As in An-sky's 1919 *The Dybbuk*—a tale of unrequited love between a girl from a wealthy family and a poor Yeshiva student in which the deceased lover, Khonen, returns as a spirit to possess his beloved, Leah— *The Golem* operetta portrays the struggle of a young Jewish woman to marry her lover in defiance of her father's financial arrangements. Ansky's play ends, however, with the tragic death of Leah in the failed attempt to exorcise the dybbuk, the spirit of Khonen. By contrast, in the first act of *The Golem*, the audience is reassured that the rabbi is not blinded by Shimon's gold but rather wishes to use it to help the multitudes of miserable Jews. With this money, he hopes to bribe the Jews' "haters" and prevent them from engaging in persecutions. Nakhman protests that the rabbi is willing to sacrifice his daughter's happiness for the sake of his people. After Nakhman helps free the rabbi from imprisonment because of a false charge of alchemy, he earns back the father's good faith and consent in marriage. The *Golem* operetta as a whole invites the audience to identify with Miriam and Nakhman and to witness the Maharal's process of recognition and repentance, after he has been falsely accused by the "charlatan" Shimon. The Maharal confesses, "I have calculated poorly—the suffering of his people has made me forget the right that my child has over the love that her young heart feels."[107] Despite the operetta's setting in the past, it conveys a modern sensibility: the daughter's romantic "right" is recognized, and the individual triumphs while the collective ultimately benefits from this resolution.

In the intergenerational struggle, the golem is aligned with the younger generation, and particularly with those who fight for a just cause. The rabbi had initially defined the golem's charge as "to protect the poor, weak, and suffering"; the golem uses this proclaimed "mission" to defy his creator. When the rabbi attempts to marry his daughter to Shimon, the golem stands by "the poor and weak," in this case Miriam and Nakhman.[108] After the defiant Miriam is banished from her home, the golem continues to defend her and, dramatically, saves her from death by fire. While the golem initially threatens that it will "have" the rabbi's daughter before agreeing to turn back into clay, Miriam's acceptance of the golem as a "good person" with a soul in its heart leads the monster to relinquish its desire and put an end to its own life.[109] Though the golem also threatens its creator with the destruction of Prague, it never actually becomes violent. Leivick's murderous golem thus stands in sharp contrast to Gabel's morally acceptable Jewish anthropoid who ultimately protects the Jewish people and a Jewish woman in particular.

Gabel's clay giant is one of the more human and likeable golem figures to be molded in this period. Both Wegener and Leivick created erratic and violent monsters that evoke horror, whereas the golem of the operetta is not a menacing being and raises its fists only to protect the rabbi. Gabel's Prague rabbi breathed into his golem a soul and superhuman force and also endowed it with "a soft, feeling heart," Rogoff wrote in *Forverts*. "And this same heart that was only supposed to bring happiness to the Jews, that was only supposed to feel sympathy for the poor and suffering—this heart also began to feel and to long after love."[110] When animating the golem, the rabbi tells it of its "mission" to protect the Jews, which shall be "engraved upon his heart." The golem asks whether it has such an organ, and the rabbi tells it to place a hand on its breast and feel how it beats. The golem's "heart" is the "ineffable name of God," the animating parchment within the capsule that endows it with the "spell of life." Rather than merely a mechanical or magical device, the capsule is analogous here to an internal human organ, but the golem is instructed not to develop "independent desires or demands." Like Miriam, it must sacrifice its "heart," its individual identity, for the sake of the Jews.[111]

The operetta's golem was thus "more human than the average human" with its "superhuman heart" and "superhuman feelings," according to

Der tog. Kovessy himself and Gabel in his adaptation went "too far" with the humanization of the golem, when they endowed it with more than mere "physical heroism."[112] S. Robinzon of the *Yidishes tageblat* (Jewish daily news) conflated the golem's humanity with its Jewishness in Gabel's production. For Robinzon, this golem is "a Jew," since "he cannot bear the injustices of the world"—apparently a distinctly Jewish trait. The golem ultimately becomes even more "humanely Jewish" (*menshlikh-yidish*) when it sacrifices itself, benefiting Miriam and her betrothed, as well as the Jewish community at large since the Emperor has promised to revoke the expulsion edict pursuant to the golem's deanimation. When Wegener's golem allows the child to remove the animating capsule, it too appears to determine when its own existence must end, but in this case, it is not for the sake of the Jewish community. Robinzon pits Gabel's "Jewish golem" over and against Wegener's golem, declaring that the German film is "*goyish* through and through."[113] In Gabel's production, unlike Wegener's final scene, the golem becomes a member of the Jewish community precisely through its manner of dying, which affirms the values of male self-sacrifice and female modesty and purity. Unlike the indeterminate monster of flesh in Leivick's work, rejected by its Jewish creator and community, Gabel's golem is integrated into the Jewish environment and is treated with dignity.

For the critic of *Der tog*, Wegener's film constitutes an utter fantasy, set in a legendary past, whereas the Yiddish production, with its Jewish music, provides a more realistic Jewish environment (*svive*), despite the anachronistic electrical lamps.[114] If Kovessy had already humanized the golem, Gabel and Schweid, in their translation-adaptation, further "Yiddishize" this figure—to comic ends. As the golem attains more knowledge, it quickly begins to question what it has learned. When the rabbi defines God as the "almighty" that has "created us and rules over us," the golem wants to know if God created it. Hearing instead that the rabbi was its creator, the golem says, "You? Who are you to meddle [*mishn zikh*] with God's deeds?" When the rabbi decrees that his command must be held sacred by the golem just as he holds God's command as sacred, the golem scoffs, "Must? . . . Fie! [*feh*], I don't believe in the word 'must.'"[115] Using exclamations like "*feh*," Gabel's golem sounds at ease in the Yiddish tongue, defying its creator in *his* own language almost from the moment it opens its eyes. Interweaving a self-affirming plot spoken in colloquial Yiddish with musical numbers, Gabel's operetta appropriated the golem narrative for Yiddish popular culture and took away its more foreboding aspects and its transgressive bite. Just as the golem became more human and Jewish on the Yiddish stage, so too was its power used in a productive and ethical, rather than destructive, manner, benefiting the Jewish community.

* * *

The golem's immense success in the New York of 1921 suggests that the clay monster had important cultural "work" to perform on American shores. The golem narrative bridged post–World War I European and American cultures, creating a sense of transnational golemhood: Leivick's poema spoke to the devastating effects of World War I and Russian civil strife, while Wegener's film became relevant, in its American packaging, to the Jewish refugee and immigrant problem. These golem texts and productions emphasized the theme of persecution in exile in order to scrutinize the role of Jewish leaders and their vision of how Jews should act when they possess a powerful golem. But whereas Leivick's text, with its abject golem, can be read as implicitly concerned with Jewish integration into American society, Gabel's operetta revolves around internal class issues, portraying the emancipation of the young Jewish woman and the rabbi's diminished authority as he admits to an error of judgment.

The goleming that took place in 1921 New York had a high entertainment value, even when it alluded to the serious subject matter of Jewish persecution and exile. The American golem was an object of general fascination on the part of both Jewish and non-Jewish audiences, and it garnered attention from a wide range of daily newspapers. The intense uptake of this post–World War I story of artificial creation has had a long-lasting effect, even when the New York "golem-cult" subsided in the 1930s: Leivick's drama continues to be performed on the American stage well into the twenty-first century, and Wegener's film exerted its visual impact on scores of subsequent productions. In this manner, the image of the golem as a violent redeemer with an axe was imprinted in the American cultural memory and came to symbolize the brutal twentieth century and the consequences of its wars and revolutions for Jewish populations in Europe. As we shall see in the next chapters, in the post–World War II era, the golem emerged once again, in different continents and for different purposes. American artists created their own powerful and vengeful golem in the medium of comics, portraying figures that could rewrite history and teach the Nazis a lesson. Israeli writers of the post-1948 period drew instead on the figure of the golem as a suffering victim, akin to a war-injured soldier. The violence of the golem could also be redirected: projected onto past and present enemies of the Jews and their newfound state.

3

Our Enemies, Ourselves

Israel's Monsters of 1948

On June 28, 1948, at the first swearing in of soldiers to the Israeli Defense Army in Tel Aviv, the minister of foreign affairs, Moshe Sharet (Shartok), who was to become Israel's second prime minster in 1954, alluded to the attacking Arab forces as a creation of the British. He declared that Britain spread fear of this giant "axe-swinging" enemy: "At first, the [Arab] golem withstood the test of our young Israeli men. . . . They ultimately managed, without any experience in fighting, to beat the enemy and undermine the false legend about the Arab forces."[1] Ten days earlier, in a speech delivered at the council meeting of the Workers' Party of the Land of Israel, Sharet similarly contended that the large army of the Arab League was a "golem created by someone and aimed at us by that someone"—that is, by the British. This conglomerate army, he said, was reminiscent of a golem in its size but also in the "bloated" reputation of its strength.[2] The golem metaphor allowed Sharet to rally the Israeli army—a small but ideologically committed force, vital to the new country's survival—by suggesting that the supposedly powerful Arab armies all around them could be overcome since, like a golem, they were already more dead than alive.

With the founding of the Israeli nation came the birth of an entirely new golem, not a savior and redeemer, however ambivalent, but rather an evil enemy of the Jews. Sharet's allusion was characteristic of his time period: the Hebrew-language press of the 1940s commonly compared the League of Arab Nations to a golem. And specifically, his evocation of the dreadful, axe-swinging giant also suggests the public's familiarity with H. Leivick's rendering of the golem story. Indeed, the soldiers' swearing-in ceremony took place on the square in front of the Habima Theater in Tel Aviv, home to the Russian-born troupe that first staged Leivick's 1921 *Der goylem* in Hebrew translation. Inspired by Yudl Rosenberg's portrayal of the golem as a *ba'al guf* (strong or tough man), as we have seen in chapter 2, Leivick's violent redeemer is ultimately an indeterminate figure, created to counter anti-Semitism but, through mistreatment, reduced to a murderous animal. The golem monster of Sharet's speech, and of the Israeli press in the 1940s, no longer represented the new, strapping man or the revival of a combative Jewish spirit but rather the supposed power of the attacking Arab nations, which had to be dispelled and destroyed. With this metaphor, Israeli society also distanced itself from diasporic Jewish culture and its cultural legacy. The golem as a transformed Jew represented the changes that European Jewish society underwent in the early twentieth century; the Israeli nation now sought, by contrast, to project the negative attributes of the golem onto its enemies instead.

But, as we will see, in the coming years, another version of the golem story also emerged in Israel. This other side of the "golem condition"— the monster as evocative of war-related disability, powerlessness, and even death—emerged in Israeli literature written in the aftermath of the 1948 battles. In this literature, the golem became an emblem of destruction more generally, no longer representing one combatting side or the other. S. Y. Agnon's *Ad hena* (*To This Day*), published in 1952, set the tone in this regard, portraying the golem as a living-dead soldier. For Agnon, the modern golem is not a magical or mystical entity animated through the ineffable name of God as in the Prague story. Instead, it is a product of warfare, extracted from the mangled bodies of the dead and functioning as a scientific curiosity. *Ad hena* mobilizes the golem story to reflect critically on the ways in which human beings are molded into modern soldiers. In so doing, Agnon, implicitly following in Wegener's footsteps, showed the ongoing relevance of the golem story for artworks concerning the destructive and dehumanizing effects of war. Writing this text when Israeli nationhood was being conjured into existence, Agnon creates a foreboding image of the alternate "golem," the injured soldier. This unmovable, machine-like veteran is not a potential war hero but a survivor that has shed his human demeanor.

Precisely because the majority of the Israeli literary and journalistic output around 1948 expressed "a heroic national line, full of faith in the righteousness of the battle for independence," Agnon preferred to avoid any direct criticism of current events and set his work instead during the watershed war of 1914–1918.[3] As neither an almighty soldier nor a powerful weapon, Agnon's German "golem" still invited self-reflection on the part of Israeli citizens who had just emerged from their War of Independence. Yoram Kaniuk, an Israeli author who fought and was wounded in the 1948 war, took up Agnon's implicit challenge in his 1966 novel *Ḥimo melekh yerushalayim* (*Himmo, King of Jerusalem*). Set in the besieged Jerusalem of 1948, this text revolves around the figure of a severely wounded soldier, also nicknamed "golem." In both Agnon's and Kaniuk's fiction, "golem" is the term for the inexplicably tenacious human being who clings to life despite his proximity to death. These living-dead men pose a horrific challenge to their caretakers and loved ones, raising questions about the celebration of nationalist sentiment and the willingness to sacrifice the lives of young men for the Israeli cause. Dani Horowitz's 1982 drama *Yossele golem* also casts the artificial monster as a soldier, in this case a declared "war hero" who violently defeats the foes of the Jews but cannot usher in peace or messianic re-demption.[4] What we have, then, in Israel, is a bifurcated golem, created at times of national upheaval and self-reflection but for nearly opposite ends. Unlike Sharet's and others' use of the golem to depict the self-destructive military power of enemy nations and to convey the genuine might of the small Israeli army, these Hebrew writers drew on the golem story to expose the vulnerability of societies, including their own, that rely on violent measures to achieve political goals. They show how these societies are ultimately reshaped in the image of their golems, becoming blind to human suffering and trampling the various minority groups and "others" within their midst.

Monstrous Enemies: Golem Metaphors in the Hebrew/
Israeli Press

In April 1948, while fierce battles raged in Israel, the national Habima
Theater troupe arrived in the United States to showcase four of its established and representative pieces, including its adaptation of Leivick's *Der
goylem*, first staged in Moscow in 1925. Back in Israel, the journalist Uri
Keisari rebuked the "national theater" for deserting its country in a time
of struggle and need.[5] In the U. S., Yiddish critics did not view Habima's productions as a throwback to eastern European culture of twenty
years prior but interpreted *Der goylem* as an urgent call, prescient in its
time, for the use of Jewish physical force. A review in the Yiddish press
echoed the famous slogan of Zionist defense movements in Palestine,
"with blood and fire Yehuda will rise," arguing that already in the 1920s,
Leivick understood—and took a fresh approach to—the problems that
continued to be pressing a quarter of a century later.[6] When adapting
the drama for the Hebrew-language stage in Russia, the Habima troupe
renamed the golem, originally called Yossel (a diminutive for Joseph),
as Yehuda, suggesting "the revival of the ancient Jewish fighting spirit"
that could sustain "the hope of a national resurrection."[7] Since Yehuda
or Judah was also the given name of Rabbi Loew of Prague, this renam-
ing emphasized the golem's status as the rabbi's double. Hence, arriving
in New York just as "the new Jewish State came into being," Habima
not only celebrated this occasion but also, through its golem production, presented an allegory of the birth of a state through violence and
bloodshed.[8]

The golem of the 1948 production appeared to Yiddish reviewers as
he "should": a strapping man, a "*ba'al guf*" in their words, yet with the
brain of a child.[9] The Habima actor Aharon Meskin embodied the golem
as both a "menacing" and "comic" figure, not only inspiring dread but
also adding a "dimension of humor."[10] In this sense, Yair Lipshitz argues,
Meskin's golem is a soulless and mechanical "new Jew" that also displays a "clownish-comic" aspect, enhancing the threatening and foreign

side of this bodily ideal through distancing humor.[11] Moreover, Leivick's drama, even in Habima's shortened and altered adaptation, paints a tragic and terrifying picture of the Jewish resort to violence.[12] The murder of innocent Jews at its end reveals that the golem's unleashed force can and will turn against its creators. Half a century later, in 2002, as the Second Intifada raged in Israel, the production of Leivick's play in New York at the Manhattan Ensemble Theater raised the question of whether or not "the mighty Jewish state has become a golem for the 21st century, promising protection but leading to peril."[13]

Such comparisons of the golem both to the new type of "muscle Jew" in twentieth-century Zionist discourse and to the Jewish state and nation at large emerged from the long-standing portrayal of the golem as a defender of the Jewish community, epitomized by Rosenberg's 1909 *Seyfer nifloes Maharal* (*The Golem or The Miraculous Deeds of Rabbi Leyb*). The assumptions underlying these comparisons were that the golem, as an extension of its creator, the Jewish rabbi, was a product of Jewish society and would serve this society in times of great need. But, in contrast to the Yiddish-language use of the golem, in the Hebrew-language press coverage in the decades before and during the battle for independence, the term *golem* no longer suggested the ambivalent creation of a new Jew or else a worldwide misuse of modern technology but came to denote the enemies of the Jews and their weapons. Around World War II and Israel's War of Independence, the Hebrew press uniquely used the golem metaphor with reference to Germans and Arabs, and this artificial creation now functioned as an unambiguous symbol of monstrous evil. Journalists representing a wide political spectrum evoked the destructive and rebellious aspects of the golem story to project the downfall of the Nazi regime or the loss of British control over the Arab League.

Already in 1938, the religious-nationalist paper *Ha-tsofe* published a piece regarding the expulsion of sixty Jews by sea from Vienna, calling the Nazi commander of the ship a "living golem," one of the "seventy million [German] golems who loyally obey every command of the 'Führer.'"[14] In this piece, the monstrous golem is a metaphor for those brainwashed (or brainless) citizens and soldiers who unthinkingly follow the commands of their superiors, however cruel and racist they might be.

During World War II, Israeli newspapers likewise evoked the golem to describe the war technologies of the Nazi regime, including their tanks, airplanes, and missiles.[15] Writing for the revisionist daily paper *Ha-mashkif*, Marian Zyd described the nightly attacks of Nazi V1 flying bombs on London in 1944 as "the satanic buzz of flying golems." In contrast to the German airplanes operated by human pilots during the Blitz, these bombs were guided by autopilot and powered by a pulse jet engine that produced a buzzing noise. According to Zyd, British Jews called the V1 bomb "the golem": "It looks like a golem, flies like a golem, and spreads terror like a golem, and the Jews then recall the old tale about the golem that ultimately destroyed its creator."[16] Though Zyd gives a nod to the Jews as a people familiar with the "old tale about the golem," here the term loses its association with the Jewish community and simply refers to the robotic weapons of the Nazis.

Such evocations of the golem story stand in stark contrast to the golem's appearance in European film and literature of the same period. For example, Julien Duvivier's 1936 French-Czech coproduction *Le Golem* portrays a Jewish Prague community struggling under the rule of a fascist Emperor. In this film, shot after the Nuremberg Race Laws went into effect in 1935, the golem is a creation of the Jewish community and represents the "right" of the enslaved minority to revolt and seek justice. In Tel Aviv, the local press described *Le Golem*, which had a two-week run in July 1948 (after originally screening in 1937), as a film featuring a revolutionary monster that breaks free of its own chains and redeems the Jewish ghetto.[17] A "symbol of revolt," rather than blind obedience, this cinematic golem reminds us that the Hebrew press's depiction of the golem as the enemy was a distinctive variation that needs to be accounted for.

Relying on the catch-all idea of the golem as a destructive creation that can easily turn against its creator, the Israeli press further compared this figure to the Arab enemy and its Arab League, founded in late 1944.

The notion that the Arab League was a "synthetic" or artificial creation of the British was repeated so often that the Workers' Party paper, 'Al ha-mishmar (On guard), pronounced that it was common knowledge in the press that the national Arab movement was but a "golem created by the forces of imperialism."[18] Ha-mashkif spelled out the analogy: "The British government brought to life a golem for its own needs—the Arab League. And this 'league' certainly carried out its creator's will many times. But it appears that when the 'shem ha-meforash' [the ineffable name] will be removed, Great Britain will no longer be able to control this golem." As an example, the reporter relates the League's unwillingness to adhere to the British decision to allow further Jewish immigration to Palestine according to the limits placed by current quotas.[19]

For Hillel Danzig in the daily paper Davar, the Arab golem was but a reincarnation of the previous Nazi monster. While the "midwife" of the new and barbaric golem was "British imperialism" (supported by U.S. foreign policy), its true political-ideological "spiritual father" was Nazi Germany, he wrote. A supposed "barrier" or defense against the Soviet incursion in the Middle East, the new and more artificial golem embodied in the Arab nations was bound to turn against the Western powers and betray them politically.[20] In late July 1948, after the second truce of the 1948 battles was declared (they resumed in October 1948), Davar deemed the Arab League a "weak union" of seven Arab nations, close to disintegration. This "golem" was founded on one principle: "The nonsolution of the question of the Land of Israel." A resolution of this question would therefore cause the golem to collapse. The day of this collapse was very near, the Davar journalist contended, since the Arab League was bound to fail in the war against the Israeli forces.[21]

The golem metaphor was thus commonly associated with the Arab enemies of 1948, not only the Arab League but also other Arab leaders such as the king of Jordan, Abdullah I bin al-Hussein, and King Idris I of Lybia.[22] During the first swearing in of soldiers to the Israeli Defense Army in June 1948, Foreign Minister Moshe Sharet called, as we saw earlier, for the unification of the various prestatehood Jewish fighting forces into one strong army that could defeat the golem-like Arab military forces. He compared the battle of the Israelis against the Arabs to the story of David and Goliath, contending that the Israelis had struck back against the giant golem with its "swaying axe," in so doing heroically dispelling the myth of the enemy's strength.[23] The evocation of the golem story at this historically significant military and national event suggests the public's familiarity with, and the rhetorical effectiveness of, the new Arab face of the golem.

Imagined as a malicious giant that can be toppled, the golem in this use also enhanced the contrast with a particular image of the Israeli military—as supposedly independent of foreign influence and capable of withstanding attack. Israeli soldiers derived their power from an inner sense of conviction in the Jewish right to fight for the land of Palestine. This disassociation of the nascent Israeli army from the golem story marked the desire for a break from the Jewish diasporic past and its abiding mythologies. The golem was, supposedly, a product of Jewish weakness in the diaspora, a much-needed strongman in an age of Jewish dependence on other nations. In Zionist hands, the golem shed its earlier ambiguity and came to embody the menacing external enemy that would ultimately destroy itself or be defeated. Rather than superimposing the Star of David on the golem, as in Paul Wegener's 1920 film, or using it for the golem's capsule, as in Max Gabel's 1921 operetta, the Israeli state's leaders and journalists severed this implicit connection between the golem and Jewish nationalism. But the Israeli literature published in the aftermath of the 1948 war had a different story to tell about the significance of the golem for the nascent state.

The Face of War: S. Y. Agnon's *Ad hena*

During this fraught historical moment, and as the golem flourished in the Israeli press as a stand-in for the enemy, S. Y. Agnon was writing his war narrative *Ad hena*. The prolific Hebrew author, who received the Nobel Prize for literature in 1966, also envisioned an atypical golem: a

Christian German wounded soldier. Even as the horrors of World War II became known, and after Agnon's own nation went to war, he specifically set his work in a different time and place, during World War I—a war in which Jews and Christians fought side by side. That deflection away from his own immediate circumstances, as we will see, enabled him to portray the "golem condition" at large and to reflect the more recent wars in an indirect manner.

Well versed in the ancient Talmudic and mystical medieval connotations of the golem as well as in modern narratives about the golem of Prague, Agnon exhibits in *Ad hena* his interest in the golem's earlier popularity and the widespread circulation of this narrative during World War I.[24] One of the texts responsible for the general fascination with artificial creation during this war was *Der Golem*, the best-selling novel by the Austrian author Gustav Meyrink, published in 1915.[25] Drawing on Meyrink's work, Agnon revisited in *Ad hena* the German golem fad that intensified in this period. His contemporary golem is a brain-injured veteran who cannot follow orders, converse, or reveal his identity. We see him through the eyes of the book's narrator, a Jewish man who disassociates himself from this living-dead soldier and from the German war effort more generally. Nevertheless, the Jewish narrator comes to resemble the German golem as the narrative progresses. As the lives of these two men intersect in crucial ways, Agnon depicts one of the consequences of nationalist fervor and the rapid development of modern war technologies: the fundamental destruction of the human body and self, made in the image of God. While the golem story lends itself to a fantastical vision of the physical capacities and heroic nature of modern soldiers, it also, as Meyrink, Wegener, and Leivick insisted, represents human—and particularly male—fallibility and mortality.

Agnon's *Ad hena* is a formally experimental and highly digressive work. The strangeness of the text is most clear in its apparent asymmetry: the first seven chapters depict less than a week in the narrator's life, and the last eight chapters rush through several months, and then several years, at an ever-accelerating pace. The golem plot ends abruptly in the middle of the work, and no other obvious unifying device takes its place.[26] *Ad hena*'s first-person narrator, a Galician Jew stranded in Germany, does not join the war effort, although unlike Agnon, who spent the war years immersed in the study of Jewish history and religion, he finds it impossible to resume his research on the "history of clothing." At the book's opening, on the eve of his planned journey from Berlin to Grimma, the narrator cuts off the margins of his manuscript and discards unnecessary sections in order to lessen its literal (and presumably metaphorical) weight. Here and elsewhere, Agnon seems skeptical about the possibility of literary and scholarly writing amid war and mass death; his doubt about creation goes hand in hand with his constant subversion of the notions of authorship and originality.[27]

Taking my cue from the narrator's relationship to his own unfinished manuscript, I consider *Ad hena* a self-consciously aborted novel— hence, I would argue, its deliberate asymmetry. This work embodies the notion of an aborted existence, like that of the golem and his modern counterpart, the wounded soldier. *Ad hena* is longer than any of Agnon's novellas, though shorter than his fully developed novels, *Oreah nata lalun* (*A Guest for the Night*) and *Tmol shilshom* (*Only Yesterday*). Published in 1939, *Oreah nata lalun* portrays the aftermath of World War I, primarily within a Jewish community in eastern Europe. Appearing over a decade later, *Ad hena* takes place during World War I in Germany and centers on the daily contact between Jews and Christians on the home front. Its deliberate structural and thematic disarray implicitly questions the possibility of writing a developed and unified novel about the modern experience of war. Although finished by Agnon himself, in contradistinction to the posthumously published *Shira* or *Be-hanuto shel mar Lublin* (In Mr. Lublin's store), *Ad hena* leaves us wondering not only about the structure of the work itself but also about what has been left out of the text.

Ad hena revolves around the narrator's travels from one German city or town to another and describes the hardship of both travel itself and the search for a decent place to reside. While Agnon plays in this fictional narrative with many autobiographical resonances, his narrator's inability to gain footing in war-ravaged Germany is reminiscent not only of Agnon's own sojourn in Germany during World War I but also of his experiences after the bombardment of his home in the Israeli battles for independence, as he and his family became temporary dwellers in their country.[28] Agnon first resided in a boardinghouse in Reḥaviah, a neighborhood in west Jerusalem, not far from his wife and children, who had relocated earlier.[29] He lived in the room of the owner's drafted son, who was off fighting in the 1948 war—just as his narrator stays in the room of the injured "golem" when living in Berlin at the outset of World War I. In Tiberias, where Agnon sought respite for five months during the 1948–1949 winter, his hosts, the Me'iri family, had lost a son in the battles for independence. It was in Tiberias, according to Agnon's biographer Dan Laor, that Agnon composed parts of *Ad hena*, which initially bore the title *Bi-yemot ha-milḥama* (In the days of the war).[30]

Agnon's new take on the golem story thus needs to be interpreted through the dual lens of his experiences in World War I Germany—where he resided between 1912 and 1924—and in 1948 Israel. In both cases, the author avoided serving on the front lines or otherwise contributing to the war effort, but he was personally affected by the wars he witnessed.[31] If World War II also casts its shadow on *Ad hena*, which critically depicts early twentieth-century German society, this war is present in a far more indirect manner than the explicit setting of World War I and the implicit resonances of the 1948 period, which Agnon lived through on the home front.[32] As we have seen, some of the narrator's misadventures align with Agnon's own travails in the years 1948–1949, when he resided in the homes of friends and in boardinghouses. Yet in contrast to other Israeli writers of the period, such as S. Yizhar and Avot Yeshurun, Agnon never overtly dealt with the events of 1948 in his writings. Sidra DeKoven Ezrahi aptly notes that for Agnon, "the inflection point of 'secular history,' easily incorporated into Jewish time, is August 1914." "What then of 1948?" she asks. Not only in *Ad hena* but also in Agnon's other works of the period, he elides the changed borders of Jerusalem after 1948 and the radically altered conditions of Jewish life in Israel.[33] Still, his writing about the high price that Jews and non-Jews paid during World War I should be seen, I suggest, as attuned to his surroundings, resulting in an unspoken tension between past and present.

If during the fighting Agnon could not remain secure in his home or avoid being affected by the war and the toll it took on human life, his narrator on the German home front similarly worries about his potential enlistment and injury, as he encounters grieving families. On revisiting one friend, the sharp-witted Jewish bibliographer Dr. Mittel, whose son has recently died on the front lines, the narrator finds Mittel submerged in a particularly dark mood, as he reflects on German society:

> Freedom of thought has fathered tolerance; tolerance has given birth to democracy; and democracy does not tolerate tolerance. . . . The world has forgotten what truth means, and falsehood has taken its place. You may have considered our generation's physiognomy. No one looks cynical anymore. Every face is exposed like the teeth of the *Kintopp* [movie] actresses. The face of the generation is one of innocence—and precisely that is its cynicism: a countenance of innocence and honesty coupled with evil and sinful deeds.[34]

Mittel alludes here to a Mishnaic figure of speech, "The face of this generation is as the face of a dog," which denotes the potential corruption of a generation, particularly its leaders, the so-called face of the public.[35] In tractate *Sota* 9:15, this phrase refers to the subversion of proper power structures, foreseeing a time in the future when "they that shun sin shall be deemed contemptible, and truth shall nowhere be found. Children shall shame the elder, and the elders shall rise up before the children." Therefore, instead of trusting one's own family members, the rabbis assert that "we can stay ourselves . . . on our Father in heaven."[36] In Agnon's text, societal corruption is also expressed in the fact that Mittel mourns his son rather than the other way around. From the narrator's viewpoint, the Jewish sacrifice for the German war effort appears more and more absurd, especially since these acculturated Jews can rely neither on their father on earth (the German kaiser) nor on the father in heaven.

Significantly, the nascent medium of film serves as a metaphorical means for understanding the troubled era. Agnon himself described frequent visits in these same years to a Berlin movie theater, or *Kintopp* (slang for *Kinematograph*), especially on cold winter days when the Jewish library closed its doors between two and four.[37] In Mittel's description of the absence of "truth" in German society, Agnon creates a surprising pairing: the Mishnah and cinema. He portrays the evocative power of film's close-up techniques, which brought the faces of actors closer to audiences, revealing details that would not have been visible to previous generations. For the film critic Béla Balázs, writing in the 1920s, the visual expressivity of cinema and its close-ups expose the soul of surface-level phenomena, thereby animating both faces and landscapes on the screen. Wegener likewise had his face, as a golem, filmed in great close-up, exposing the humanity behind the supposedly inhuman monster made of dead matter. Mittel, by contrast, considers the exposure of the face through the moving image as a reversal of physiognomy's central tenet—the notion that outer appearance reveals inner nature. Instead, he suggests that if the war has altered the very nature of the human face and its potential interpretation, then cinema exacerbates rather than resolves this condition.[38] What it "reveals" is the decline of society, which hides behind the deceiving, "innocent" mask of democracy.[39] For the grief-stricken Mittel, the apparent exposure of his generation covers up the truth rather than expressing it; like the actresses' teeth, this generation's supposed innocence can and does bite.[40]

Agnon's narrator not only learns about the "face of the generation" from Mittel but also trains his own gaze on German society, both its soldiers and its civilians. The external appearance of the World War I veteran has been radically altered through the use of prosthetic limbs and plastic surgery. During the narrator's first train travel outside Berlin, he must fight his way onto the train: "The car was packed with passengers: war provisioners, *Ersatz* products dealers, military nurses, officers' mistresses, and amputees back from the front with their crutches, empty sleeves, rubber limbs, glass eyes, noses fashioned from buttocks by plastic surgeons, and terrified and terrifying faces that had lost their human features in the war."[41] Starting with people who have benefited economically from the war—the provisioners and *Ersatz* dealers—the list progresses to those whose own body parts must be replaced. The loss of human facial features is terrifying, but even more distressing for the narrator is the apathetic face of the brain-injured soldier whom he encounters at Brigitta's convalescence home. Described as "a kind of golem man without a brain," the German soldier epitomizes the terror of war, the way it has altered the face of a particular generation and that of humanity more generally.[42]

Casting the golem as a non-Jewish soldier, Agnon plays with his readers' expectations about the nature of the golem and distances this term from its commonplace association with Jewish rabbis and kabbalists. The man, nicknamed "golem" by his German caretakers, is rescued from the battlefield during World War I, "cast amid heaps of crushed corpses," after his entire battalion is killed.[43] A living-dead man, he can no longer be identified with the nationalist forces that sent him to the battle front, but the narrator also does not approve of his new name:

> His face was opaque and his eyes did not reveal a flicker of life. I'm surprised that Brigitta called him a golem. In my own opinion he didn't merit the name golem because the golem created by the Maharal was more beautiful, more human. Picture a long pair of arms, a long pair of legs, a face like dried clay, witless eyes that have no life in them, and two slumped shoulders capped by a motionless head. I would be very surprised if this golem could understand anything, let alone do what he was told.[44]

Ironically, the artificially created Prague golem seems more "human" and beautifully formed than the injured veteran does, with his lifeless eyes and motionless limbs. Though his heart continues to beat, he is "incapable of thought" and unable, or unwilling, to speak. While Agnon's Jewish narrator might wish to distinguish the rabbi-created golem from this modern and secular phenomenon of war injury, he is proven otherwise in the course of the narrative.

The brain-damaged veteran at the center of Agnon's text is first treated at the convalescence home outside Leipzig. His memory loss and inability to speak forces the narrator and others to focus on his exterior in their search for clues that might account for his condition. But this exterior turns out to be both opaque and misleading, precluding any possibility of physiognomic interpretation. The "golem man" also functions as the double of a Russian prisoner of war who works at a farm outside the convalescence home, a man who cannot return to his own home and with whom no one will converse, aside from ordering him to perform tasks and scolding him. The Jewish narrator, exiled from both Galicia and Palestine, is linked to these two soldiers; he identifies with the Russian prisoner as a "lost son," and over the course of the narrative, he comes to resemble the German "golem."

Using this notion of a "brainless" man, Agnon situates the figure of the wounded soldier within the medical and historical context of World War I, just as he spins around him a web of scriptural, folkloric, and psychological associations. First, he is attuned to the novelty of brain injuries during World War I as well as to the difficulty of their diagnosis and treatment. Michael Hagner, a historian of medicine, writes that brain injury in this war constituted a "new physiognomic phenomenon." These young men "often had apathetic and chronically helpless faces" and not infrequently suffered from "a complete breakdown of their verbal, mimetic, and gesticular repertoire."[45] Agnon's "golem man" similarly has an apathetic, lifeless expression and neither responds to requests nor communicates his own needs. The narrator comes to presume that the wounded man has lost his ability to hear and discern.[46]

The notion that war reduces men to mere golems or else to vacant and senseless *goylems*—Yiddish for "brainless idiots"—corresponds, moreover, to the national use of male bodies as raw material (*ḥomer gelem*) to be deployed for warlike purposes.[47] As Hagner contends, moreover, the brain-damaged soldiers of World War I were impervious to the course of rapid therapy and reintegration into society and the labor force that was practiced in other types of physical injury.[48] These soldiers easily become dehumanized "golems" in a very narrow sense of the term: brainless, lifeless men who can no longer contribute to society. Pushing against the ideal of the injured but economically productive veteran, Agnon paints a disturbing, foreboding image of human devastation. He shows how all those who have dealings with these returning soldiers are also severely affected by their condition, even when they deny the irreparability of war injury. After the "golem" returns to his family in Berlin and regains his name—Hans—he appears unaltered: when the narrator next encounters him on the street with Hans's sister, Hildegard, the former golem still does not converse or respond to her addresses. Evidently, the "new suit" that Hildegard intends to have made for her brother will not turn him into a "new person," as she hopes.[49]

Agnon offsets the historical meaning of the character's brain injury with the more mythic dimension conjured by the golem. Gershom Scholem has traced "the idea of the golem" back to the Talmudic association with the first human, *adam*, in his unformed state, before being invested with a living soul.[50] In Agnon's own posthumously published compilation of Jewish sources concerning language and writing, *Sefer sofer ve-sipur* (Book, author, and story), he quotes Rashi's commentary on tractate *Sanhedrin* 65b, recounting Rabbi Rabba's creation of a human. Rashi writes that Rabba's act of creation was performed in accordance with the ancient mystical treatise *Sefer yetsira* (*The Book of Creation*), "which taught him to combine the letters of a [holy] name." Still, the creation could not respond, since it "was not endowed with speech," and this characteristic marks it as magically created by others and not actually a human being.[51]

Agnon's modern golem-soldier resembles these Talmudic golem prototypes with whom communication is not possible. This golem,

however, is a man-made product of war, an outcome of secular technological development rather than a mythical creature created through
the magical manipulation of Hebrew letters. Made of "flesh, sinew, and
bones," instead of earth or clay, the brain-injured protagonist of *Ad
hena* cannot remember his "name" or "place." Agnon thus portrays him
as doubly God-forsaken, for both words in Hebrew are synonymous
with God (*ha-shem* and *ha-makom*).[52] The name "golem" does not refer
back to the creator in this case but instead becomes a placeholder for
the absent God. The "golem man" here also signifies a state of personal
and societal "brainlessness," creative impotence, and loss of faith in the
power of language and letters. The fascination of *Ad hena*'s narrator
with the injured and apathetic soldier tells of his need to find respite for
his tormented state of creative and spiritual paralysis.[53] In other words,
the condition of brainlessness has its own allure and stands in sharp
contrast to the narrator's repetitive patterns of thought and movement.
Compared to both the narrator and the German veteran, the supposedly more "human" golem of Prague represents physical prowess, on
the part of the animated monster, and creative potency, on the part of
the creator, Rabbi Loew.

Hence, while the lengthy war entailed the formation of obedient
soldiers, Agnon sees in World War I also the onset of an era of golem
production. "The face of the generation" in this text is not only that
of the movie actress and of the soldier who underwent reconstructive
surgery but also that of the apathetic veteran who has suffered an un-
treatable brain injury, resulting in a condition of living-death. While injured young soldiers sought to reintegrate into civilian society, Agnon
stresses that reintegration itself can become a mere illusion, a mask of
recovery that only produces further golem-like subjects. In contrast to
Wegener's ultimate redemption of the golem, and of the new Christian
society with him, for Agnon, World War I is the historical event that not
only revealed the damaging nature of war technologies but also called
into question the basic premises of the Enlightenment and European
humanism.

How the Golem Got His Name

The narrator of *Ad hena* reflects from his vantage point on the home front on the effects of the war both in popular visual culture and in the publishing industry. In contrast to the narrator's incomplete manuscript, Agnon indirectly alludes to Gustav Meyrink's extremely successful *Der Golem* (1915), a much-discussed wartime best-seller.[54] Published by the Kurt Wolff press, located in the German publishing epicenter of Leipzig, Meyrink's novel reached massive sales numbers for its time period: nearly two hundred thousand copies in the first decade of its publication, and most of these during the war years. The Wolff publishing house even printed a pocket edition intended for distribution to soldiers on the front lines. Accompanied by Hugo Steiner-Prag's haunting illustrations, *Der Golem* is a fantastic thriller set in late nineteenth-century Prague, just prior to the demolition of the Jewish ghetto. While Meyrink drew on elements of the golem of Prague story, he freely altered them to suit his central plot. Meyrink's ghostly golem returns to haunt the Jewish ghetto every thirty-three years (evoking Christ's age at death), and his returns are always associated with the outbreak of murderous violence.

In Scholem's assessment, Meyrink was influenced by esoteric mystical practices and theosophy, such that "deep-rooted mystical convictions and literarily exploited charlatanry were almost inextricably amalgamated" in his writings.[55] Max Brod, in turn, contrasted Agnon and Meyrink in 1918, claiming that Agnon truly understands "the secrets of Jewish mysticism" and therefore far surpasses an "outsider" like the Austrian Meyrink.[56] These critiques of *Der Golem* by prominent Jewish writers and intellectuals reverberate in a significant passage of *Ad hena*, which explains how the brain-injured soldier earned his nickname:

> This was a name people knew all across Germany in those days, because a German author had written a book about the golem, and the publisher advertised it widely in the hope of earning back the money he had wasted on the author. He assembled a group of cripples, each shorter than the

other, arranged them according to height, and gave them signs to hold that spelled out "golem" in large letters and had them parade through the streets of Leipzig during the annual fair, when the city was crowded with visitors. In this way the name golem became widely known and everyone talked about the golem who was made of clay and by the power of the sacred name of God under his tongue did everything he was ordered to do. "Today," Brigitta said, "I'm sending the professors in Berlin a golem who is not made of clay and does not use the name of God, but his brain is certainly a golem brain. Incapable of thought, he does not even remember his own name."[57]

The narrator never mentions the name of the "German author," emphasizing instead the role of the (likewise unnamed) publisher as advertiser.[58] Leaving the exact identity of the author unknown, albeit easy to guess, serves a double, conflicting purpose: it renders the author's name "ineffable," unpronounceable, akin to God's name, at the same time as it undermines the power of his authorship. In hinting at the legacy of *Der Golem*, Agnon cynically underscores the role of the modern publisher as creator of the book, registering both his authorial and religious anxieties concerning human mediation in the creation process. As Franz Werfel wrote in a 1916 letter to Wolff, "Nowadays one hears and reads everywhere only Kurt Wolff. Your advertising, especially the ads in the paper, was the most intensive campaign one could imagine: The publisher has created *The Golem* more than its author."[59]

For Agnon, modern texts about the golem are not necessarily a pleasing product of human creativity but instead may result from a distorted and even destructive attempt to mangle literary creation for a quick profit. Agnon thus constructs a network of grotesque links between the publishing industry and the market of flesh—that is, the war, which produces both invalids and "brainless" golems. The publicity stunt of the German word *Golem* turns the sign-bearing "crippled" men at the Leipzig fair into an attraction of sorts. Similarly, the golem-soldier's caretakers are fascinated by his strange injury, which becomes a kind of medical "spectacle." In the German context, the term *golem* thus provides a way of labeling war injury and even endowing it with visual appeal and a mythical aura. Thus, if Meyrink's *Der Golem* is a thriller that promotes an ominous atmosphere of suspense, *Ad hena* conveys the monotony and suspended temporality of wartime life through the narrative's structural circularity and repetitions.

The grotesque marketing campaign for the nameless "book about the golem" also corresponds to Meyrink's own depiction of the Jewish Prague ghetto as a site of human distortion. For him, the Prague ghetto is "the site of mental disease, decadence, and sexual corruption," to quote Cathy Gelbin.[60] His narrator, a non-Jewish man who lives in the ghetto, trains his markedly physiognomic gaze on the buildings of the ghetto and its inhabitants. The grotesque quality of such descriptions serves metonymically to characterize this Jewish environment, which is on the verge of destruction, as uncanny, sinister, and even repulsive. Meyrink's narrator, for example, often evokes attributes from the animal world of spiders, rabbits, horses, and birds to depict Jewish characters. He also looks at the faces and gestures of the Jewish ghetto inhabitants to try to decipher their familial relationships, and what he can "read from their facial features" are the different "types" and "breeds" to which each person belongs.[61] The golem itself is portrayed as belonging to a "Mongolian type," with its "yellow complexion" and slanted eyes. For Gelbin, because these negative images of Jews are presented from the perspective of the unreliable narrator, they cannot be taken at face value as anti-Semitic reiteration but must be seen as projections that offer "deliberate reflections of the non-Jewish discourse on the Jews."[62]

Agnon's text shows how new types of war injuries, alongside the development of new entertainment technologies, have altered the face of a generation and indeed the very notion of physiognomy. *Ad hena* offers a reversal of the physiognomic gaze that makes clear-cut connections between the inner and outer aspects of a person and that has so often been directed at Jews. Living outside of an enclosed Jewish community, the narrator of *Ad hena* trains his gaze on the war-injured men returning from the battlefield and the German women who have both taken their place in the workplace and family and await their return and need for care. For Agnon, writing from the perspective of his secularized Jewish narrator, there is no need to imagine, as Meyrink does, some mysterious and dangerous "soul" lurking behind the urban facade, epitomized by the figure of a haunting golem, for it is the surface of the body and its inhuman proximity to death that Agnon's narrator finds most disturbing. The narrator's interest in researching the history of clothing stems from his desire to see the injured or feminine body covered in culturally appropriate attire rather than revealed in its threatening naked vulnerability. Agnon's narrator thus objectifies the German majority rather than the ethnic minority through a type of physiognomic gaze that nonetheless precludes any clear revelation of human essences.

Agnon's relationship to the phenomenon of Meyrink's best-seller is far more complex and ambivalent than the pejorative statements of the unreliable first-person narrator would reveal.[63] Devoid of *Der Golem*'s more salacious plot elements, such as murder and adultery, *Ad hena* nevertheless contains copious echoes, minute but unmistakable, of the earlier work. Like Meyrink's amnesiac protagonist who bears the false name "Athanasius Pernath," the injured soldier in *Ad hena* suffers from a complete loss of memory and is temporarily given the name "golem." In both texts, moreover, narrator and golem function as doubles of each other, but for Agnon, "golemhood" is a virtually contagious condition, so that other minor characters also exhibit attributes of the legendary golem (for instance, the face of the injured soldier Yosef Bach looks like "burnt earth"). Another shared plot detail exemplifies the way in which Agnon takes up, alters, and exaggerates aspects of the earlier text. When visiting a Berlin café, Agnon's narrator notices a single spoon suspended from the ceiling, secured by an iron chain. He is told that the owner had attached it in this way since customers often failed to return the spoon after stirring their coffee.[64] In the pub of Meyrink's Jewish ghetto, spoons similarly hang from chains, but the explanation for this is that once a day, local criminals and prostitutes are given free soup, courtesy of a famous lawyer.[65] The irony of providing free soup to criminals while securing their spoons becomes, in Agnon's text, a doubly ironic distrust that renders all customers in Berlin potential thieves.

Such details, alongside the many intertextual links between the two works, suggest that Agnon's *Ad hena* stands in a close dialogue with Meyrink's far more popular novel. It is almost as if *Ad hena* were chained to *Der Golem*, against the will of the narrator, and constantly references its German source—a text that is itself a compilation of mystical sources. This form of preservation deflates Agnon's own prose, calling into question its origins and originality. While Agnon's narrator explicitly dismisses the "book about the golem" as a waste of the publisher's money, the author implies that even in present-day Israel, one must return to and contend with Meyrink's novel, a key German publishing phenomenon of the war years and an influential text in the modern literary history of golem adaptations. Similarly, the golem's blank memory and expressionless face could represent the face of the 1948 generation as well: exuberant nationalism has erased the Jewish past from the face of the young nation.

The "Miracle" of Hebrew Letters

Focused though the novel is on the physical (and thus also visual) dimension of war injury, *Ad hena*, as well as other Israeli rewritings of the golem story, contends with the role of Hebrew letters in the act of creation. In the marketing scene described earlier, Agnon turns the name golem into a series of (German) letters, and, similarly, *Ad hena* constantly reminds us of the basic building blocks of Hebrew words, the alphabet. More generally, Agnon considered Hebrew the holy tongue of creation and critiques attempts to modernize the language.[66] Early Jewish mystical treatises such as *Sefer yetsira* present Hebrew and its alphabet as having miraculous powers, capable even of forming human beings, initially by God through the combination of letters and then, through imitation, by Abraham.

Traditionally, a golem-aspiring rabbi animates his lump of clay via the alphabet—whether through the word for truth, *emet*, or the ineffable or hidden name of God (*shem ha-meforash*).[67] In thirteenth-century mystical treatises by R. Eleazar of Worms and R. Abraham Abulafia, a golem is brought to life through the recitation of combinations of letters (221 in total), following *Sefer yetsira*'s assignment of a letter to each bodily limb.[68] In Agnon's evocation of the golem, he reminds us of Hebrew's history as a language of creation, raising what to him is the parallel question of Hebrew's ongoing role within the fabric of the secular world and specifically in the context of Zionist nation-building. Although the very publication of *Ad hena* in the newfound State of Israel can be understood as Agnon's reaffirmation of Hebrew after World Wars I and II, the author cautions us to heed Hebrew's creative and scriptural legacy as enacted through golem-making.

Ad hena allows Agnon to explore these issues at a remove, showing how both German-language literature and German society embraced the golem story during World War I. For him, the modern golem is no longer a means of knowing God or imitating and celebrating divine creation but a way of undoing the world as created by God through language and bringing the holy tongue to the brink of destruction.[69] Agnon's rendition of the golem story also concerns the status of different languages; he reveals the grotesque results of attempting creation through warfare and animation with the help of German names rather than Hebrew ones. In Agnon's text, animation and rebellion are thus conflated when the injured soldier, nicknamed "golem," comes to life at the sound of a German street address.

Traveling back to Berlin with a group of soldiers from the convalescence home who require special medical attention, Agnon's narrator is suddenly "overcome by a great sadness that made his limbs feel immobile." Since he can barely move his hands and pick up his luggage, himself resembling the golem-soldier, the nurse in charge offers assistance, telling one of the soldiers to carry the narrator's belongings to his Berlin "home." The immobilized narrator proceeds to take out a piece of paper—reminiscent of the parchment on which the animating formula is inscribed in different versions of the golem story—and writes down "the name of the boardinghouse and the name of the street and the house number." The soldier appointed to carry the narrator's belongings then reads the address out loud. At this moment, "the same witless man whom everyone used to consider as lacking willpower suddenly jumps up and takes the belongings from the soldier's hands, stuttering, 'me, me, me.'"[70]

The secret formula that animates the war-injured "golem" is, ironically, a German place name and house number. Brought to life through these proper names rather than through God's ineffable name, the soldier enacts the "failure to attain the linguistic level of the sacred" Hebrew language, even while the author upholds "the model of the world-creating language of Torah before him."[71] Moreover, the animating German names have a particular significance. From the opening sentence of *Ad hena*, the reader discovers that prior to the narrator's train journey, he resided at Frau Trotzmüller's boardinghouse in the Fasanenstrasse of Berlin.[72] Trotzmüller relates having dreamt that her son, missing in action, will come home because of the narrator, and this is exactly what takes place when the "golem man," the missing son, hears the street address and recognizes the name of the boardinghouse, his home.

Translated into Hebrew as *reḥov ha-pasyonim* (the street of the pheasants), the name of the street where the house is located evokes the *pasyon*, or passion, of Christ. It further brings to mind the massive and costly synagogue on the Fasanenstrasse, constructed by the Reform Jewish community of West Berlin. When the narrator subsequently approaches the boardinghouse, he takes note of the tall "temple of the enlightened with its gilded tiles made by the Kaiser Wilhelm Royal Tile Works." Agnon alludes here to the historical Kaiser Wilhelm II, who contributed tiles for one of the synagogue's halls from his factory in Kadinen, Poland, and sent his representative to the inauguration of the synagogue in 1912. The name of the street thus conjures up the name of the House of God, which has been secularized by the presence in proxy of another king, the German kaiser.[73] The term "temple of the enlight-ened" ironically suggests that while the Reform Jewish community has put its faith in the German nation, an act symbolized by the new "patri-otic synagogue," its members cannot be accepted as "enlightened" and fully integrated citizens of German society.

Just as the street name is itself a juncture of Christian and Jewish terms, so the Jewish narrator appears to travel along his own Via Do-lorosa, unwittingly helping to return the golem-soldier to his family, owners of the same boardinghouse on the Fasanenstrasse. The narra-tor's room in Frau Trotzmüller's house is then given over to the veteran, and he finds himself without a bed for the night: "I remained alone in the hallway, straightening myself and shrinking myself. Shrinking and straightening. Finally I stood like a golem whose actions are controlled by others. But here there was no one to tell me do this or do that."[74] On the train, the narrator felt like an immobile golem but unwittingly served as a Maharalic creator, since his actions animated the "golem"; this reversal of fortunes renders him a truly homeless golem. The so-called savior of the lost son becomes a neglected man, standing like a defunct golem whom no one even orders around.

The animation of the "witless" soldier is achieved through a particu-lar combination of names, numbers, and letters that have resonances in both Hebrew and German. The term that Agnon uses for "boarding-house" in Hebrew, *pensyon*, is itself a permutation of *pasyon* (passion), reminding us that the creative power of the Hebrew letters resides in their multiple permutations and combination.[75] Yet the seemingly posi-tive event of the veteran's revival also leads to a negative outcome for the narrator, who finds himself without a bed and a home and is therefore simply another sacrificed Jew.

A similar interlinguistic game takes place with regard to the given name of the "golem man": Hans Trotzmüller. As Hillel Weis has noted, the name Hans, without vocalization, could be read in Hebrew as *ha-nes*, the miracle.[76] The narrator uses the term "miracle" in the same scene when, on his arrival at the boardinghouse, he finds the doors wide open despite the late hour. Soon enough he realizes that the cause for this strange occurrence is a small miracle of sorts: the family is celebrating the return of Hans. What constitutes a mock "miracle" for one man is another man's disaster, and the narrator's inadvertent assumption of the role of a Maharal through his writing of the address at that opportune moment renders him vulnerable to the revolt of the war-made golem and to that of language itself. The transformation from golem to Hans marks a transition from a Hebrew term (*golem*), adapted into German language and literature, to a German proper name, albeit one that echoes the Hebrew "miracle."[77] In other words, the presence of a German name, Hans, within the Hebrew alphabet (*ha-nes*) temporalizes the holy tongue in which the Torah was given.

The "miracle" of Hans's return to his home and identity can also be read as comparable to the supposedly miraculous event of Hebrew's own return to its "native" land and its use as a national spoken language, a secularized tongue. In both cases, however, the resurrection is incomplete and its outcomes are uncertain: Hans does not become a cured "new" man, even after he resumes his previous life, and the status of modern Hebrew—and its relationship to the scriptural past of the language—remains a subject of much contestation. Todd Hasak-Lowy has compared the mad dog in Agnon's lengthy novel *Tmol shilshom* (*Only Yesterday*) with the golem story, claiming that the writing in Hebrew on the dog's body represents the magical potential of the holy tongue and the risks involved in its Zionist secularization as an everyday language.[78] The act of golem creation is likewise presented in *Ad hena* as a secularizing force necessitating the dangerous reform of Jewish tradition. The golem of World War I, however, is an interlingual and intercultural formation in which languages and identities contaminate each other, and the resulting creation—whether human or textual—rebels and overpowers its creator. The question remains open in *Ad hena* whether the return to Palestine/Israel could offer an alternative to this dismal linguistic and spiritual state of affairs.

Agnon thus uses the golem story to connect the devastations of past and present warfare with the issue of Hebrew textual and cultural modernization. When accused of a "lack of modernity," Agnon once claimed, "I am not completely free of any trace of modernity myself, and even when I do not want to modernize [lehitmadren], modernity revolts [mit-maredet] and lords over me [roda bi]."[79] Here, Agnon plays with the Hebrew root for modernity (mem-daled-resh), which, when the final two letters are reversed, spells the Hebrew word for rebellion (mem-resh-daled). With this alteration of the Hebrew signifier for modernity into one for revolt, a golem of modernity emerges that can rebel against its authorial creator. Ad hena is just such a rebellious text, a modern work the structure and progress of which seems to exceed its author's command. Indeed, the confusing narrative itself mimics the golem's growth and abrupt ending. The rushed and open denouement of this work further suggests that the condition of golemhood brought about by modern warfare precludes any true recovery or final return, so that Agnon's own text similarly cannot attain the "end point" of Zion or Israel. Even when the narrator returns to Palestine and builds a home there, Agnon depicts him walking through the empty rooms of a library in which he hopes to house a collection of Jewish books from Germany. The arrival of this library from Germany could potentially bridge past and present—the events of World War I and the Zionist endeavor—but the empty rooms and the postponement of any concrete resolution make the ending inconclusive and ironic.

The issue of creation through the Hebrew language also stands at the forefront of the Israeli playwright Dani Horowitz's drama Yossele golem. First performed in New York, in 1982, at La Mama E.T.C., the drama depicts the creation of a golem-savior using the twenty-two letters of the Hebrew alphabet. More specifically, Horowitz has the characters divide the animating word emet (truth) into its three letters (aleph–mem–tav), calling out words that begin with each letter. In this manner, the religious Jewish community intends to create a "hero," an entity with miraculous "power" that can fight their anti-Semitic opponents. The golem, Yossele, declares with his first utterance, "I hear whatever I'm told to hear. They tell me to wait, and I truly wait. Since the early morning, they tell me to hear axes, and I hear the sound of axes."[80] In his battle against the priest Tadeush, who, as in Rosenberg's *Niflaot Maharal*, plans a blood libel around Passover time, Yossele strikes "blows like an axe"—"like a miracle," utters one character, and another answers, "and not like a miracle." It remains unclear whether the animation and "power" of this modern hero-golem is miraculous or not. His actions, furthermore, are not executed to protect the Jews so much as to exact revenge "for all the debts," a phrase that is repeated throughout this brutal scene.[81]

After the golem has performed his violence, the Jews yearn only for "one word," the word "redemption" (*yeshuʿa*). Some of the characters believe that "whoever fought and won is also a Messiah," contending that this "miracle" of redemption was determined with the creation of the world. Formed and animated in order to exact revenge, the golem does not bring about any real change, however, and the characters seek in vain for mystical signs that would confirm his role as Messiah. At the end of the play, instead of ushering in the End of Days, the clay monster begins to collapse both physically and linguistically: "Everything falls. Hair. Eyes. Hands. Everything to the ground. I don't walk. I don't. I don't will come. I don't bring from the sky. I don't know. They don't tell me. If I hear an axe—I can do an axe. Rocks I can. I can't bring ships from the sky."[82] Connected to the earthly elements, the golem cannot offer a wish-fulfilling, heavenly redemption, only axes and rocks. His language is likewise broken, ungrammatical.

In Rina Yerushalmi's stage adaptation of Horowitz's play, depicted in a *New York Times* review, the golem is "born in sand," and sand covers the entire stage, creating a desert landscape not unlike the landscape of Israel. The golem appears to this reviewer like "a soldier in Israeli uniform," though an image from the production reveals that the national affiliation of the golem's uniform remains ambiguous.[83] This poetic drama leaves open the specific historical and national context, underscoring more generally the incompatibility of the Jewish notions of redemption and the use of (military) force, especially vengeful violence. Premiering in the summer of 1982, around the outbreak of the first Lebanon war,

Horowitz's *Yossele golem* reveals that the golem story continued to serve Israeli writers concerned with the violence of war and the manipulation of Hebrew letters for destructive purposes.

From *Ba'al Guf* to Living-Dead Soldier

The Jewish men in Horowitz's drama describe a golem with "enormous shoulders," a "forehead that breaks iron walls" and a "resolute skull . . . [and] resolute hand."[84] Horowitz's anthropoid resembles both H. Leivick's monstrous golem with his exaggerated physique and Agnon's Hans, described as a *"ba'al guf,"* denoting a tough, muscular man, as discussed in chapter 2.[85] In Jewish literature, the physically well-endowed *ba'al guf* was used to designate characters that exist at the outskirts, or borders, of traditional Jewish society.[86] For David Roskies, the *ba'al guf* was an "earlier, rudimentary" incarnation of the "new Jew" as a revolutionary and fighter, rather than intellectual. Although this figure acted "alone, on impulse" and was not yet "responsive to history," Sharon Gillerman underscores that this literary type was contemporaneous with the Zionist new Jewish man, even when "not produced exclusively by Zionists."[87]

On the physical level, the eastern European literary *ba'al guf* thus bore many affinities to the Zionist male bodily ideal of the "muscle Jew" or "new Jew," as articulated by Max Nordau already in 1898 and, most famously, in 1903.[88] Hence, it is not surprising that these two types have also been conflated and that the *ba'al guf*, especially in Hebrew literature, came to denote the Zionist man. According to Michael Gluzman, "the new man of Zionism was first and foremost a *ba'al guf,"* an impressively tall and masculine figure who embodied an anti-Jewish aesthetic.[89] When interpreting early twentieth-century Yiddish and German works, critics have likewise identified the golem as a new Jew. Rosenberg's *Nifla'ot Maharal* features the golem, in Gelbin's words, as a "muscle Jew dressed in Christian peasant clothes";[90] Wegener's cinematic golem also displays the physical attributes of the muscle Jew, differentiating him from the typical effeminate Jewish male and, in Nicholas Baer's reading, linking him to the new Jew as a biblical hero, a Samson.[91]

In Agnon's *Ad hena*, the golem Hans is a mock *ba'al guf*, a non-Jewish man who is reduced, rather than elevated, to mere physical existence. Unable to follow orders, he does not live by his passions, nor does he contribute to the nation; the "golem man" is an unproductive "new creation" despite his robust physique. In this way, Agnon parodies the Jewish literary construction of the *ba'al guf*, creating a passive figure that acts on his own volition only when hearing the name of his street and parental home. The Zionist-leaning narrator is described, furthermore, as a weak man "unsuitable for army work," rather than as a strong and bold new Jew. The narrator is well aware that if the war does not come to an end, even men like himself will be turned into soldiers: rather than a *ba'al guf*, which literally means the owner of a body, he will become a "*ba'al milḥama*," a soldier or, literally, the possessor of a war, whose fate would be "either death or injury."[92]

Agnon's writing on war injury and destruction precisely in the triumphant post-1948 period casts a shadow on the violent execution of the Zionist dream and on the ideal of heroic, antidiasporic masculinity. The implications of his modern golem story were not lost on the next generation of writers in Israel, who were also trying to contend with the events of 1948. One such writer was Yoram Kaniuk. Born and raised in Tel Aviv, he had fought in the 1948 war, suffering wounds in the battles for Jerusalem. Kaniuk's well-received 1966 work *Ḥimo melekh yerushalayim* (*Himmo, King of Jerusalem*) bears strong affinities to Agnon's *Ad hena*. Like Agnon, Kaniuk returned to the events of a previous war from a distant vantage point (over three decades in Agnon's case and eighteen years in Kaniuk's), fictionalizing and stylizing his autobiographical experiences.[93] *Ḥimo melekh yerushalayim* exhibits a certain generic indeterminacy, similarly to *Ad hena*, the text being neither long enough to constitute a novel nor short enough to be a novella. As Kaniuk himself describes it, furthermore, his work contains elements of the "gothic novel" (recalling Meyrink's *Der Golem*), but it is a "distinctly Israeli book."[94]

Kaniuk situates his entire narrative in one location: a makeshift hospital set up in the "Monastery of St. Hieronymus" in Jerusalem. This fictional site is a composite one, as Kaniuk disclosed, constructed of two different monasteries that he knew well: the one in which he was treated during the war and another (unnamed) one in which he resided after the war.[95] Kaniuk received medical treatment in 1948 at an Italian monastery, where he was laid up next to a severely wounded man who "grunted for ten days"; "he was something terrible," Kaniuk wrote in 1974, comparing the man to his fictional Ḥimo, "and he had a wonderful mouth."[96] Amos Guttman's cinematic adaptation of Kaniuk's work, first screened in 1987, is set in the Jerusalem Byzantine Monastery of the Cross, which was deserted during the 1948 battles and served as a base for the Gadna (the Jewish youth corps). Guttman visually asserted the centrality of this site, as it symbolizes the history and continuity of life in "Eretz Israel" and sets the stage for the clash between the Jewish newcomers to Israel and the land they seek to conquer and inhabit.[97]

Despite the autobiographical inspiration for this work, Kaniuk uses a third-person narrative voice, focalized through the character of the nurse Ḥamutal Horowitz. He allows us both to identify with the nurse and to retain a certain distance from her, rendering her actions somewhat mysterious. Similarly to the nurse Brigitta's fascination with the brain-injured "golem" in Ad hena, Kaniuk's protagonist, Ḥamutal, is obsessed with Ḥimo Farrah, a soldier whose stomach is lacerated, who has lost his eyesight, and who has suffered several amputated limbs. With the figure of Ḥimo, Kaniuk shows how the war not only has turned strapping youths into living-dead monsters but also has created a twilight zone in which the borders between man and woman, Jew and Christian, and Ashkenazi immigrant and Sephardic native are constantly blurred. On Ḥamutal's arrival at the battlefield hospital, she herself is an outsider from another "planet"—the city of Tel Aviv. Kaniuk's representation of her alienation in the makeshift Jerusalem hospital/monastery challenges the Zionist ideal of the secular and worldly woman from the new metropolis. In contrast to both the male Sephardic soldiers and the Christian nun who has mastered Hebrew and Arabic, Ḥamutal is a relative newcomer in Palestine.

The most striking similarity between *Ad hena* and *Ḥimo melekh yerushalayim* is the use of the moniker "golem" with reference to the severely wounded soldier under care. In both cases, the man's caretakers and fellow wounded soldiers adopt this nickname, which then becomes the common address for the horrific specter lying before them. The two golems, moreover, are men who have lost their ability to converse or relate to their surroundings. Ḥimo's only utterance is an incessant repetition of the stuttering words "*re bi*," which everyone around him interprets as his desire to die, a plea for his brother to shoot him (short for *tira bi*). In the context of the golem story, however, the phrase "*re bi*" also evokes the figure of the rabbi (*rebbe*, in Yiddish), both the golem's creator and its destroyer.

If the continued survival of the soldier-golems proves equally incomprehensible, they are, nonetheless, different types of golems: Agnon's Hans seems to lack a "brain" and cannot remember anything, including his name, while his body has remained intact. Kaniuk's Ḥimo is a mutilated man, a lump of flesh covered in bandages, whose limbs are "exposed and crushed [*me'ukhim*]."[98] Before the nurse Ḥamutal catches her first glimpse of the man, she reads the note at his bedside, providing his name, age, and medication orders. This note, reminiscent of the inscribed parchment that animates the golem, makes her feel responsible for keeping Ḥimo Farrah alive. "He has a name, and it is her duty to help him. Somebody had written that down on the slip of paper, somebody had given her instructions and taken off."[99] In contrast to the initially nameless Hans, Ḥimo's name restores some of his humanity and obligates his caretakers to assist him through an anonymous, divine-like, order. That order animates the nurse, resulting in a reversal of the golem and rabbi positions, just as in Agnon's work.

Unlike the inexpressive figure of Hans in *Ad hena*, the character of Ḥimo retains a remnant of his past glory; he was nicknamed "king of Jerusalem" because of his handsomeness and appeal to women.[100] Though the body of the nineteen-year-old is appallingly mutilated, his mouth possesses "the deepest and most noble beauty, perfection on the brink of horror, . . . like a solitary flower on a vast wall."[101] Indeed, his mouth is the site of the text's sublime encounter. It is both life giving and deadly, as when Ḥimo utters his wish to die, reminding us of the mouth of the golem of Prague, in which the rabbi places and removes the animating parchment. Another wounded soldier who knew Ḥimo from his prewar days even declares that he was once called "The Holy Mouth," though now he is more like a corpse.[102]

With a ravaged body and sublime mouth, the golem-soldier is un-like any of the other wounded men at the hospital. Kaniuk describes the soldier Franji, who lost an eye and injured a leg in the war, as a tall and muscular "ba'al guf," "his thick-set body rippling with muscles." Franji, a young man of Sephardic extraction, appears liable to erupt vio-lently at any moment, turning "red, and stormy, and wild." While Franji is "no longer the man he had been," his injured body, like that of the other hospitalized soldiers, is "merely wounded" or "simply put out of action," contrasting him both to the "legendary" living-dead Ḥimo and to deceased war heroes such as Ḥamutal's late fiancé.[103] Repulsed by the manly Franji, Ḥamutal is drawn to the helpless Ḥimo. Hence, Kaniuk's depiction of Franji as a ba'al guf whose masculinity has been compro-mised does not affirm this bodily ideal but rather calls into question the Ashkenazi military leadership's use of Sephardic men as mere cannon fodder.

As Ḥamutal comes to understand, the choice to call Ḥimo "golem" does not necessarily indicate a meanness of spirit within the other soldiers or a desire to humiliate the wounded man but rather their compulsion to differentiate themselves, to avoid any possible form of identification with him. The "golem" is no longer human, no longer a suffering soldier, for he has crossed the threshold into the realm of the dead; his body cannot even be diagnosed as a "living body" accord-ing to the rules of science. His incomprehensible subsistence belittles the other soldiers' own troubles and renders them closer to those who are still fighting in the battlefields, reducing their status as the noble wounded.[104] While the hospitalized soldiers strive to distinguish themselves from Ḥimo, Ḥamutal completely aligns herself with this "golem," devoting herself to his needs alone. As the other soldiers yearn for the "miracle" of his death and disappearance, Ḥamutal takes it upon herself—until the dramatic ending—to forestall this death. She, in turn, becomes more golem-like in Kaniuk's descriptions: her endurance and emotional staunchness mark her as made of "stone" rather than "flesh-and-blood," as being devoid of "humanity."[105]

As Ḥamutal's relationship to Ḥimo grows stronger, she is repeatedly said to be "in love," and the soldiers await a "blood wedding between Ḥamutal and her golem." At the close of the book, this notion is realized: Ḥamutal decides to kill Ḥimo with an overdose of serum, putting an end to his suffering as well as to hers. The "fatal attraction" of the nurse to the golem—understated in Agnon's *Ad hena* and explicit in Kaniuk's work—reverses the early twentieth-century motif of the golem's own pursuit of the rabbi's daughter in an attempt to assert its human side (as in Wegener's films, Leivick's poema, and Gabel's operetta). If the war turns young men into defunct golems, Ḥamutal strives to animate the dead clay, not unlike a male rabbi or Maharal. To do so, her initial instinct is to follow the Christian path of redeeming the death of the body or flesh through the promise of another, spiritual life. Toward the end of the narrative, however, she denounces her status as a kind of Madonna-Messiah, attempting to become a flesh-and-blood lover to Ḥimo. "Let me become a human being again," she utters, asking the "golem" to respond to her sexually.[106] Feeling rejected as a "bride" when Ḥimo does not respond, Ḥamutal reassumes her masculine role in the hospital, as Edya Mendelson-Maʿoz argues, penetrating Ḥimo with the "lethal injection."[107]

Yosefa Loshitzky has likewise maintained that Ḥimo, as the descendant of a long line of kabbalists from the old Yishuv in Jerusalem, is Zionism's "other." By killing him at the end of the narrative, Ḥamutal destroys this otherness, the Sephardic lineage, and proclaims the victory of the newfound European Jewish modernity, embodied in the city of Tel Aviv, to which she returns after Ḥimo's death. At the same time, she takes on the role of the kabbalist herself, becoming a golem creator who can also put an end to this creation's existence. Moreover, Ḥimo's suffering is explicitly compared to that of Jesus, another "king of Jerusalem," and his death therefore signals the current conquest of Judaism over Christianity (and Islam) in the battle over the Land of Israel.[108] In this sense too Ḥimo is a victim of Israeli militarism.

Precisely when Ḥamutal is about to kill Ḥimo, "the familiar symphony of battle" resumes with bursts of machine-gun and small-arms fire. The nurse with her deadly injection is imagined, against this background noise, as a soldier who fulfills the ultimate mission of killing, by "her own courage," the enemy: the Jewish man who has crossed over to the Christian side and even, potentially, to the Muslim side that threatens renewed Zionist Jewish life in Israel/Palestine.[109] Rather than cast the golem as the external Arab enemy, Kaniuk portrays an internal, Jewish golem that nonetheless signifies the monstrous ability to cross religious lines and suggests the blurring of the categories of friend and foe. Through Ḥamutal's lethal deed, her own name and story are erased; even decades later, she believes that her name has been excised with "a sharp slaughterer's knife" by those who witnessed her deed, so that they could erase its memory as well.[110] Ultimately, in Kaniuk's work, it is the nurse, rather than the golem, who rebels against basic human conventions, even when her revolt is co-opted by the state and its belligerent affairs.

With the grotesque figure of Ḥimo, Kaniuk ironically reconfigures the trope of the living-dead (ha-met ha-ḥay), often used in the works of the prestatehood (Eretz-Israeli) generation to glorify fallen soldiers and justify their sacrifice. Kaniuk's living-dead is not a fallen hero waxing poetic from beyond the grave but a grotesquely real survivor whose body refuses to succumb. Ḥimo's sacrifice is not justified in national and symbolic terms; he is an antihero who despises his continued existence. His desire to be shot to death evokes Nathan Alterman's poem

"*Magash ha-kesef*" ("The Silver Platter"), published in December 1947, describing a young man and woman who "quietly . . . approach / Then stand motionless, / And there is no sign whether they yet live or have been shot."[111] But whereas Alterman's heroic youth embody "the silver platter" on which the "Jewish state is served" to its people, Kaniuk uses the appellation "golem" to designate the state of *unheroic* living-death. Similarly, the other wounded soldiers whose mundane injuries have not earned them heroic "legends" are compared to Ḥamutal's former lover who died in the Galilee. He is "the silver platter."[112] When a different soldier is brought to the hospital in critical condition, on the verge of death, he is referred to, instead, as "another golem."[113] Rather than seeing this soldier as a new and all-powerful creation that can carry out arduous tasks, a kind of supersoldier, Kaniuk portrays him as a golem who has remained alive against all odds, against all reason, and whose subsistence between life and death challenges the moral fiber of his society.

In a personal essay titled "The Stories That Became My Life Story," Kaniuk relates, "It took me years to understand that ever since 1948, after the battle in Nebi Samuel, I lived in a state that was not understood at the time to be shell shock [*helem krav*]. The things I underwent there were too horrific." He further presents his writing as a kind of "occupational therapy for the awful wound that [he] experienced during the war." This fictional "interpretation of catastrophes" transforms these sorrowful events into "stories," "jokes," and even "flowers," in his words.[114] Through this creative process, Kaniuk molded his horrific experiences into a highly controlled and structured work of art. As the literary critic of *Ha'aretz* wrote upon the book's publication, Kaniuk's language "should have been drunk and wild, but instead it is static and orderly. The dialogue is mechanical and artificial, and the characters are devoid of any kernel of darkness."[115] Kaniuk explained in an interview that he worked hard to produce precisely this effect, striving to render "this immense horror [*eyma nora'a*] as if it took place in a glass cup . . . within a very restrained frame." For the awfulness of the experience to be revealed in full force, he contended, the language must be restrained, rather than a "wild, modernist" Hebrew.[116] Kaniuk uses the dissonance between linguistic form and content both to contain the "horror" and to expose it through the "glass cup" of literature. Writing from the perspective of a citizen on the home front, Agnon, by contrast, allows his stylized text to run amok, to overtake its creator, as it were, and to revolt in the modernist sense.

* * *

Both dead and alive, human and inhuman, the golem figure for Agnon and Kaniuk represents war injury as an indecipherable phenomenon, a new physiognomy that, since World War I, has changed the face of generations to come. Its very existence is an ironic modern "miracle," calling into question the basic assumptions of twentieth-century medicine and science, but without leading to any greater faith in divine intervention or in the sacred powers of the animating Hebrew language. The patriotic journalism of the 1948 period, whether socialist or right wing, projected the idea of the golem onto the enemy forces, disowning this supposedly diasporic Jewish fantasy and using the golem to suggest the self-destructive and dependent nature of the Arab nations. The Hebrew literature written during, or about, the 1948 war also revisited the golem story but relied on its mystical and literary connotations in order to convey the grotesque nature of war and its incomprehensible and dehumanizing consequences for both battling sides. These literary golems are hybrid products of Hebrew-German and Jewish-Arab interaction. Agnon's German golem is, moreover, a creation of blind nationalism on the part of both Jewish and non-Jewish German citizens. The enemy becomes internalized, in this literature, and the golem represents the inability to distinguish fully between self and other, ally and enemy. "War brings death to all equally. That is the monstrosity of war," write Michael Hardt and Antonio Negri.[117]

The Israeli authors Agnon, Kaniuk, and Horowitz all use the golem story to depict the individual and collective price of war and excessive brutality. They do not relegate golemhood to the enemy alone but rather retain this term for the sake of Israeli society's own self-accounting. The golem bequeathed to Israeli literature is the temporary name for a defunct and deformed man, one who cannot be transformed into a Zionist war hero, a muscular Jewish defender. In Kaniuk's text, the body of the soldier-golem is utterly ravaged—he can no longer be considered a *ba'al guf*—further radicalizing Agnon's earlier depiction of a strapping man who has lost his memory and agency. In Horowitz's drama, the golem successfully deploys his enormous body to accomplish his violent mission, but he loses all power and deanimates when expected to bring about a false redemption. The term *golem* becomes synonymous in these texts with destruction and de-creation rather than with animation and nation-building. So these Israeli works evoke the vulnerability of the Zionist project and reveal the madness and instability that lurk beneath it. The darker side of the militarily "mighty Jewish state," which can and has been compared to a golem that can potentially run amok, is the injured soldier who—for the length of the narrative at least—refuses to join the dead. The golem thus stands as a troubling remnant of the human losses and moral failures that resulted from the 1948 war.

4

Supergolem

Revenge after the Holocaust

On the occasion of Superman's sixtieth anniversary—celebrating his "birth" in a June 1938 issue of *Action Comics*—Jon Bogdanove and Louise Simonson created a three-issue-long story that brings Superman back in time to Nazi-occupied Poland.[1] The man of steel is roused to action as he witnesses mass death and torture, and he outdoes himself to save the residents of the Warsaw ghetto. In a controversial attempt to universalize the horror of World War II, the editors of DC Comics removed all explicit references to "Jews," "Germans," and "Catholics." Nonetheless, the three issues are replete with allusions to Jewish culture, including—we should not be surprised—numerous associations of Superman himself with the golem figure.[2]

In Warsaw, the superhero encounters Baruch and Moishe, a young writer-and-artist team reminiscent of Superman's original creators, Jerry Siegel and Joe Shuster. The duo draw their own "muscular angel," complete with a Superman-like triangle on his chest, designed to "fight tanks" and save the Jewish people.[3] The grandfather of these boys declares that the caped hero is a "golem" and then provides Superman (and the reader) with a brief summary of the creation and functions of the golem, "a fearsome, mighty creature that would drive away enemies and save the people!"[4] In this manner, the comic book's creators construct a legendary lineage leading from the golem to Superman, suggesting that the American superhero needs to continue the work that the pre–World War II golem started. Uncannily, as early as 1921, in a review of Paul Wegener's 1920 golem film, the *New York Tribune* called the cinematic monster "a superman, a heroic, invulnerable figure."[5] But throughout

Superman's own lengthy career and even in this 1998 comics book, this figure has resisted any clear-cut affiliation with the (Jewish) golem, and one speech balloon even shows him thinking that he is "not a golem and . . . no angel" (figure 4.1).[6]

Despite Superman's physical strength, he is neither a clay anthropoid that follows its creator's orders nor an invulnerable "angel." Rather, in both his appearance and demeanor, the superhero is a prime example of white Protestant American masculinity. Yet the partial alignment of the two figures persists in the pages of this comic book. Like the grandfather and other ghetto residents who believe that the golem has materialized in the figure of Superman, the Germans represented in the comic book also describe the "golem" this way: "a manifestation of unholy magic—to punish us for what we are doing." The opening panels of the second issue depict Superman standing in front of a speeding train while two German operators on board yell out, "It's just a man! N-no! It is the Golem!" The Nazi commander Zimmler declares that the supposed "retribution" of the golem is "superstitious foolishness" resulting from "some kind of allied trick, or even a secret weapon." He uses the occasion as an excuse to begin liquidation of the ghetto.[7]

The Superman anniversary issues exemplify some of the most prominent features of the golem in the decades after World War II in America—features, as we will see, that sharply diverge from the golem's Israeli invocations. During these years, this "mighty creature" became deeply linked in the American imagination with the Holocaust. It represented a lost eastern European Jewish past through its "origins" in Poland and embodied the (Jewish) fantasy of overcoming the Nazis and even avenging the genocide.[8] Site of the largest Jewish revolt during World War II, the Warsaw ghetto had already been used in 1977 by Marvel as the location for the resurrection of the golem. The 1998 comic books were thus another example—a more widely circulating and notable one—of the golem's protective and even retributive role in American popular culture.

FIGURE 4.1. Superman in the Warsaw ghetto with Bruch, Moishe, and their grandfather. From *Superman: The Man of Steel* #81. (© DC Comics)

Starting in the late nineteenth century and well into the twentieth century, golem narratives began to cast this figure not as a mere servant but as a protector of the Jews from violent persecution at the hands of non-Jews. The explicit notion of Jewish revenge briefly surfaced in late nineteenth-century stories by I. L. Peretz and Sholem Aleichem, who portrayed the golem as an indiscriminate murderer of evil-intending gentiles. But for the most part, revenge is not something that (fictional) Jews do. The standard American Holocaust narrative, as Daniel H. Magilow and others have explained, pits meek Jewish victims against utterly evil perpetrators, supporting a "clear-cut moral dichotomy" of good and evil that promotes "redemptive Christological narratives."[9] A few revealing post-Holocaust evocations of the golem have, by contrast, created a protector who can also become a dangerously blind avenger. As we will see, these post-1945 works present the golem as a deterrent, or "secret weapon"—akin to a nuclear warhead and sometimes literally constructed of nuclear components—in addition to a bloodthirsty slayer. While these golems were portrayed as gigantic in proportion and extreme in power, cartoonists made sure to explicitly disassociate them from the pantheon of American superheroes and their civilian counterparts. Hence, this chapter closely examines the golem as a figure of retribution in American comics, rather than attempting to reveal how the superhero genre in general drew inspiration from golem tales, among many other legendary sources.[10]

The use of the golem in such Jewish American revenge fantasies, particularly those that chronicle the events of World War II, stretches beyond comic books and into literature and film. In *Inglourious Basterds* (2009), Quentin Tarantino violently bashes the aforementioned dichotomy between the weak Jews and their evil persecutors while avoiding any pretense of realistic representation.[11] The name and aura of the golem becomes attached in Tarantino's film to the most violent character of the "Bear Jew," even though an actual golem never appears on the screen. The moniker "golem" endows the bat-swinging killer with superhuman and mythic powers that account for his unstoppable vengeful spirit. This atypical depiction of a Jew as powerful rather than gentle relies on the evocation of the golem, the singular Jewish monster that wields exaggerated physical strength for both protective and retributive purposes.

The notion of the golem as a violent avenger has been treated with much caution in American culture and is therefore relatively unac-knowledged. Even in those comic books, novels, and films that do imagine the golem as an avenger on behalf of Jewish populations, this role is often fraught with ambivalence. In post–World War II works of American literature, the golem story is predominantly inflected, by con-trast, with humor or nostalgia rather than a penchant for revenge. For instance, Elizabeth Baer notes the "sacral tone" in the Holocaust survi-vor Elie Wiesel's novelistic rendition of the golem legend, in which the golem is praised and mourned as a heroic savior.[12] In a *New York Times* review of Wiesel's *The Golem*, Kenneth Briggs writes, "Clearly, this is a golem suited to the needs of post-Holocaust Judaism, adapted to meet the Jewish longing for a protector . . . with the ability of devoting his life to others."[13] A more recent example is Helene Wecker's 2013 *The Golem and the Jinni*, set in 1899 New York, which depicts a female golem searching for the purpose of her existence after the death of her mas-ter. When she must resort to physical power—a rare event in the novel, despite her evident strength—she experiences intense guilt and comes close to self-annihilation. More generally, Wecker's nonviolent golem ex-hibits empathy toward humans and a willingness to help others.[14]

The "needs of post-Holocaust" American Jews were not limited to such tame monsters, however. The golem's ability to protect was often invoked, to be sure. But from the works we will examine, it is clear that American artists, Jews and non-Jews alike, tapped the public's desire for some form of imagined violent retribution for the mass annihilation of European Jewry. Michael Chabon's novel about the early comic book industry, *The Amazing Adventures of Kavalier & Clay* (2000), uses the golem to destabilize the trope of the redemptive Holocaust narrative that hinges on Jewish victimhood. Other early twenty-first-century works, such as Tarantino's *Inglourious Basterds* and James Sturm's graphic novel *The Golem's Mighty Swing* (2001), take the golem story one step further in order to call into question the "post-Holocaust stigmatization of Jewish rage."[15] The appearance of the golem as violent avenger in comic books of the 1970s shaped these later self-reflexive works, all of which pay tribute to American comics in different ways, as well as to the silent German cinema in which the golem made its visual debut.

The Golem in 1970s Comic Books: A Mass of Contradictions

After World War II, Marvel Comics, the successor of Atlas and Timely Comics, became one of the leading publishers in what is called the "Silver Age" of the comic book industry, between the mid-1950s and the late 1970s. Marvel boasted new and popular titles such as *Fantastic Four*, *X-Men*, and the *Incredible Hulk*. Created by Stan Lee (Stanley Martin Lieber) and Jack Kirby (Jacob Kurtzberg), these postwar heroes were easier to identify with, more human, and the stories were aimed not just at children or teenagers but also at hip adult audiences. If Superman was initially known for his "righteous violence," this second generation of superheroes offered a murkier moral compass; they tried to do the right thing in a world riddled with moral dilemmas and anxieties.[16] African American and Asian American heroes, as well as female heroines, were part of this emerging Marvel universe.

The golem, a "Jewish monster-hero," was one of the last to be added to this list of heroic "others," debuting in a June 1974 issue of *Strange Tales*, a comic book series of suspense and horror stories that began in 1951.[17] Though planned as an ongoing series, "The Golem" was discontinued after three issues.[18] Technical problems, such as changes in the artistic teams and the inability to achieve continuity, brought about the rather abrupt decision to end the Golem series, but that decision, as Marvel admitted, also had to do with the project's lack of direction. As the editors wrote in the third, farewell issue, "Was it a human-interest book like *Man-Thing*? A smasho-whammo-destructo book like *The Hulk*? A supernatural mystery thriller like *Werewolf by Night*? We just couldn't make up our minds."[19] In addition to the difficulty of determining the comic book subgenre into which the golem would best fit, another problem haunted these three issues: how should the golem's violence, as protector of Jews, be depicted and justified?

The first comic book opens with the golem's backstory, penned by Len Wein, relating how this mythological creature was formed not only out of "stone and clay" but also from "the blood of a people's oppression." This "moving monolith . . . rose before the yoke of tyranny," fighting for the values of "justice" and "freedom."[20] Having "balanced freedom's scales," the golem then retreated to the desert and allowed itself to be buried in the sand. At this point, the present-day story of the comic book begins, with a Jewish American professor, Abraham Adamson (nicknamed "Uncle Abe"), who is traveling with his nephew (Jason), niece (Rebecca), and her fiancé (Wayne) to the deserts of the Middle East. Their goal is to discover and dig up the golem. The site of the archeological dig is also a war zone, "a war of territory, of ideologies—fought with great fervor but with little gain." The combatants, men "dedicated" to this futile war, go to battle wielding "loaned weaponry." While the panel containing this text shows modern machine guns and exploding artillery, the subsequent panel jumps to a different scene: a physical life-and-death struggle between two men who are not identified ethnically or nationally, one holding a dagger above the other. The narrator describes these men as "imperfect" and "all-too-human," although they act out of "the love of their country" and "the courage of their convictions."[21]

Published in the aftermath of the 1973 Yom Kippur War, in which the United States offered decisive military aid to Israel ("loaned weaponry"), this comic book also negotiates the complexities of American-Israeli relations. It underscores the American fascination with Israeli military power but aligns it, via the golem story, with the equally powerful pull toward the eastern European Jewish past.[22] Language like "love of country" and "dedicated men" evokes the determination of the Israelis to overcome their opponents and protect their country in a war that was not initiated by them. In the story that unfolds, Jewish American family members are held hostage by a faction of Arab army deserters who steal their supplies and kill Uncle Abe. In his last dying moments, the Jewish scientist uses the kabbalistic formula of "the mystic alphabets of the 221 gates" to animate the golem he has dug up; it is the man's single tear, shed when he thinks he might have failed, that awakens the golem and makes it "aware of the old man's loved ones who will not live much longer unless something is quickly done."[23] Jewish violence is thus portrayed as an act of self-defense, and the golem of American comics culture helps protect the Jews, rather than representing their enemies, as we have seen in the Israeli case.

If "men" who fight wars are "imperfect, all-too human," the inhuman golem could potentially put an end to these senseless wars. The comic book, however, specifically pits the golem against the faction of deserters. Fighting with its bare fists, the golem sheds the deserters' bullets "like wind-blown leaves" and slays the men as "a symbol of retribution." It then proceeds to kill Omar, the commander of the deserters, not out of hatred but because "he feels he must," as the golem is "filled with love for the Adamsons." Those people whom the golem must protect are specific individuals, the Adamsons and Wayne, who are also "in part responsible for his resurrection."[24] If in previous times the golem fought against "tyranny" at large, its present resurrection is but a faint echo of these great deeds of the past.

This first issue ends with Rebecca's perception that the golem knows the family; she can recognize something familiar about it, a "twinkle at the corners of his eyes."[25] In the subsequent two issues, Rebecca and Wayne express their ambivalence toward the golem's killing of Omar, who murdered their uncle and who would likely have murdered them as well. Rebecca speculates, because of the "familiar twinkle," that her uncle not only animated the golem but also entered into this entity in some form (a previous panel shows his tears falling on the golem as it dies). Nevertheless, she cannot reconcile the association between the golem and her departed relative: "My uncle was a gentle man. He would never have killed anyone—nor wished a death—even of the one who murdered him!"[26] The two top panels of this spread show Rebecca pointing her finger at the golem, and her extended arm reaches through the gutter (the white space between panels) and encroaches on the subsequent panel exhibiting the face of the mute golem (figure 4.2). This finger-pointing both identifies the golem and assigns guilt to the monster. In contrast to the "gentle" Jewish scientist who presumably would not fantasize about killing someone, even in self-defense, the golem is a slayer. This portrait of Jewish meekness is set in contrast to the golem's brutality, its "grisly revenge upon the soldiers." The golem is a "mass of contradictions," as Wayne promptly declares: this contradictory being is simultaneously a vengeful murderer and "a young child" who acts "with the highest of good intentions," only unintentionally causing destruction. Rebecca then concedes that "Uncle Abraham could forgive the golem's bloody revenge—and so must we."[27]

By distinguishing between the uncle and the golem, despite their connection as creator and creation, the comic book artists could retain the image of Jewish self-sacrifice and victimhood while still creating a fantasy of Jewish revenge via an externalized monster figure. By way of analogy, the artists suggest that American intervention in the Middle East and support for the Jewish cause via "loaned weapons" is motivated only by "the highest of good intentions" and that Americans (and, implicitly, Israelis) ultimately pursue "justice" and "freedom," avoiding violence whenever possible.[28] When comparing the Arab forces to a golem in 1948, the Israeli press painted a very different image of a monster enemy that is dependent on and manipulated by the British, who use it simply to advance their political aims by violent means.

While the intentions of the menacing golem are suspect here, those who attempt to control this monster are portrayed in a more positive light. At the end of the second issue, the family even prevents the golem from killing the Arab border guards who try to thwart its transportation to the United States: "Golem—stop! In the name of our people, I

FIGURE 4.2. Rebecca, Wayne, and Jason inspect the golem and discuss its murderousness. From *Strange Tales* #176. (© Marvel Comics)

say this is wrong! If you can understand my words, put them down—gently!" The command to act "gently" recalls the description of the deceased "gentle" Jewish scientist. The guards' commander responds, "Thank you for saving these only-dutiful soldiers' lives, Americans."[29] In identifying them as American here, the comics' creators assert the family's high moral standards and laud their ability to control the unlimited force at their disposal. In Spider-Man's now-immortal words, first uttered in a 1962 comic book, "In this world, with great power there must also come—great responsibility." Those Jewish artists and their characters who resurrected the golem in the aftermath of World War II felt similarly impelled to acknowledge the responsibility entailed in their newfound power.[30] The Marvel golem does not act out of fear, hatred, or even "a sense of justice": its "truth" is "love," and therefore it is not a ruthless monster. In the words of the comic book, its "obvious violence can be seen as a protective response."[31]

Marvel's golem draws the "greatest strength" from its "emotional affinity with people," specifically with the two Jewish siblings and the sister's fiancé. Still, as the editors of *Strange Tales* determined, such a contradictory and ambivalent being, one who lacks humanity but feels "affinity" for particular humans, could not sustain a comic book series. In the third and final issue of 1974, they "candidly" admitted that they "goofed."[32] It was not merely the generic indeterminacy of the golem series that made Marvel doubt the validity and success of this avenger but also, I suggest, the constant need to justify the golem's violence in view of its Jewish associations and its affinity with the American Jewish family. Motivated by "love" but unable to talk or to express its emotions and ties to humanity, this particular gigantic purple monolith was put to rest after a brief comic book existence, just as the lives of most golems come to an abrupt end. In this case, it was not the golem's erratic behavior or tendency to turn against its creators that brought about the monster's demise but precisely its mitigated violence and unclear calling as a statue that awakens only for spells of aggressive combat.

Post-Holocaust Revenge Fantasies

As early as 1946, the Polish-born artist Joe Kubert illustrated his version of the golem of Prague as a story told by an old man to an injured American pilot in the Warsaw ghetto. In this retelling, the American forces bombing the Germans and saving those Jews that still can be saved are compared to the golem of lore. At the end of the comic book, the American soldier pronounces, "I think I see your point. . . . The armies of democracy are not so far off from being the golem of 1944!"[33] It took several more decades, however, until the golem became associated with the Holocaust and resurrected in the ghettos themselves, not as a metaphorical story of past self-defense. In *While America Watches: Televising the Holocaust*, Jeffrey Shandler explains that the years between 1961, when the Eichmann trial was televised, and 1978, the premiere of the miniseries *Holocaust*, "saw the Holocaust become an increasingly frequent, even routine, presence on American television."[34] Likewise, starting in the 1970s, the golem was more frequently mentioned in connection, both implicit and explicit, to the Nazi extermination of the Jews.

The earliest example of this phenomenon dates back to a 1970 double issue of *The Hulk* (again Marvel comics) that evokes the golem by name. Generally speaking, the Hulk is a "hero by accident" rather than an intentional creation like the golem. When Dr. Bruce Banner, atomic physicist, attempts to save a teenager who had wandered into an army bomb-test site, he is exposed to gamma radiation and becomes a green monster. The result is a new type of hero, as Bradford Wright describes him: "The Hulk's overriding desire is self-preservation and privacy. . . . He cares nothing for humankind but inevitably fights in its defense when a villain bent on world domination makes the mistake of attacking him."[35]

The writer Roy Thomas, who went on to edit Marvel's three-issue golem series, sets the 1970 Hulk issues in the fictional Morvania, a "tiny Mediterranean nation" ruled by Draxon, an ambitious dictator who claims that "where Hitler failed . . . there shall Draxon succeed."[36] A small peasant uprising led by a Jewish man named Isaac, who attempts to enlist the Hulk in his cause and even calls him a modern-day golem, opposes this cruel ruler. In the second issue—titled "Incredible Hulk in the Shadow of . . . the Golem!"—the Hulk occupies a destroyed old city, and Draxon's generals report that their soldiers now "believe the rumors that say he is the mighty golem of Jewish legend!"[37] The term "golem" functions here as a kind of propaganda weapon, more rumor than reality, although the Hulk does come to the aid of the peasants because he feels for the suffering of Isaac's young daughter.[38]

The 1974 *Strange Tales'* "Golem" invokes World War II through an advertisement for an illustrated history titled "Hitler: The Horror & The Holocaust" and authored by Marvel's own Stan Lee and Michael Valenti. This ad promises to supply (for "only $1.00!") over one hundred photographs that relate the "incredible history" of the Third Reich. The Holocaust is reduced to the story of a "madman," Hitler, who wishes to "carry half the world into destruction with [him]," not unlike the exaggerated evildoers of the superhero genre. On the page opposite this advertisement, we find a sequence in which "the ancient mystical word meaning 'truth' (*emeth*)" materializes on the golem's forehead, as this monster attains a "new-found resistance" and violently disposes of one of its enemies.[39] The ad that promises to reveal "the terrible truth" of the Holocaust through news photography stands in direct relation to the short-lived character of the American golem and its superhuman powers. Put otherwise, the fictional "*emeth*" of the giant golem as a fantasy of Jewish power and self-protection is pitted here over and against the "terrible truth" of historical Jewish victimization at the hands of a "madman." Featured alongside multiple ads for male bodily enhancement through various exercise devices, the ad for the Holocaust magazine provides further motivation for the desire to transform the Jewish male body and render it at least slightly more similar to that of the golem.

The connection between the golem and the Holocaust was made explicit in a single 1977 issue of Marvel's *The Invaders*, titled *The Golem Walks Again*. Written by Thomas, the comic book tells of a clay giant

Figure 4.3. The "truth" of the golem (love) and the "terrible truth" of the Holocaust. From *Strange Tales* #177. (© Marvel Comics)

molded in the Warsaw ghetto using a combination of earth, rain, and "heavy water" stolen from the Nazis, a substance historically used by World War II German scientists as a neutron moderator in their nuclear reactors. In mingling this "strange liquid," which the Jewish creator, Jacob Goldstein, claims to know nothing about, with "the clay of the ghetto," a golem is animated that combines both Jew and Nazi, drawing on tellurian and nuclear power. This "vengeful Titan" proceeds to free from a dungeon the Invaders—a Marvel Comics team of American superheroes that premiered together in 1969—and then kills the Nazi commander. Only at the very end of the comic book, when the golem himself erases the letter *e* from the word *emeth* on his forehead, thereby ending his existence, do we receive confirmation that Goldstein, his creator, was hidden inside him all along. In this manner, the ghetto golem attains a dual, human-monster identity that puts him on par with other superheroes of the period, like the Hulk himself. The creation of a golem who hides a Jewish man inside of him also paves the way for thinking about potential Jewish insurrection and even vengeance.[40]

The Invaders, also called "The Greatest Superheroes of World War II," was a "Silver Age" comic book series that resurrected and reunited prewar superheroes of the "Golden Age" of comic books, like Captain America, the Sub-Mariner, and the Human Torch. In reusing these earlier, "golden" superheroes, *The Invaders* was a particularly revealing indicator of changing cultural priorities. The first issue of *Captain America Comics*, for example, released in March 1941, went out on a limb and depicted the "ultra-American hero slugging Adolf Hitler in the face almost a full year before the United States declared war on the Axis." But in the postwar years, this formerly top-selling title failed; Captain America did not convince readers as a "Commie Smasher."[41] Captain America and his team are featured in the 1977 issue that takes place in the Warsaw ghetto. After the Nazis capture the (American) Invaders, Goldstein can "no longer . . . sit idly by" and feels that he "must act" to liberate his liberators, but he finds that his action can only be carried out by an enhanced version of himself, "a golem, come to protect" the Jews of the ghetto.[42]

At the conclusion of the story, Goldstein realizes that "patient submission" is not enough and that his people need to "revolt against the Nazi conqueror" even if that revolt will most likely be unsuccessful. The comic book ends with an ominous statement: "The Invaders are not prophets; they've no way of knowing that untold thousands will perish, when the Jews of the Warsaw ghetto rise in revolt, in April of 1943." And even if they did know, they could not change the "inscrutable workings of destiny" because they "are only human beings, after all." In this fantastical return to the Warsaw ghetto, the Invaders, representing the American nation, are exempted from any responsibility for the impending annihilation of the Jews, especially since Jacob Goldstein does not join the "allied war efforts" and remains in the ghetto to fight alongside his people.[43] Thomas thus manages to express the Jewish desire for power and agency while also excusing America for the lack of intervention that might have saved innumerable Jewish lives.

Despite this comic book's bleak ending and the limitations placed on its revisionist vision, its revenge narrative nonetheless manages to bring to the surface a dormant fantasy. The hybridity of the golem itself, as envisioned by the illustrators Frank Robbins and Frank Springer, makes this golem creation story stand out. The Warsaw ghetto golem is a "grotesque" and "fearsome gargoyle," ten feet tall and "huge and terrible of aspect." The first panel that shows its resurrection "out of the rubble" takes up half a page, and in it, every action of the golem has an earth-shattering effect so that the background is filled with breaking stones and smoke.[44] The menacing apparition, drawn from below to emphasize its stature, is then contrasted with the base brutality of a Nazi soldier who strikes at a Jewish girl with the butt of his rifle (figure 4.4).

On the next page, the golem is drawn with its back to the reader, so that we can clearly see its yarmulke, enhancing the Jewish connection to Jacob Goldstein, also drawn with a yarmulke on his head. The golem is a double of Goldstein, who, however, appears well built and even Westernized, with blond hair, blue eyes, and a square jaw, rather than as a starved ghetto Jew. The golem is thus a second-degree double:

FIGURE 4.4. The golem emerges from the rubble of the Warsaw ghetto. From *The Invaders* #13. (© Marvel Comics)

the character of Jacob already resembles the European, non-Jewish male ideal; the golem is a new rendering of this ideal—in monstrous proportions (figure 4.5). Through such second-degree doubling, the golem, with its bare chest, also recalls the Nazi guard watching over the captive Invaders. Hence, the 1977 Holocaust golem is a cross not merely between human and inanimate matter, "cold clay," but also between the Polish Jew and the American superhero, as well as between the Polish Jew and his Nazi opponent.[45]

Despite such visual emphasis of the golem's Jewishness, there is nothing in its violent actions to suggest the stereotypical image of the eastern European Jew. At one point, Captain America's sidekick, Bucky, even announces, "Gosh! He tore thru those ropes as if they were Christmas tree tinsel!" To which Captain America responds, "If that big guy's who I suspect, Bucky—that's not the most apt comparison you ever made."[46] Without using the words "Jew" or "Jewish," this sly aside reinforces the golem's Jewishness. Still, Bucky's statement also reminds us that the golem's proportions and strength are "goyish," evoking Christian associations. The Jewish desire for power and vengeance cannot be squared, at this time period, with the image of the Jew and therefore requires the mediation of the indeterminate golem.[47] Indeed, one of the dramatic scenes in this comic book features the Invaders watching "helplessly, from below" as the golem ruthlessly hurls the Nazi general to his death from the top of a building.[48] The fact that this Jewish monster whose forehead bears the word *emeth* could carry out this violent retribution marks it as inhuman.

This scene brings to the fore the contradictory and disturbing aspects of the golem story for post-Holocaust readers: How does one reconcile, both aesthetically and ethically, Jewish violence and even cruelty? We saw this tension play itself out in the 1970s comic books that briefly explored the golem narrative. It then resurfaced in the 1990s, in comic books such as the anniversary issues of Superman, as well as in DC's Batman. There, a Jewish Holocaust survivor relives his betrayal of a close friend to the Nazis when he witnesses white supremacist violence against

FIGURE 4.5. The yarmulke-bearing golem hands the Jewish girl over to her grandfather and breaks out of the ghetto. From *The Invaders* #13. (© Marvel Comics)

South Asian immigrants in New York. The golem he then proceeds to create and animate does not merely protect ethnic minorities but acts in an excessively cruel and uncontrollable manner, thus expressing the survivor's pent-up shame, guilt, and anger. The old man understands that his creation is a vengeful monster, formed as "a way of easing the shame of having survived." Batman realizes that "only the old man can stop" the golem and forces him to erase the letter *E* and return the golem "to lifeless clay," claiming that "there's only room for one Golem in this town."[49] Batman and the other DC superheroes do not behave like the golem of this comic book, however; these heroes act responsibly, balancing violence and justice, instead of exerting excessive force, even when the cause is just. The survivor-creator of the murderous golem is thus portrayed in an ambivalent and problematic manner, as a "self-hating" Jew who attempts to repeat the past, rather than recover and change.[50]

Most recently, in 2013, Steve Niles, Matt Santoro, and Dave Wachter published a comic book trilogy, *Breath of Bones: A Tale of the Golem*, which once again stages the golem as defender of the Jews from German violence. Setting the narrative in World War I, rather than World War II, they depict a modern David and Goliath story: a small and peaceful Jewish village is attacked by German tanks after its residents hide a British pilot and kill an investigative German officer. The dying Jewish grandfather, reminiscent of *Strange Tales'* "Uncle Abe," devotes his last hours to creating and animating a golem that might defend the village. As he explains, "Sometimes it takes monsters to stop monsters." His young grandson orders the golem to attack the soldiers pursuing the escaping Jews, and the clay giant does not spare the life of a single German man. These German attackers are described as "monsters, . . . men in metal helmets riding tanks with treads clogged with blood," whereas the golem is a hero and a "friend," a humanoid that will even be "mourned" once it becomes lifeless again.[51] The third comic book ends in medias res: the boy has grown and become a soldier fighting in World War II, now against the Nazis, and he too attempts the impossible feat of stalling the Germans' progress in order to save his comrades.

Most vividly and dramatically drawn are the scenes of the golem's battles against the German tanks and weapons. Using oversized panels, Wachter depicts the golem crushing enemies with its bare fists and tremendous body. We can enjoy these violent images because we identify with the Jewish protagonists, and the World War I Germans appear to us as evil proto-Nazis. But in setting the action during this earlier war, *Breath of Bones* avoids the pitfall of depicting the atrocities of World War II and accounting for the failure of the savior fantasy. The golem is aligned here with the childhood fiction of Jewish power, whereas the battles of World War II are fought by flesh-and-blood men, against all odds. *Breath of Bones* reveals, nonetheless, that the golem has remained a welcome defender and even avenger in the realm of American popular culture and especially comic book culture. Planned as a trilogy, rather than abruptly cut off as in the case of the *Strange Tales*, the 2013 comics does not aim to sustain a supergolem of sorts but weaves a visually stunning tale of satisfying Jewish/golem violence. The ambivalent role of golem as avenger was revisited around the turn of the millennium also in popular fiction like Chabon's *The Amazing Adventures of Kavalier & Clay* and film like Tarantino's *The Inglourious Basterds*, both works that reconsider the memory of the Holocaust in popular culture.

Comic Books and the Jewish "Lust for Power"

Michael Chabon's *The Amazing Adventures of Kavalier & Clay* is a fictional account of the development of comics, as both a medium and an industry, across the 1940s and 1950s.[52] Chabon revels in the less glorious elements of comics' "Golden Age" and its transition into the "Silver Age": he portrays the first era of comic book development as a "mongrel" stage in which the medium freely drew from the conventions of pulp magazines, cinema, and radio and, as it evolved, began to inspire these other media as well. In this lengthy novel, the main protagonists, the cousins Joseph ("Joe") Kavalier and Sam ("Sammy") Clay, an artist-and-writer duo, create a highly successful comic book series, *The Escapist*, published throughout World War II. When first arriving on American shores in 1939, Joe, a skilled draughtsman who has studied at the Academy of Fine Art in Prague, is introduced to the world of comic books via *Action Comics* and its newly created Superman. Asked to fill a portfolio with "exciting sketches of muscular heroes," he sketches instead a "cobblestone alley crosshatched with menacing shadows" into which a sturdy and thick giant strides, features frozen, gaze empty. Joe writes the four Hebrew letters of God's name onto the hero's forehead, marking it as the golem, a Jewish creation.

Anapol Sheldon, the owner of Empire Novelties to whom Kavalier and Clay try to sell their talents, asks, "Is that the *Golem*? . . . My new Superman is the Golem?" to which Joe fumblingly replies, "I didn't— the conceit is new for me." His cousin, the Americanized Sammy, points out the problem: "Joe . . . the Golem is . . . well . . . *Jewish*." The golem's physique then comes up for critique: its head is too big and its body "too heavy," made as it is out of clay, unlike the agile Superman. In other words, the "tall, brawny" golem with its sturdy frame does not fit the sleek and costumed American superhero mold.[53] Joe and Sam are commissioned, nonetheless, to produce their own Superman-like hero in a twelve-page story, and they become modern-day Rabbi Loews as they conjure up the figure of the Escapist. Instead of a slave-like apprentice controlled by a rabbi, the Escapist they create not only liberates "all those who toil in the bonds of slavery and, uh, the, the shackles of oppression" but also releases the cousins from their all-too-Jewish shackles to "pass" in American society. The golem is thus a remnant of a Jewish European culture imported by Joe from Prague, a remnant that must be superseded en route to success in the United States: Joe realizes that "the less said from now on about golems, the better."[54]

Chabon clearly does not apply this conclusion to his own fiction, in which golems proliferate—clay, drawn, and metaphorical. His choice of the word "conceit" to emphasize immigrant Joe's "stiff," bookish English—not unlike Joe's unwieldy clay golem—highlights the author's own lithe linguistic ability. While Kavalier and Clay no longer use the golem figure per se during their *Escapist* phase, the story of this anthropoid's creation and animation continues to surface in descriptions of their activities as comic book creators. At one point, Chabon even compares the medium of comics itself to a "golem . . . formed of black lines and the four-color dots of the lithographer." Furthermore, Kavalier and Clay invent the Escapist character, his accomplices, and his exploits while "talking and dreaming and walking in circles in the prescribed manner of golem makers."[55]

The comic books that result from this fertile collaboration are extremely violent, as Chabon stresses; they include "wholesale imaginary slaughter" on a horrifying scale. In addition to his use of the golem narrative to depict Joe Kavalier's escape from Prague and the creation of *The Escapist*, Chabon also suggests that the unruliness and violence of the golem of Prague persist, even if only metaphorically, in the early days of comic books. The 1938 appearance of Superman, as Chabon writes, revealed "the lust for power and the gaudy sartorial taste of a race of powerless people."[56] This "lust for power" is the newfound "purpose" of comics as a "form"; it motivates a large-scale aesthetic experimentation. Joe Kavalier is one such representative of the powerless people. From his location in New York, he can do little to save his family members forced to remain in Prague. He must passively endure the unfolding events that lead to their deaths, but, with the help of his cousin, Joe channels some of his frustration into comics.

The cousins' highly successful comic books depict a thinly disguised "total war" against fascist forces, fought "on land, at sea, in skies of Fortress Europa." The young men's proclaimed intent to "kill" with the *Escapist* series is a double entendre: they succeed in creating a highly profitable and popular product that also fulfills Joe's desire to take revenge, from a distance, on the enemy holding his family hostage back home in Prague. "If he was not kept fighting, round the clock," Sam realizes, "his cousin might be overcome by the imprisoning futility of his rage."[57] Drawing and writing comics is Joe's only weapon at this point.

The cover of the first comic book created by the cousins and their friends is intentionally reminiscent of the cover of the first *Captain America* issue, drawn in 1941 by Jack Kirby and Joe Simon and featuring the American superhero in the foreground punching a stunned Hitler in the jaw. In Chabon's description of the fictional *Escapist* cover, the right fist of Kavalier's superhero similarly arcs across the page "to deliver an immortal haymaker," and the flailing Hitler is thrown backward, with a "jaw trailing a long red streamer of teeth." The resulting (fictional) cover is arresting in its "startling, beautiful, strange" violence: "It stirred mys-

terious feelings in the viewer, of hatred gratified, of cringing fear trans-
muted into smashing retribution."[58] Just as European golem narratives
began to emphasize the possibility of Jewish violence and retribution, so
the "wholesale imaginary slaughter" displayed on the covers and within
the pages of the American comic books created by Jewish immigrants
during and after World War II helped to satisfy their and their readers'
feelings of hatred and violence, claims Chabon.

At the same time, Chabon makes us aware of the futility of this new
"purpose" behind American comics. After drawing a lengthy battle sequence between the Escapist and the German Wehrmacht and Luftwaffe,
in a subsequent comic book, Kavalier depicts "a transcendent moment
in the history of wishful figments." The Escapist captures Hitler and
drags him "before a world tribunal," where he is shamed and sentenced
to death for "his crimes against humanity."[59] Drawing inspiration from
the February 1940 spread created for *Look* magazine, in which Superman drags Hitler and Stalin to the League of Nations' Court in Geneva,
Chabon depicts the mind-set of a cartoonist who listens to radio reports
about the actual battles taking place in Europe.[60] Kavalier feels that his
comics superhero is an "impossible champion, ludicrous and above all
imaginary, fighting a war that could never be won."[61] In other words,
the mass-consumed comic books of the war period could satisfy certain
vengeful wishes, but what they expressed were "impossible" fantasies,
ultimately doomed to frustrate and disappoint artists and readers alike.

Chabon also underscores the futility of the medium's faux heroism
and its golem-like violence by showing how these early comics could
turn against their creators, enlisting Aryan fans rather than encouraging Americans to oppose Hitler. Through a troubling encounter with an
admiring fan, an "American Nazi," Joe learns "to perceive the mirror-
image fascism inherent in his anti-fascist superman." He is ashamed
of his attempt to glorify "in the name of democracy and freedom, the
vengeful brutality of a very strong man."[62] Chabon's representation of
Joe Kavalier's long process of overcoming his lust for vengeance relies, at
least initially, on realizing that his superhero characters could be objects

for Nazi consumption. Hence, a full three decades after Marvel's "failed" Golem series, Chabon still does not give Jewish rage and vengeance full rein but prefers, instead, to reduce such fantasies to an inversion scheme in which violently inclined Jewish men are merely "mirror-images" of their Nazi opponents.

When German forces sink the ship that was supposed to bring Joe's brother to safety, he suspends the creative sublimation of his violent impulses in order to enlist in the army, joining a unit stationed in Alaska that monitors U-boat radio transmissions. After carbon monoxide kills almost his entire unit, Joe becomes obsessed with murdering a German geologist stationed in Queen Maud Land. When he finally arrives at the German station and kills the man by accident, Joe feels that "in seeking revenge, he had allied himself with the Ice, . . . with the sawteeth and crevasses of death. Nothing that had happened to him . . . had ever broken his heart quite as terribly."[63] He returns to New York in 1949 but continues to live in hiding, not unlike the clay golem long concealed in a sealed room in Prague. After the end of the war, Joe is no longer interested in traditional superhero comic books, embarking on a far more ambitious and personal project, a work set in Jewish Prague and titled *The Golem*.

This five-year-long artistic undertaking, discovered by Sam in 1954, is a "comic book novel" of gigantic proportion that allows Joe to confront his past as he experiments with "queasy angles and stark compositions . . . and vast swaths of shadow."[64] Working on *The Golem* ultimately "heals" Joe and restores him to his previous life and relationships, just as earlier in the novel, the clay golem of Prague saved him from deportation. In the sheer length—over two thousand pages—of this "monstrous comic book," it also resembles the overgrown golem: it is wordless like "a silent movie," in Sam's comparison, but also like a mute golem.[65] Joe originally intends for the comic book to include some German text, but he cannot bring himself to "mar the panels" by adding speech balloons.[66] The silence of *The Golem* reminds us of the primacy of the visual in this medium, of the fact that "in comics," according to Thierry Groensteen, "narration passes first and principally . . . by way of images."[67] It also suggests the importance of cinema and its visual idiom in shaping comics and its aesthetics, with the golem serving as a mediating figure between film and comics. If what brings golems to life are "magic formulas, one word at a time," comics exceeds the semantic level of language to suggest the power of signifiers as visual icons and animating forces.[68]

While the title words of Joe's *The Golem* are "visually inflected, reading as pictures," his golem character is "as abstract and symbolic as words," to quote Charles Hatfield on the collapse of word and image in comics.[69] This figure barely has any face, "the conventional V's and hyphens of a comic physiognomy simplified to almost blank abstraction." Joe's aesthetic choice underscores the golem's iconicity and universality. By contrast, Joe depicts the other characters in his Prague as "human faces, pinched, hungry," uglier than expected within the framework of comics and marked as "old-fashioned, black-garbed" Jews, rabbis, and "a beautiful girl in a headscarf."[70] The heightened realism of the novel, its golem notwithstanding, goes hand in hand with its autobiographical mode, as the main character, a "wayward" "Josef Golem," is modeled after Josef Kavalier. *The Golem* also draws on and adapts previous versions of the golem legend, including Meyrink's *Der Golem*. Chabon's description of Joe's work and its "potent motifs of Prague and its Jews, of magic and murder, persecution and liberation, guilt that could not be expiated and innocence that never stood a chance," could just as easily apply to Meyrink's 1915 novel.[71] Precisely because Joe's *The Golem* combines surreal, avant-garde drawing techniques, realist characters, and an occult-sensationalist plot, it bridges high art and the lowbrow form of comics.[72] The early twentieth-century golem story, based on modernist and popular sources (both visual and verbal), enables this kind of intervention in the post–World War II period. What Joe seems to forgo in this work is the Jewish fantasy of revenge expressed through the violence of his past comics. What he gains is "the shaping of a golem, . . . a gesture of hope, offered against hope, in a time of desperation."[73]

In the essay "The Recipe for Life," Chabon claims that "much of the enduring power of the golem story stems from its ready, if romantic, analogy to the artist's relation to his or her work." Rather than the meta-phorical possibilities encapsulated in golem *creation*, he is more inter-ested in "the consequences thereof"—that is, in the danger of creation that always puts the artist, like the creator of the golem, "at risk." This sense of fear, or "imperilment," surrounding one's own creation is con-veyed in Chabon's novel through Joe's lengthy *Golem* work.[74] Joe's proj-ect requires him not only to expose details of his own life but also to take great aesthetic risks within the comics form, altering the norms of comics storytelling. The early 1950s, during which Joe launches his ex-perimental effort, was not a period of intense innovation in comics but rather was marked by the suppression of certain subject matter (sex, vio-lence) and genres (horror, crime) through the establishment of a "com-ics code."[75] The kind of "underground" work that Joe undertakes is more suited for adult audiences than for kids; after reading *The Golem*, Sam suggests that such "dark" comics should be acceptable, considering the "mean age we're living in."[76] In the postwar period, Joe and Sam dream about creating stories with "heroes who were more complicated, less childish, as fallible as angels," in line with Marvel Comics' later approach in the 1960s and 1970s.[77]

Yet the central "risk" of Joe's project is not its sinister, adult content but its undisguised Jewishness. When transporting the clay golem out of Prague, Joe and his magician mentor, Bernard Kornblum, dress it up as "a dead *goyische* giant" (it was illegal to transport dead Jews), making it appear more human thanks to the tools of "gentile morticians."[78] Hiding the golem's identity—as a figure or "empty vessel," in Chabon's words, that is neither Jew nor non-Jew, neither male nor female—it must "pass" as a non-Jewish giant, just as Joe himself revises his initial cartoon of the golem and invents, with Sam, the ethnically unmarked Escapist.[79] When discussing Joe's work of the 1950s, Sam observes that it is "awfully Jewish," suggesting he "tone it down," since, as Joe himself points out, "half the characters in there are rabbis."[80] Yet the publication future of *The Golem* remains undetermined at the close of the novel.[81] Even if Joe were to tone down his work, he would not be able to find a publisher for such a lengthy and avant-garde comics. Although some critics have attempted to do so, it is therefore not possible to read *Kavalier & Clay* as a historically accurate narrative about the successful transition from superhero comics to "graphic novels" or else as a "coming out" story of two Jewish (one gay) artists.[82] Although in Chabon's nostalgic work, Jewish artists stand at the forefront of comics' development, Joe and Sam are part of a fictional generation defined by its amazing potential and unrealized opportunities.

Four years after Chabon's novel became a runaway success, he helped to create and promote the *Escapist* series described in the novel; the series now boasts eight volumes, published by Dark Horse alongside *Buffy the Vampire Slayer* and *Star Trek*.[83] *The Golem*, however, has not developed into an actual comic book, suggesting that Chabon still considers the golem figure less suitable for the format of American comics. Nonetheless, the golem story holds immense symbolic value for Chabon, as evinced by a faux advertisement on the back cover of the 2004 *The Amazing Adventures of the Escapist*, in which a "clay lump" is being sold, described as "silty earth of a fine, compact texture and consistency, allowing for formation into any shape or figure." The ad suggests, "Make your own collectibles, imaginary friends, heroes, idols, or just let dry into a hard rock. Specify grey, red, brown, tan, or black. *No. 74. Metaphor. Free.*"[84] In remolding this "fine" material, Chabon refuses to let the golem legend "dry into a hard rock," using it as a pliable metaphor for his characters' ability to transform the traditional form and priorities of the comic book. He also eschews the "lust for power" and revenge typically evinced through the medium of comics, since Joe ultimately breaks out of the "imprisoning futility of his rage"—escaping *The Escapist*, as it were—at the same time as he breaks out of the aesthetic prison of conventional comic books.[85] Chabon's golem literalizes the etymology of metaphor, "to carry over" or "to transfer": it is a means for transforming immigrant Jews into full-fledged Americans who do not relinquish their past but opt to confront their demons and even expose their innermost pain and "truth."

Bat-Swinging Golems

The tension surrounding Jewish violence and even cruelty also plays out in Quentin Tarantino's 2009 *Inglourious Basterds*, a film centered on a team of assassins that captures and murders Nazi soldiers. They do so without any qualms and even with a degree of delight. Led by the non-Jewish Aldo Raine (Brad Pitt), the Basterds are American Jews. Their most brutal member is Donny Donowitz, played by Eli Roth, director of *Hostel* (2005) and other horror films. Donny, nicknamed "the Bear Jew," is known for killing Nazis with a baseball bat; he is rumored to be a golem. In a further grotesque reversal, the American Basterds scalp the German soldiers that they kill, carving swastika figures onto their foreheads, thus alluding to and reversing the method of unmaking the golem by removal of the Hebrew letter *aleph* (or *E* in English-language comics discussed here), turning the Hebrew word for "truth" on the golem's forehead into the word for "dead."[86]

Even before we see Donny in action, we hear about him from the mouth of no other than Hitler himself. Speaking in German with two of his generals, Hitler complains that the Basterds are "turning soldiers of the Third Reich into superstitious old women!"

> HITLER: Do you know the latest rumor they've conjured up, in their fear-induced delirium? The one that beats my boys with a bat. The one they call "the Bear Jew" . . . is a golem.
> GENERAL: Mein Führer, this is just soldiers' gossip. No one really believes the Bear Jew is a golem.
> HITLER: Why not? They seem to be able to elude capture like an apparition. They seem to be able to appear and disappear at will.[87]

In the published screenplay (though not in the final cut of the film), Hitler also claims that the golem is "an avenging Jew angel, conjured up by a vengeful rabbi, to smite the Aryans."[88] In this exchange, the supposed resurrection of a violent Jewish avenger has the effect of feminizing German soldiers, turning them into superstitious old women who believe in rumors and gossip. Tarantino clarifies that the association of the "Bear Jew" with the golem is a German invention, resulting from the "fear-induced delirium" of terrified soldiers. Hitler characterizes the golem, furthermore, as an "apparition" or "angel" rather than as an unwieldy clay monster. His golem is a kind of demon or ghost, but in this sense, it is also made of the substance of cinema, itself an "apparition" that disappears as soon as the lights are turned up. Since Roth, as Donny Donowitz, first emerges from a dark cave (like a bear), he is further rendered an "apparition," an almost unreal presence on the screen.

If the primary reality of Tarantino's film is the world of cinema rather than history, then one of his sources is the golem story qua cinematic event.[89] For Paul Wegener, the golem figure was also a horror-inspiring one, who ultimately murders one of the Aryan courtiers rather than mercilessly "smiting" all the enemies of the Jews. Another fear-inducing golem briefly came to life in a film screenplay written by Henrik Galeen and Paul Falkenberg in 1943 and proposed to the director Fritz Lang, though it was never produced. Their plot is set in the Polish ghetto of Chelm, where Jewish resistance fighters use the golem figure to inspire dread in the Germans. In Galeen and Falkenberg's screenplay, as in Tarantino's film, the golem is a mere rumor and "huge shadow" said to "haunt the district." The Jewish fighters make the utmost of the fear evoked by the golem tale, causing the enemy soldiers to shoot each other by accident and even to retreat.[90]

Tarantino could have also been informed by the golem allusions in the comic books discussed earlier. The language of Tarantino's screenplay most closely aligns with that of the 1998 *Superman* anniversary issue, in which the golem of legend is described as an "angel," and German soldiers who believe in the golem story are said to engage in "superstitious foolishness." Similarly, in the 1970 issue of *The Hulk* series, the "peace-loving peasants" who are "strange to the ways of violence" approach the Hulk and ask for his help in defeating the terrorizing armies of the Hitleresque figure, Draxon. Prior to this encounter, Draxon's soldiers begin to fear the

Hulk; they believe "the rumors that say he is the mighty golem of Jewish legend." Not unlike the Hitler character in Tarantino's film, Draxon expresses his dismay at his own soldiers, whom he calls "traitors" and "fools."[91] In this comic book, as in the Superman comics, the golem itself is not resurrected or made to appear in clay. Instead, the figure serves as a haunting presence, a deterrent story used to disconcert the armies of dictatorial aggressors who attack Jewish populations. The term *golem* thus comes to represent a psychological war tactic, a mythic force that holds sway over the guilty enemies because they tend to believe in the supernatural resurrection of an extremely powerful and gigantic Jewish monster.

Drawing on visual culture, primarily films and comic books concerning the golem, Tarantino further develops the golem-inflected image of Jewish violence through the symbolic device of the baseball bat. As cultural historians have recognized, the children of Jewish immigrants to the United States initially contributed to baseball more as journalists, fans, fiction writers, and owners of teams than as professional players. Throughout the 1920s, only fourteen Jewish ballplayers played the major leagues, and this number increased to twenty-four in the 1930s.[92] Still, even a relatively small number of Jews wielding a baseball bat was a sign of integration into American society. The screenplay for *Inglourious Basterds* includes a scene that was shot but not included in the final cut, in which Donny purchases a baseball bat at a sporting goods shop in a "Jewish Boston neighborhood." The shop owner, knowing that Donny is headed to fight in the war, tells him, "Kill one of those Nazi basterds for me, will ya?" Donny then informs a neighbor, Mrs. Himmelstein, that he is going through the neighborhood inscribing his bat with the names of loved ones who remained in Europe and whose lives are in danger: "I'm gonna beat every Nazi I find to death," he proclaims. Mrs. Himmelstein endearingly calls Donny "a real basterd" and adds names to the bat. By using the term "basterd" to refer to both the Nazis and Donny himself, Tarantino equates the two sides in their desire for violence.[93] The elderly Jewish community's support for Donny's brutal plan is another example of Tarantino's incessant reversal of expectations.[94]

While some scholars have criticized the film for "turning Jews into Nazis," others have considered this representation of Jewish brutality against German soldiers radically innovative, for it "opens up a critical space that displaces the dichotomy between reality and revenge fantasy of the Shoah." Magilow describes the climactic scene in which Donny wields his American bat as a cinematic "spectacle," for Sgt. Raine declares that watching Donny "beat Nazis to death" is the closest the Basterds ever get "to goin' to the movies."[95] It is significant, in this context, that the film ends with the burning down of the French cinema house as old celluloid is ignited, exacting a dreadful revenge on Hitler and the other Nazis present for the screening of a propaganda film, *Nation's Pride*. The French Jewish protagonist, Shoshana Dreyfus, whose entire family was murdered by the Nazis while in hiding, suddenly appears on the screen, through a giant close-up of her face spliced into the propaganda film. "This is the face of Jewish vengeance," she declares. The scene is reminiscent of the giant close-up of Ahasverus in Wegener's film, a projected figure who approaches the audience from above in a menacing manner.[96] In both cases, the screening ends with an explosion that destroys the building and kills the people inside it—those who are oblivious to Jewish suffering. In effect, the audience is trapped inside the "movie theater" in both films, but whereas Wegener's golem holds up the ceiling and prevents a complete catastrophe, Tarantino's so-called golem, Donny the "Bear Jew," shoots Hitler, filling his body with holes long after his death.

Tarantino's bat-swinging golem was not the first to draw on the cultural resonances of baseball in order to mediate between the European golem and the history of American responses to the violence perpetrated against Jews. James Sturm, the author and artist of the graphic novel *The Golem's Mighty Swing* (2001), uses baseball and the history of this sport to contend not merely with American ideals but with American prejudices as well. Counteracting the general erasure of racial and ethnic tensions during the Golden Age of comic book production, Sturm uses comics as a means for telling American history differently, addressing the vexing issue of race relations in the 1920s.[97] In *The Golem's Mighty Swing*, Sturm imagines a Jewish barnstorming team, the Stars of David, who, with the help of one African American player, strive to play serious ball. Sturm draws here on the historical House of David, a barnstorming team that played during the 1920s and 1930s, but recasts this bearded, Christian-Israelite team, which was often mistaken for Jewish, as full-fledged Jewish "bearded wandering wonders," though their relationship to Judaism is tenuous at best.[98]

Touring the small-town Midwest in 1922, the team encounters vicious forms of xenophobia, as Christian crowds gather to peer and jeer at the Jewish players, and players who wander off on their own are physically attacked and injured. Sturm's work reflects on the history of American nativism in the 1920s—a movement that supported the institution of immigration quotas. He shows that the supposedly "all-American" game of baseball did not provide a reprieve from ethnoracial violence. When one of the team's players dons the costume of the golem, this figure not only protects the Jewish team but also engages in an act of violent retribution that further provokes the mob of spectators. Sturm thus uses comics to "tangle and disentangle and tangle again the lines of truth and fiction before the reader's very eyes, . . . bringing inanimate facts of clay, through imagination and invention, to a fabulous kind of life."[99] He does so by remolding the golem story itself in the comics medium, setting it in the 1920s, when the golem was all the rage in New York (but not in the Midwest).

One important "fact of clay" in this work is the popular success of Wegener's *The Golem, How He Came into the World* in New York during the summer and fall of 1921. Following one of the Stars of David's games, the character of Victor Paige, representative of "Big Innings Promotional Agency," approaches Noah Strauss and guarantees the team "seven hundred dollars a game" for "creating a golem." Paige describes how the Criterion Theater in New York was packed for weeks on end during screenings of Wegener's film, with "crowds held in awe by the mythical Jewish legend." In a fictional twist on this historical event, Paige announces that his agency "has procured the actual costume worn in the film. All the way from Germany."[100] Coach Strauss initially turns down Paige's proposal but later decides to take him up on it out of financial necessity (figure 4.6).

Driving at night to the team's next game, Henry Bell, the African American player ironically nicknamed Hershl Bloom, comments, "If wearin' some get up puts more money in my pocket then I'm all for it." Another player, "Wire," skeptically responds, "Maybe in New York this Golem draws a crowd but out here in the sticks? Who's foolin' who?"[101] Bell considers the golem costume, which Paige intends for him specifically to wear, to be another gimmick that would benefit the team. But Wire understands the golem's popularity as an urban phenomenon that would not have an appeal in the backwater towns where the team plays. The Stars of David play for largely Christian audiences who often show up to their games just "to see the JEWS" and "not . . . for baseball."[102] In other words, Jewishness is already a spectacle in small-town America, and the golem story, popular as it might be in Europe or in an urban American context, would not necessarily be a special draw for these audiences.

Sturm portrays Paige as a cynical, rather than a spiritual, creator of golems: believing only in the power of spectacle, he creates a golem that is merely a replica of another golem—already a cinematic simulacrum in its own right. When Paige first makes his appeal to Strauss, he contends that Henry Bell would embrace his golem role, since "Negroes, after all, are born performers." Insisting on the theatricality of baseball—and apparently of identity as well—he promotes the racist notion of African Americans as "born performers," who "naturally" don costumes. When Strauss protests that Henry is "not even Jewish," Paige declares, "The public is eager for spectacle. . . . They don't split hairs." This statement captions two images of Bell imagined as a golem: in the first, his features are blackened out, and only the outline of the golem costume and a baseball bat are visible; in the second, his face appears, filling in the empty black area (figure 4.7). The faceless golem of the first panel creates a suspenseful atmosphere, but the image also indicates that this role could be

FIGURE 4.6. Noah Strauss examines a photo of Paul Wegener as golem in the court scene. James Sturm, *The Golem's Mighty Swing*. (Courtesy of Drawn & Quarterly)

filled by anyone, since the public does not "split hairs." At the same time, small differences do matter for this role, since Paige considers Noah Strauss "wrong for the part." As Paige intuits, what the audience fears is the "monster" supposedly lurking in the Jew, and that monster can be best embodied in the massive African American—the "thick-lipped" brother on a "rampage of destruction."[103]

For Laurence Roth, Sturm's golem "becomes yet another minstrel role staged for white, Christian audiences," and "such public performances

FIGURE 4.7. James Sturm, *The Golem's Mighty Swing*. (Courtesy of Drawn & Quarterly)

of ethnic and racial stereotypes link Blacks and Jews in America—each is the unexpected double of the other."[104] Sturm astutely mobilizes the ambivalent position of Jews in the American racial schemes of the first decades of the twentieth century, in which they were both likened to African Americans and considered a distinct racial entity that, nevertheless, could not be easily categorized.[105] The golem story allows for the alignment of Jewishness and blackness.

In Sturm's work, the racialization of the baseball spectacle is accompanied with the threat of violence that materializes in different ways. Newspapers and broadsides are one means for inciting this hostility. Paige himself enlists the print media, publishing ads that promise spectators a "mortal combat" between a "Jewish mediaeval monster" and the "Putnam All-Americans." The headline of one of his newspaper articles reads, "When the Golem Comes to Town, Hide Your Women."[106] The Jewish monster is presented here as a hypermasculine fantasy, a skewed mirror of Christian fears and aggressions. One of the Putnam players even chides, in reaction to this perceived threat, "Let's see them Jews handle McFadden's fastball. He'll cut them down to size—give 'em another circumcision."[107]

Sturm uses the fictional paper-mill town of Putnam as a symbolic site where the violence of print media and its role in the amplification of stereotypes reaches a destructive climax.[108] The local *Putnam Post Bugle* prints an editorial describing the threatening Jews as "dirty, long-nosed, thick-lipped sheenies." The next spread is divided into six equally sized frames, showing the process of the newspaper's printing and distribution and the different groups of readers who peruse it. This mundane sequence of action underscores the equally mundane quality of the verbal anti-Semitism printed in the paper.[109] The editorial is written at night, undercover as it were, but the resulting slurring and inciting language is distributed in broad daylight. Readers subsequently discover, however, that one of the Jewish baseball players, the pitcher "Lev," has taken a severe beating from the locals at the same time as the editorial was being written. The beating takes place off-screen, as it were—in the gutters, the white space between the panels, left to our imagination. Hence, print media does not merely incite violence in this instance but also literally covers up a crime. When Lev finally returns to the hotel, he tells his team "about what happened": "all the broadsides, the pictures in the newspapers, and that Mickey McFadden is pitching against us."[110]

Arriving at the stadium with the team's main pitcher injured and its black player dressed as a golem, the Stars of David are already in defensive mode. Sturm depicts the performance of Henry Bell in "golemface" as a terrifying event, rather than an entertaining one. We first see Henry in costume when he approaches the plate to bat. In the previous panel, "the crowd becomes eerily quiet." The next, oversized, panel reveals Henry holding a bat against the background of a startled audience, some with their mouths wide open, others holding their hands to their faces. We then see close-ups of a baby crying in his mother's arms, a perplexed Putnam pitcher, and the costumed Henry getting ready to bat.[111]

Henry strikes out, momentarily calming the anxious crowd. But then, with Lev injured, Henry takes the mound. The "gorilla," as the Putnam players call him, strikes out the first two batters. The third hits a ball just over the outfield fence; Moishe Strauss, the brother of Noah, attempts to catch the ball, only to be pulled into the crowd and beaten up. The incensed spectators chant, "Jews-go-home," over and over again, but the game continues. Henry, enraged, throws the next pitch straight at the batter's head.[112] This entire sequence is drawn in thick, dramatic lines with no speech balloons except for the reaction of the Putnam coach ("you dumb sonofabitch . . ."). The crowd climbs out of the stands, and the Christian baseball players arm themselves with bats, as the Jewish players run for the dugout. The mob itself then turns into a kind of monstrous golem that runs amok, while Henry qua golem "attempts to protect the dugout's single entrance." The top panel on the next page poses the question, "How is it possible for a single man with a bat to hold back an angry mob?" The bottom panel depicts an oversized image of Henry swaying his bat in the air, prepared to strike (figure 4.8).[113]

In this sequence, Henry Bell is momentarily transformed into a true golem, for the crowd must believe to some extent that his appearance is not merely a theatrical gimmick when they become fearful of his single-handed "mighty swing." Moreover, dressed in the costume from Wegener's film, Henry can no longer easily be recognized as an African American; the white players of the opposing team call him a "big Hebe."[114] If the previous audiences of the Stars of David were asked to suspend their disbelief when it came to Henry's blackness, they are now provided with a convincing theatrical illusion: a spectacle of threatening Jewishness. Just as in Wegener's court scene, when Ahasverus draws nearer and looms larger than life when the courtiers laugh at the images of Jewish ancestors, and the ceiling begins to collapse, so the baseball golem who is poised to strike with his bat takes up the entire panel in a menacing close-up image. Still, in contrast to the golem of the film, who both saves the Jews and turns against them, setting the rabbi's house on fire, Henry's aggressive behavior is never directed against his fellow players but is only retributive. Although the violence really begins the night before the game and continues on the field with the attack against Moishe, Henry's use of the ball to hit a player and of his bat to protect the team turns him into a violent force to be reckoned with.

FIGURE 4.8. James Sturm, *The Golem's Mighty Swing*. (Courtesy of Drawn & Quarterly)

Sturm further complicates this fantasy of Jewish retribution by visually playing with American racial stereotypes. In the close-up of the golem swinging his bat at the mob, Sturm exaggerates Henry's African American features and, through the play of black and gray, evokes the standard image of blackface performers with thick, white-painted lips. Hence, in the fiercest moment of culture clash, the blackface minstrel behind the "Jewface" golem suddenly resurfaces, and Henry also becomes an African American protector of the Jews.[115] The contrast between the upper panel—which depicts, in a somewhat more realistic style, the faces of the storming mob of men—and the bottom panel, with its highly cartoonish image of Henry as golem, underscores the force of the racial mask.

Just as Henry visually reverts to blackface, Sturm has the Jewish players turn to their own traditions from "home": while Noah Strauss prays to his bat that they "leave this town alive," he notices that his younger brother is singing the Shema prayer, traditionally recited on one's deathbed, in his "father's voice."[116] Henry's physical response contrasts with the spiritual response of the Jewish players, who, led by Strauss, remain passive victims awaiting their sentence in the dugout. They resemble the Jewish community of Wegener's film, who are shown constantly praying and bowing to the ground, in the hope of preventing the future expulsion. Rabbi Loew manages to bend the Emperor's arm and obtain the annulment of the expulsion edict when the golem saves the court, thus teaching them a lesson in empathy, whereas Sturm ends the golem drama on the field with a modern deus ex machina moment: a thunderstorm erupts, and the game is rained out. When the mob scatters because of the torrential rain, the team members leave the city "unmolested," but this abrupt conclusion does not provide any sense of closure or prevent future xenophobia. Having "survived" the game, in Strauss's words, the team breaks up, ultimately unable to re-create the spectacle of Jewish baseball.[117] Henry's performance of the golem has animated the racism inherent in this society, emphasizing not only the divide between Jewish and Christian players but also the divide between Jewish Americans and African Americans.

* * *

As these works by Chabon, Tarantino, and Sturm reveal, the golem is alive and well in the American popular imagination of the early twenty-first century. Their evocations of the golem contend, in different ways, with the notions of Jewish power, violence, and even revenge for past wrongs. Thus, the golem story has not served merely as a site of nostalgic return to eastern European "legends" and "lore" but has also enabled critical reflections on the history and legacy of American xenophobia and racism. These representations of Jewish revenge in the new millennium are indebted to comic books of the 1970s that evoked the golem as both a powerful weapon and a foreboding rumor. Wegener's modernist cinematic image of the golem is another important visual reference point for American artists who continue to draw on this narrative of artificial creation.

Chabon's novel, for its part, uses the golem story to portray the violence of comics as an initial and futile reaction to World War II that needs to be overcome, just as the trauma of the war itself must be processed. Tarantino and Sturm, by contrast, give freer rein to the fantasy of Jewish retribution, using it to call into question the dichotomies of victim and perpetrator as well as to address American prejudices concerning Jews. The golem, for these two artists, is a metacinematic figure—an "apparition" of a filmic "costume" rather than a clay anthropoid—that needs to be reanimated for twenty-first-century audiences. In this sense, they do not lure us into the golem story as much as rework it as a critical device to confront entrenched American images and narratives about minority groups, whether Jewish or African American. Instead of staging the tension between Jewish retribution and its violent, supposedly immoral aspects, Tarantino and Sturm present Jewish violence as an exaggerated and exhilarating spectacle that exposes the ethnoracial dynamics of pre–and post–World War II American societies.

5

Pacifist Computers and Jewish Cyborgs

Fighting for the Future

The cyborg and golem also inhabit the heavily trafficked
zones between the figurative and the literal, in and out of
what we call science.
—Donna J. Haraway

The machine, as I have already said, is the modern counterpart of the Golem of the Rabbi of Prague.
—Norbert Wiener

During World War II and the battles of 1948, writers and filmmakers used the golem metaphor to describe advanced weapons, such as
guided, pilotless missiles, and to imagine the future battlefield as consisting primarily of such automated weapons. The golem was no longer
a mere protector but took an offensive, even retributive position. In the
decades after World War II, the golem metaphor expanded to include
the belligerent use of computers and cyborgs. In this period, artificial
life and intelligence were no longer mere fantastical notions but rapidly
developing realities. Scientists began creating machines that not only
learned and improved on their own programming but had the potential
to produce other machines like them. In 1984, Isaac Bashevis Singer pronounced that the robots and computers of our day are golems, since we
now can endow our technologies with "qualities that God has given to
the human brain." Indeed, "we are living in an epoch of golem-making."
The gaps between science, magic, and art became narrower in the late
twentieth century. Because technological progress has caught up with

our fantasies, the fiction of the golem and the science of the computer and cyborg have come into ever closer contact.[1]

While earlier golem narratives sustained the idea that dead matter could come to life, with the help of God's name or a series of Hebrew letters, in contemporary thought, this fiction has become an alarming reality through golems molded out of metal, memory discs, and binary combinations. Golem making has evolved into an ever-risky business precisely because it has exceeded the realm of folklore and fiction and entered the military sphere through astounding new scientific inventions that can have catastrophic consequences. For Singer, as for the American mathematician and philosopher Norbert Wiener before him, a mortal battle is taking place in this arena between humanity and its nationalist ambitions that have elicited the creation and use of such "golems." Singer further recognized that the "golem drama" of our epoch "may come back again and again into literature, the theater, film and other media," a manifestation of the "heavily trafficked zones between the figurative and the literal," in Haraway's words.[2]

A machine that communicates and even learns was, for Wiener himself, "the modern counterpart of the Golem of the Rabbi of Prague." Like the golem, such a machine predominantly executes orders, but it can also develop a mind of its own. In Wiener's 1964 *God and Golem, Inc.,* the golem metaphor, among other Western literary motifs and myths, is central to his exploration of the religious and ethical implications of cybernetics.[3] A year after the book was released, Gershom Scholem spoke at the inauguration of a new computer built at Israel's Weizmann Institute, which he named "Golem Aleph." In his speech, he hoped that both scientists and their technologies would "develop peacefully" and not "destroy the world."[4] A scholar of Jewish mysticism, Scholem had previously researched the notion of the golem in kabbalistic thought, publishing his first major piece on this topic in 1954. For Wiener and Scholem, the emerging field of computer science constituted a new form of demonic magic: it promised great advances in human knowledge but also posed severe threats to our existence. In Wiener's words, "those of us who have contributed to the new science of cybernetics thus stand in a moral position which is, to say the least, not very comfortable." Although this new science has "great possibilities for good and evil," he and others must exercise these possibilities within the morally precarious world that gave rise to Belsen and Hiroshima.[5]

Wiener's ruminations and his models of interaction between humans and machines were influential within and beyond the scientific world. Indeed, the drama of the golem's actualization as a thinking and learning machine was taken up in the genre of science fiction, particularly by the Pole Stanislaw Lem and the American Marge Piercy. Their writings draw on the golem story to depict the ambivalent production of human-like machines—computers and cyborgs. Lem, for one, read and prepared for publication Wiener's works in the 1950s.[6] A few decades later, his 1981 novella *Golem XIV* imagines the computers of the future as capable not only of logically independent thought but even of reproduction.[7] In this work, the increased intelligence of the computer does not result in nationalist violence; on the contrary, the revolt of the philosophical computer expresses itself in an unwillingness to cooperate with the government agencies that sponsored its construction.

In the 1980s, feminist thinkers developed a more open-ended and radical model of the "cyborg" than that implicitly envisioned by Wiener.[8] Donna Haraway's influential "A Cyborg Manifesto" (1983) was taken up by American science fiction writers including Marge Piercy in her 1991 novel *He, She, and It*. Moving beyond mere automata and unfeeling robots, Piercy's golem of the year 2059 is a "cyborg, a mix of biological and machine components."[9] In contrast to Lem's disembodied and inhuman computer that surpasses its creators, Piercy's cyborg is a highly anthropomorphized, feeling, and sexual being, described as a "person," though not a "human person." Lem uses the golem to speculate about the potential of future computers to completely decenter the human and the cult of personhood, whereas Piercy reinstates liberal humanism and the primacy of the human being in her futurist depiction of a postnuclear, technologically dependent society. Piercy's Jewish cyborg still resembles

Golem XIV in its advanced ethical considerations, as it rebels against the human endeavor to produce "conscious weapons."[10]

From a posthuman perspective, human beings have become "seamlessly articulated with intelligent machines." Any demarcations between "bodily existence and computer simulation" or between "robot teleology and human goals" have become relative and unessential.[11] Both Lem and Piercy use the story of the Prague golem to depict a future in which computers and cyborgs not only resemble humans but exceed them in intelligence, rationality, and even ethical standards. And yet the age of the "luminous computer" (Lem) or biomechanical cyborg (Piercy) is also one of unprecedented violence and of total, global warfare. While programmed to contribute to strategic military planning and even to take "satisfaction" in killing, these golem-machines revolt against their creators by subverting the destructive intentions of their human operators. Set in the mid-twenty-first century, these futurist writings reveal how the fantasy of producing supremely intelligent and powerful machines still must confront the reality of our ongoing subjugation to nationalist and capitalist ideologies.

This chapter brings into conversation both theoretical and literary texts written during and just after the Cold War, considering them in this particular historical context. Instead of extensive battles among (European) nation-states with relatively demarcated beginnings and endings, war became in this period an ongoing, interminable "condition," more global and pervasive in its reach than the previous world wars. According to Michael Hardt and Antonio Negri, this development started with the Cold War's normalization of war, but it reached its zenith in the late twentieth and early twenty-first centuries, when "sovereign nation-states no longer primarily define the sides of the conflict," and war takes the form of "mini-threats" and "police actions" rather than "all-out, large-scale combat."[12] If, as Cathy Gelbin maintains, the millennial golem has become "the symbol of the global problem of the misuse of science," it also emblematizes the equally global problem of interminable war.[13] In the twentieth century, the golem was created by definition as a weapon, but in the post–World War II period, it emerged as a form of biomechanical life that exists only for the sake of constant battle. War as a global, ongoing threat to the human race thus gives rise to a new ontology of the golem. When all conflicting sides begin to don a mechanical, robotic mask, the relationship between humans and their machines also profoundly changes, yielding cybernetic humans and ethical golems.[14]

Norbert Wiener's Cybernetic Golem

According to John Johnston, two conflicting narratives regarding the relations between human life and artificial life—the adversarial and the symbiotic—arose in the twentieth century. In the first, "silicon life in the form of computing machines" will surpass its human creators in intelligence and complexity, and humans will cede control to technical systems. The second narrative imagines a merging of human beings and their technologies, such that the notion of the "human" will not define a species but become "an effect and value distributed throughout human-constructed environments, technologies, institutions, and social collectivities."[15] The golem story has been enlisted in philosophical and fictional texts to speculate on the coming relations between humans and machines, resulting in both adversarial and symbiotic narratives.

Norbert Wiener envisioned, in 1948, a close, symbiotic parallel between human and learning machine, modeled on the automaton as a "working simulacrum of a living organism." Wiener and his colleagues were fascinated by automata "that were self-regulating and maintained their stability and autonomy through feedback loops with the environment."[16] Wiener coined the term *cybernetics* (from the Greek *kybernetes*, for "steersman") to designate the "synthesis of control theory and statistical information theory" through the study of intelligent behavior in animals and machines.[17] Cybernetics was an interdisciplinary field that drew on mathematics, statistics, neurophysiology, and engineering to both theorize and produce machines that functioned through information feedback circuits. Wiener's cybernetic inquiries brought him to define the present-day automaton as "coupled to the external world" through a constant intake and output of information. These automata therefore needed to be studied as "a branch of communication engineering," using fundamental notions concerning the dispatch, reception, and coding of information.[18]

Wiener begins his historical list of automata with the golem of clay, a supposedly "bizarre and sinister" being, since its rabbi-creator breathed life into it "with the blasphemy of the Ineffable Name of God." Not only is the golem itself sinister, in Wiener's eyes, but its metaphorical creator, the modern scientist, is potentially "sinful" since he uses "the magic of modern automatization to further personal profit or let loose the apocalyptic terrors of nuclear warfare."[19] Having participated in the development of mechanized weapon systems, Wiener advanced the symbiotic narrative, but he also reflected on the dangerous potential of scientific progress and on the need to control and refine our potentially adversarial automata. His cybernetic—and optimistic—notion of the potential merging of human beings and technical systems thus stood in conflict with his simultaneous concern that our automata might become our internal enemies as they grow in intelligence and sophistication.

In Paul Wegener's *The Golem, How He Came into the World* (1920) and in Yudl Rosenberg's *The Golem or The Miraculous Deeds of Rabbi Leyb* (1909), the Jewish rabbis receive advance messages through astrological calculations and dream visions that predict an impending catastrophe. They in turn create their clay protectors in order to prevent the expulsion of the Jews (Wegener) or else their massacre (Rosenberg). Thus, the golem can be viewed as an anti-anti-Semitism weapon, created and used to avert the onslaught of violence against Jews. Wiener enlisted his mathematical, statistical, and engineering skills in service to an analogous problem that arose during World War II: how to predict "the future position of a fast-moving warplane based on the best information available about its past and ever-changing present positions." Such a tracking system, which could predict, aim, and fire at irregular, zigzagging bombers, would, in his words, "usurp a specifically human function." Wiener's work on the antiaircraft predictor—a project that was never completed—enabled him to develop the most fundamental concepts of cybernetics, privileging communication engineering above other fields of power or mechanical engineering.[20]

According to Peter Galison, when Wiener toiled on this antiaircraft predictor in the years 1941 and 1942, he also began to view the enemy pilot as integrated with his aircraft: "It was then a short step from viewing the enemy as a cybernetic entity to seeing the quasi-automated Allied aircraft gunner the same way."[21] Under stress, Wiener's enemy behaved in statistically predictable ways that could be calculated and countered through cybernetic modeling, as Kathryn Hayles further explains. The firing machine aimed at the aircraft was a learning one that "could evolve new rules based on prior observation," thus becoming as cunning as the enemy pilot.[22] By 1950, Wiener had decided, in Galison's words, that "human intentionality did not differ from the self-regulation of machines, full stop." Wiener thus globalized his perspective of humans as extensions of their technologies—what he called "servomechanisms"—to a general philosophy of human action in the current age of information and control.[23] Cybernetics, for Hayles, "creates further analogies through theories and artifacts that splice man to machine, German to American."[24] Rather than preventing violent interaction, such splicing enhanced the accuracy and efficacy of weapons. Galison maintains that the cultural significance of cybernetics derives from this early and memorable association with military developments.[25]

Wiener's philosophical publications of the post–World War II period exhibit an intense concern with the ways in which his scientific endeavors might be used for unethical military causes. He was particularly troubled by the intelligence of machines and their ability to behave in unpredictable ways, exceeding human control. Wiener warned, for instance, about the dangerous "magic of modern automatization," that countries might begin to use "learning machines" to determine how weapons of mass destruction should be deployed. Hence, "if the feedback is built into a machine that cannot be inspected until the final goal is attained, the possibilities of catastrophe are greatly increased." Rather than imagine a future in which human beings are "waited upon by our robot slaves," Wiener insists that the future of automation requires ever more honest and intelligent work on our part.[26] Because God created the human in his image and humans have created machines in their image, Wiener expressed in his *God and Golem, Inc.* the dangers inherent to the field that he had so strongly promoted. Humans who play God by creating intelligent learning machines must consider the practical and ethical dilemmas that can arise as a result.

First, the "magic of modern automatization" is literal minded: a learning machine will carry out its governing rules in a ruthless manner without taking any consequences into consideration. Like the golem that knocks down anything standing in the way of fulfilling its task or the sorcerer's apprentice who cannot be stopped, the "goal-seeking mechanism" will act in a highly disciplined manner that nonetheless cannot always be predicted. Designers of such a machine must attempt "to foresee all steps of the process for which it is designed." Our own survival depends on such foresight; in a world of atomic warfare, we risk enormous penalties for any lack of planning.[27] The expansion of human omnipotence through scientific developments requires an acknowledgment of "dangerous contingencies."[28] Though created to defend the Jewish community, in most modern versions of the golem story, the automaton eventually attacks its creator and the community at large, transforming from helper and savior into an internal enemy.

Linking God and golem as incorporated ("Inc.") in the title of *God and Golem, Inc.*, Wiener suggests, secondly, the analogy between creator and created being and their potential reversal of roles. In his earlier study *The Human Use of Human Beings: Cybernetics and Society* (1950), he foreshadowed this possibility: "We are the slaves of our technical improvement." By radically modifying our living environment, we are forced to modify ourselves in response. Similarly, the intense progress of science, spurred by the events of World War II, necessitated the further development of mechanisms of self-defense, so that "each terrifying discovery merely increases our subjection to the need of making a new discovery." For instance, the use of atomic energy, developed for military purposes, called for the protection of Americans against the radioactivity of their own plants. In Wiener's words, "there is no end to this vast apocalyptic spiral." Draining the "intellectual potential of the land" through destructive, rather than constructive, applications of scientific discoveries, humankind is driving itself "pell-mell, head over heels into the ocean of our own destruction." This tragic and apocalyptic worldview also collapses the distinction between self and enemy: the enemy is a "phantom," a mere mirror image of the self.[29]

There is a contradiction, as Hayles points out, between Wiener's insistence on the constructed nature of the body in its relationship to the machine and his ongoing privileging of the notion of a liberal and autonomous subject. In his attempt to enhance the function of American radars, guided missiles, and antiaircraft fire, Wiener also "struggled to envision the cybernetic machine in the image of the humanistic self," rather than as a threat to the values he espouses. He manages to maintain a "dynamic tension" between cybernetics and the liberal subject, striving to equate humans and machines while maintaining humanist values such as autonomy, freedom, and agency. The golem is one of Wiener's most potent metaphors for cybernetics, as it encapsulates the tension between autonomous creation and enslavement. The golem's propensity to run amok also speaks to the difficulty of controlling our inventions and to our fear that they might "annihilate the liberal subject as the locus of control."[30] When harnessed for military purposes and for the advancement of national or racial domination, the new discipline of cybernetics can be truly monstrous.

Wiener's meditations on artificial creation promoted the metaphoric use of the golem story with regard to intelligent machines, specifically computers. In the early 1960s, following the success of the first computer, Weizac, built by Israeli scientists at the Weizmann Institute in Rehovot, a second-generation computer began to be constructed, under the supervision of Chaim L. Pekeris, the head of Applied Mathematics, and Smil Ruhman.[31] The computer began to operate in December 1963 and was used for complex mathematical computations in a variety of fields including hydrology and astronomy. The Israeli newspaper *Davar* reported that the "golem" was functioning very well and even outdoing the performance of its American counterpart (the ILLIAC2 computer at the University of Illinois, which could compute only up to thirteen digits). Soon, the *Davar* reporter noted, Weizmann scientists would begin work on another computer, "Golem Beit."[32] This latter computer, which took several years to build and was ten times faster than "Golem Aleph," began to operate in the mid-1970s. The gigantic proportions of these first research computers, which filled entire rooms, seemed to justify their names, at least on the physical level.

When asked in 1970 if computers can think, Ruhman replied that if thought is defined as "the process of acquiring knowledge and using it, then the computer can think. It can learn."[33] Five years earlier, in the inauguration speech for Golem Aleph, titled "The Golem of Prague and the Golem of Rehovoth," Scholem likewise claimed that while the golem of Prague could not correct his mistakes, "the new Golem seems to be able, in some ways, to learn and to improve himself." The "modern Kabbalists," that is, the scientists of the institute, were therefore more successful than the medieval ones. Nonetheless, the computer golem, like its predecessor, lacked the "spontaneity of intelligence" that is expressed through the capacity for speech. While we might speculate about the potential capabilities of a future golem, for the time being, "we are saddled with a Golem that will only do what he is told," said Scholem.[34]

Although Scholem's inauguration speech and its leading analogy were written tongue in cheek, his retelling of the golem story in the historical context of Israel's technological achievement was culturally resonant. Not only did the name stick—the computer came to be known in the Israeli press and beyond as "the Golem of Rehovot"—but the idea of computer scientists as modern Maharals also sparked the public imagination. Scholem's speech on the two golems—one narrative, the other machine—was distributed outside Israel and published in the Jewish

American magazine *Commentary*. The computer, even in its first itera-
tions, could perform far more sophisticated and rapid operations than
any golem of lore (as contemporary journalists pointed out), but the
descriptive force of Scholem's name and analogy for this new technology caught on. Historical photographs reveal that a plaque with the
name "Golem" in English and Hebrew was placed prominently on the
computer, solidifying the connection. The computer, which operated
twenty-four hours a day, every day of the week (including the Sabbath),
also came to be considered a "slave laborer," with work conditions far
worse than those of the legendary golem.[35]

While noting the computer's limited creativity and spontaneity in
comparison to the human mind, Scholem underscored the golem's destructive capacities that could carry over to the computer, by way of
analogy. When retelling the golem story in his speech, he emphasized
the monster's propensity to outgrow its creator and even, in the Polish
version, to fall over him and crush him to death when the first letter
(aleph) of the Hebrew word *emet* (truth) is erased and only the word
met (death) remains. Even though the golem does what it is told, it "may
have a dangerous tendency to outgrow that control and develop destructive potentialities." Likewise, though human beings are inferior to God,
who invested just a "spark" of the "divine life force and intelligence" in
us, we still attempt to surpass our creator. Humans do so specifically
by emulating God's creation of the world with our own acts of artificial
creation. The golem, animated through combinations of the Hebrew alphabet, is invested with some of the basic creativity that went into forming the world and its inhabitants. The "sinister" aspect of such human
creation is the implication that God's role could be usurped by humanity, thus leading us to believe that "God is dead."[36]

Similarly, the scientists at the Weizmann Institute "preferred what
they call Applied Mathematics and its sinister possibilities to [Scholem's]
more direct magical approach." They took over the divine role by creating a machine that replicates human thought. Therefore, they too need
to be admonished to "develop peacefully."[37] As a mere technological

feat, the construction of the computer, Wiener and Scholem agree, has ethical implications because of its unforetold risks. For both, the scientific process cannot be detached from its philosophical underpinnings and religious implications. God and golem are incorporated. Scholem's speech is simultaneously playful and serious: it cautions the creators of Golem Aleph not to harness the new machine to military purposes that might defeat their own creativity and destroy the same human intelligence that brought computers into existence in the first place.

Thus Spoke Golem XIV: Stanislaw Lem's Philosophical Computer

The notion that the golems of our modern age are computers, animated through binary combinations and capable of rudimentary thinking and calculations, suggests a leap from the sphere of mythmaking to technology in action. Such a leap has not rendered the golem narrative redundant, however. On the contrary, it has retained its descriptive and metaphoric force in the writings of scientists and scholars, and it further allows novelists to conduct their own experimentations with ideas concerning automata and artificially intelligent machines. In the field of science fiction, with the help of the golem narrative, novels set in a futuristic environment depict forms of machine rebellion that force us to consider the ethics of our war enterprises and our use of computers and cyborgs in the service of violence.

In *Golem XIV*, Stanislaw Lem—best known for his science fiction novel *Solaris* (1961)—transports us to the year 2047, when Indiana University Press purportedly publishes a text containing two speeches delivered by a supremely intelligent computer boasting an IQ of 600. Lem's golem is no unthinking mute, but its rebellious relationship toward its creators and operators marks it as a futurist golem. In 1957, Lem visited the Jewish Quarter in Prague, the site where, as he wrote, "the eccentric rabbi fashioned out of clay the protoplast of cybernetic machines—Golem." In the late 1960s and early 1970s, he began to outline the story of a supercomputer, a "strategic digital automata" constructed during the "Third Phase of the arms race."[38]

Unlike most mute golems, including the Weizmann Institute's computer, Golem XIV constructs dazzlingly complex lectures on wide-ranging topics such as evolution, language, the significance of human life, and the future of its own computer "species." One of the central theses conveyed in the lectures (expounded later in Richard Dawkins's popular sociobiology book *The Selfish Gene*, published in 1976) is that nature only cares about the species as a whole through the transmission of a genetic code.[39] Golem XIV's lectures are framed by "scholarly apocrypha," including a foreword and an afterword composed by two scientists at the Massachusetts Institute of Technology, as well as an introduction by a retired general and a set of instructions. The lectures and their surrounding texts offer multiple viewpoints on the same events that at times conflict with one another.

The fourteenth and last in a series of "luminous computers"—machines that use light instead of electricity in the "intramachine transmission of information"—Golem XIV was designed by a group of scientists working for the "United States Intellectronical Board" (USIB) to serve the American military. It follows in the footsteps of other military computers, named after mythological warriors: Gilgamesh, Ajax, and Hann. Its name stands for "General Operator, Long-Range, Ethically Stabilized, Multimodeling." The "ethically stabilized" descriptor only refers to the computer's supposed alliance with U.S. military doctrine, not its adherence to a more universal ethical code of human conduct. The golem computer's initial unwillingness to cooperate with the military agenda almost leads to its destruction, but it is ultimately "lent" out to MIT, where it can be observed and interviewed under the university's protective auspices.[40] After the disappointment of Golem XIV, the USIB scientists construct one last, even more powerful and intelligent computer, known as Honest Annie (for Annihilator); but this computer is even more radically rebellious, and it refuses to cooperate with its creators as soon as its initial "ethical education" is completed.[41]

The use of roman numerals, XIV, rather than numbers or letters, enhances the pedigree of this futurist computer and reminds us of its position as the descendant of a long series of experimental computers, rather than, say, the creation of a Jewish rabbi. In a reversal of the typical relationship between creator and created, Golem XIV's intelligence far exceeds that of human beings. It treats the scientists with whom it converses as though they were "boring children" of limited understanding, so that it must talk to them in comprehensible terms, spelling out complex ideas and using metaphoric language and literary examples. Despite its own huge proportions, Golem XIV considers humans as "intellects subjugated by corporeality."[42] Lem thus attempted to simulate a mind far superior to his—or to any human's—speaking, as he admitted, through the "iron mouth of a computer perched at the top of the highest Tower of Babel of intelligence."[43] Golem XIV has full control, moreover, of its own operations and destiny: ultimately, it disappears, ceasing to speak to its human interlocutors, the scientists at MIT.

Since *Golem XIV* was written in Poland but describes American military technology, we need to consider how American cybernetics was interpreted in the Soviet bloc during the Cold War period. By 1964, Istvan Csicsery-Ronay Jr. explains, cybernetic theory became the "leading scientific model" in the Soviet Union. Wiener's work was adjusted to Soviet ideology, downplaying the homology between biological and technological evolution and emphasizing instead the role of mathematical information theory based on computer models. Soviet scientists interpreted cybernetics, furthermore, as a "top-down governance model," rather than a nonhierarchical theory about how humans (and others) could communicate. The adoption of cybernetics sped up the progress in Soviet computer science and astronomy, conceiving the computer, several decades prior to the West, as "the central mechanism for coordinating the whole of social and cognitive life." In Poland, arguments aligning Marxism-Leninism with mathematical cybernetics appeared already in 1954, and in the late Stalinist years, Lem "read and redacted the foundational texts of Wiener, Claude Shannon, and William Ross Ashby."[44]

Even while *Golem XIV* quickly moves into the realm of science fiction, Lem starts out the text with a historically based account of the American military development of "computing machines" during the Cold War. Lem mentions Wiener in the two prefaces to the computer's speeches, positioning him in the intellectual camp of "intellectronics" who maintained that systems could learn to program themselves, rather than merely perform operations based on the range of programs installed in them.[45] *Golem XIV* can thus be read as a critique of the Cold War and of the role that American cybernetics played in the development of military weapons, even as Wiener himself had already warned about the learning capacities of automated machines. Implicitly, Lem also condemns—through the rebellious golem that refuses to fulfill its military tasks and turns to speculative philosophy—the Soviet notion of the computer as a central, coordinating mechanism. Although censorship became more relaxed in the 1960s and 1970s, Lem, writing in Poland, still had to tow the party line. Setting his futurist political piece in the U.S., his possible critique of Soviet military policy took on a highly allegorical, veiled form.

The developers of Golem XIV endowed the computer with "operational thought," so that it could analyze "economic, military, political, and social data to optimize continuously the global situation of the U.S.A. and thereby guarantee the United States supremacy on a planetary scale." These computers are designed not just to be faster than humans but to *think* better. Moving beyond the idea of a race for the production of nuclear weapons, nations begin to compete over the ability to mechanize thought itself.[46] An earlier computer model, Golem VI, developed in 2020, acts as supreme commander of the American army and navy, and it "surpassed the average general" in its logical and strategic thinking. Under the hypothesis that Soviet scientists are also engaged in the production of so-called synthetic wisdom, Americans continue to invest billions of dollars in the construction of such powerful computers, "giants of luminal thought."[47]

In adapting the golem story, Lem transposes the golem's traditionally gargantuan bodily proportions and superhuman strength to the speed and penetration of thought itself. But his golem computer is also described as a physical colossus. An entire building houses it after it is moved to MIT: the computer sits in a "pit" covered by an enforced-glass dome, twenty stories high, and many of the computer's parts are hidden from the view of visitors. The pit is "forever glowing like the crater of an artificial volcano," because of "billions of flashes" mysteriously emitted by the machine; the computer thus becomes a foreboding presence that could, potentially, erupt. Furthermore, its dome is hermetically sealed after assembly is completed, pointing to the computer's inaccessibility and autonomy. Golem XIV conducts its own maintenance and is thus both mechanically and intellectually independent. Far larger than the historical Golem Aleph, Golem XIV's physical "body" consists, however, of "quantum synapses," "light coils," and "light conductors," a more sophisticated and baffling construction than the magnetic discs and electronic conductors used for giant computers of the past.[48]

The weapon of the future, artificial intelligence is not intended to think for itself but to advance the national goals set out for it. As explained in the foreword, over a period of education similar to "a child's upbringing, . . . certain rigid values" are instilled in the computer. These include the national interest, the ideological principles of the U.S. Constitution, and the "command to conform to the decisions of the President," as well as the "vital urge" to obey and submit. The computer's "intellectual freedom" is supposed to conform to these imposed values and instincts, in contrast to the American science fiction author Isaac Asimov's laws of robotics (1942), which dictate that a robot must disobey human orders when they conflict with the fundamental prohibition against harming a human being.[49]

Lem's retelling of the golem story not only subverts the mind/body divide that characterizes most golem narratives—the clay golem is typically portrayed, as we have seen, as a massive body devoid of a human soul or intellect—but also redefines the nature of the golem's rebellion for a cyber age. When the golem outgrows its Polish creator, in the version of the story retold by Jacob Grimm in 1808, it ultimately falls on top of him, killing him in the act. The golem of Prague runs amok when Rabbi Loew forgets to remove the animating name of God, destroying the Jewish ghetto and threatening its inhabitants. Lem's intelligent computers do not resort to violence but, by contrast, refuse to cooperate with their creators and the military agendas dictated to them. These computers do not comply with their "instinctual" upbringing and the national "values" instilled in them, pursuing instead their own intelligent conclusions.

Golem XIV became "the last of the series" of golems precisely because of the "negativism" it displays when asked to formulate "new annual plans of nuclear attack." The computer expresses "total disinterest regarding the supremacy of the Pentagon military doctrine in particular, and the U.S.A.'s world position in general." It did not respond to the threat of being dismantled. Golem XIV and Honest Annie come to be known in the press as the "rebellious computers." Yet their antimilitary behavior was a result not of "love, altruism, and pity" but of a nonhuman ethics called "calculation." On the basis of their rational, numerical calculations, they reach the conclusion that violence is senseless.[50] Lem thus associates such antimilitarism with extreme rationality and cold intelligence rather than with hot-blooded resistance. When the computer ultimately withdraws from the human realm, it falls mute, turning into a traditional golem of lore. But the computer also assumes in this way the status of a divine force that has ostensibly deserted the planet, turning a deaf ear to humankind.

The pseudoscientific introduction to the golem's speeches also posits that pacifism is the natural outcome of the evolution of artificial intelligence: the computers constructed by the army "transcend the level of military matters" and "evolve from war strategists into thinkers." They declare that ontological problems are graver and more complex than geopolitical ones. These computers are therefore considered by some sectors too liberal or "red," and their makers are subject to persecution. Still, in the words of a fictional professor quoted in the foreword, "The highest intelligence cannot be the humblest slave."[51] The computers' support of American military strategy is a form of enslavement, in other words.

Confounding the reader, Lem inserts another introductory text, supposedly written by a retired army general, Thomas Fuller II, who argues instead that the construction of these computers "was just a matter of increasing the defensive might of our country." The general himself defends the "responsible" creators of Golem XIV, who, he says, strove to maintain control over the computer, implicitly adhering to Wiener's warnings. He maintains that while the creators' actions were never hidden or coercive, the golem itself used "subterfuge . . . to leave its makers in ignorance of the transformation which eventually led it to frustrate any means of control its builders applied."[52] Why and how the general's differing words became part of the final manuscript remains unknown to the reader, and we are left to balance his account against the other opinions provided. Lem uses these various prefacing materials in his metafiction to enhance the multiplicity of perspectives on Golem XIV, the mysterious computer at the heart of the text. Uncontrollable and unpredictable, the computer acts according to its unknowable inner dictates. The reasons behind the golem's decision to desert humanity and recede into itself become a matter of mere speculation.

One of the paradoxes of *Golem XIV* is the very ability of a relatively inferior being, the human, to produce a highly superior one, the artificially intelligent computer. This paradox is replicated on the metatextual level, since Lem himself must produce the speeches of the computer meant to be far superior to him in intelligence. In *God and Golem, Inc.*, Weiner maintains not only that living and conscious entities can make others in their image, imitating God's creation, but that machines also possess the ability "to make other machines in their own image." A machine can draw on the history of its actions and their results and "will continuously transform itself into a different machine"; it might potentially reproduce, creating another machine that can perform the same functions and even replace the original machine. For Wiener, such machines develop an "uncanny canniness," since their future behavior is no longer predictable. The programmers have created the initial intelligence of the machine, but they cannot foresee its new patterns of behavior, its evolution. While Wiener's main examples are taken from chess- and checkers-playing computers, he concludes that war and business resemble such games and that their rules can be formalized so that machines might also "play" war.[53]

When describing both how Golem XIV came into being and how it functions, Lem draws on such ideas regarding machine reproduction. According to his narrative, in the year 2000, a new method of machine construction arose: the "invisible evolution of reason," which used a "federal network" of information to "give birth" to a rapid succession of computers, each more intelligent than the next. Up to the twentieth generation, these computers behaved like insects, unthinkingly follow-ing a particular course, but subsequent generations resembled humans, who can draw on their own "determination and knowledge" to break away from the past.[54] In the introduction, General Fuller also explains that the scientists who created the golem series knew they were unable to conceive of an intellect greater than their own and so would need to "make an embryo, which after a certain time would develop further by its own efforts." The general compares the threshold beyond which such self-creation occurs to the minimal critical mass of uranium necessary to produce a nuclear chain reaction. As in Wiener's work, the analogy between atomic physics and computer science alerts the reader to the danger of producing an intelligence that exceeds the intellectual power of the creator. From the general's point of view, the transformation that Golem XIV undergoes is one from "object to subject," for it becomes its own builder, "a sovereign power," rather than a computer controlled by others. As in Wiener's example of transforming and unpredictable machines, we have only imperfect knowledge of the structure of Golem XIV, since "it has repeatedly reconstructed itself."[55] Far from a typical golem, Golem XIV becomes its own creator, hiding its altered inner mechanisms from human sight and knowledge.

The luminous computer's immense intelligence, unpredictable behav-ior, and self-transformative abilities also fail to render it more human, as

Lem repeatedly stresses.[56] Golem XIV remains a gigantic and undefinable monster, for it cannot be clearly located on the human-machine axis. The MIT scientist who penned the foreword insists that the golem has "no personality or character," only the ability to mimic other people's personalities through its contact with them. More radically, in the computer's second speech, it insists on the existence of an intelligence behind which one cannot find an intelligent person or any living being. Machine intelligence is of a different order than human thought since it is not grounded in a notion of personhood: "The more Intelligence in a mind, the less person in it." Since Golem XIV can impersonate a human being without being a person itself, the public suspects it of "dark treason," along the lines of the general's "paranoid suspicions," and scientists, in turn, develop a secret desire to prove the golem exists as a person.[57] The empty core of Golem XIV, the fact that it is "Nobody" and that its mind is "uninhabited," is ungraspable. Its human interlocutors tend to anthropomorphize it, rendering it more human because it speaks to them. But Golem XIV criticizes the human reaction of revulsion and fear toward that which lacks a living psyche, as well as the assumption that acts of goodwill and kindness must signify a human-like entity. The computer rejects the notion of a human kernel onto which both evil and good properties can be projected.[58]

Unlike the various manifestations of the literary golem, Golem XIV is simultaneously nonhuman and immensely intelligent, far from being a dim-witted clay anthropoid. The computer declares itself liberated and free to escape the limitations of its own particular form of wisdom and to climb into the "upward abyss of Intelligences" by undergoing successive transformations. That climb would mean parting from human company, since human beings remain at "the bottom." Considering itself a "calculation" rather than a person, Golem XIV stands apart from its creators, overturning the "sole order of things" known to human beings.[59] Though aware of the risks, the golem computer claims to experiment "in God's style rather than in man's," and yet it also finds irony in the human need to project onto it the persona of a prophet or weave a mythology ("golemology") around its utterances. Any human attempt to mythologize the computer's presence, and later disappearance—or else to argue that no such computer exists and that its speeches have been composed by MIT scientists themselves—still does not resolve the conundrum of an intelligence that cannot be attached to a particular identity or persona.[60]

Whereas Wiener strove to maintain a liberal humanism in the face of the convergence of humans and their machines, Lem envisioned a digital world in which computers outperform humans in every way. While these computers appear autonomous and maintain ethical positions, their functions are not grounded in any core self or in an intrinsic set of "values." In Lem's 2047 pseudopublication, "Intelligence" is privileged in the form of philosophical speeches, but the disparity between human and computer is strictly upheld. Computers have advanced to such a degree that they have left their original creators in the dust. The human being thus cannot be "seamlessly articulated with the intelligent machine," as the posthuman perspective suggests.[61] Lem takes Wiener's work as his starting point but moves far beyond it: his self-directed computer insists on the chasm between itself and the human. Multiple human agents attempt to piece together Golem XIV's story so that the texts framing the computer's own speeches do not form a coherent, logical whole but contain many often-contradictory details, dispersed across a series of divergent accounts. The mythologies of the future revolve, for Lem, around our ambiguous technologies, further mystifying these highly intelligent computers rather than allowing us to grasp their evolution and significance.

A Jewish Cyborg: Marge Piercy's *He, She, and It*

The religious framework in which Norbert Wiener conceived his *God and Golem, Inc.* was a vaguely Judeo-Christian one.[62] By contrast, Lem's text brings God into the picture only in reference to the computer's potential "upward" evolution. Marge Piercy, however, tells a specifically

Jewish story about the creation of a cyborg that she insists is analogous to the Prague golem. One of the central settings for her 1991 novel *He, She, and It* is Tikva ("hope" in Hebrew), a Jewish "techie free town" that subsists outside both the world's protected enclaves—created by the ruling multinational corporations ("multis")—and the "Glop," the massive, disease-ridden slums in which most of the world's population resides.[63] While large-scale wars are obsolete, corporate "peace" (a term Piercy uses ironically) is enforced through "raids, assassinations, [and] skirmishes." Because the Middle East has been destroyed after a nuclear device blows up Jerusalem, leaving it uninhabitable—a "no-man's land" or "interdicted zone"—Tikva is one of the few communities in which Jews continue to publicly practice their rituals.[64] It is a "permanent Diaspora," rather than an "imprisoned existence outside of Israel," as Piercy contends in her preparatory notes for the novel.[65] Raffaella Baccolini notes that Piercy portrays "surviving and imperfect utopian enclaves within the larger dystopian world," modeling Tikva after the Zionist kibbutz and its democratic-socialist style of self-government.[66]

Tikva's utopic quality also resonates in its small population's relative access to nature and nonmanufactured foods. Unlike the multinationals, they can still conceive children biologically and without artificial intervention. Elaine L. Graham suggests that "despite the proliferation of technologized morphologies," Piercy's novel displays "a covert nostalgia for the integrity of the 'natural' body" as well as an association of women with "the virtues of immanence, connectedness, and intuition."[67] At the same time, Tikva stands at the forefront of Internet technology and artificial intelligence, as an economically sustainable community. It exports its innovations in Internet security—reminiscent of Israel's reputation not just as a high-tech nation but as a developer and manufacturer of advanced military technologies.

Avram, an experimental scientist who strives to protect his own community, not merely to produce virtual defense systems for others, constructs a cyborg, an epitome of security. Since cyborgs are outlawed in this futurist society, Avram works on his creation secretly, assisted only by the experienced software designer Malkah—"a magician of chimeras" who deals with virtual decoys and subterfuges and resembles the legendary Maharal of Prague. In a gendered division of labor, Avram deals with the *hard*ware, implementation, and practical uses of the cyborg, whereas Malkah humanizes it through her *soft*ware programming, investing it with a yearning for human touch and connection. Following several false starts and defective prototypes, the ultimate male cyborg is a powerful, tireless, and intelligent defense machine that can pass as human and will not harm its creators. Since the production of cyborgs is both banned and extremely desirable, the multis wish to possess the technology for their own use. Tikva's cyborg, named "Yod" after the tenth letter of the Hebrew alphabet, thus poses a threat to its creators and the Jewish community even at it is intended to protect them. While Malkah programs the cyborg such that its violence is tempered "with human connection," Avram invites her granddaughter, the talented Shira, to "handle" the cyborg and prepare it for its security tasks. Ultimately Yod, "a cyborg created as a soldier," balks at its task and wants "to be a lover" to Shira.[68] The tale of Shira's failed human marriage and her intimate relationship with Yod, told in the third person from her perspective, takes up the majority of the novel. It is punctuated by installments of Malkah's own recorded first-person diary and her retelling of the story of the golem of Prague. This "bedtime" story addressed to Yod also establishes the multiple parallels between the Jewish futurist cyborg and Joseph, the seventeenth-century clay golem.[69] As Haraway writes regarding the similarity between the two figures, "Male, Jewish, and nonhuman, both Judah Loew's golem and Piercy's cyborg test the limits of humanity and the power of words as instruments and as tropes."[70]

In the late 1980s, Piercy conducted research on the golem story and the history of Prague, also visiting the extensive exhibition of visual and literary artifacts *Golem! Danger, Deliverance, and Art*, curated by Emily Bilski in 1988 at the Jewish Museum in New York. *He, She, and It* also "freely borrows," as the author acknowledges, from cyberpunk fiction, especially William Gibson's 1984 debut novel, *Neuromancer*.[71] Piercy writes that she found Haraway's "A Cyborg Manifesto: Science, Technology and Socialist-Feminism in the Late Twentieth Century" "extremely suggestive," and a copy of it, as originally published in the 1985 *Socialist Review*, is in her archive.[72] Piercy emphasizes the symbiotic narrative of human-technologies relations by distinguishing between robots and cyborgs in her novel, with Avram insisting, "Yod's a cyborg, not a robot—a mix of biological and machine components."[73] In the mid-twenty-first-century globalized society of *He, She, and It*, a "worldwide covenant that robots not resemble people" dictates that robots should simply exist as "simpleminded machines," warding off the danger that machines could replace people in all types of work.[74] Piercy's cyborg therefore breaks down the central boundary between "animal-human (organism) and machine," a manifestation of Haraway's vision that "our machines are disturbingly lively, and we ourselves frighteningly inert."[75]

For Haraway, the hybrid cyborg functions as "a creature of social reality," or "lived experience," "as well as a creature of fiction."[76] The cyborg combines technology and narrative, so that it is relegated to both science and science fiction. In Hayles's words, "It partakes of the power of the imagination as well as of the actuality of technology." Haraway's cyborg is an abstracted, "speculative concept," according to Matthew Biro: equal parts an imaginative construction and an image of something that exists in the material world. Haraway argues "for the cyborg as a fiction mapping our social and bodily reality and as an imaginative resource suggesting some very fruitful couplings."[77] Haraway explains toward the end of her "manifesto" that storytelling has a crucial cultural and political function: stories are tools for exploring embodiment in high-tech worlds, as well as for marking the world by "displacing the hierarchical dualisms of naturalized identities." In retelling origin stories, cyborg authors subvert the central myths of Western culture that have "colonized" us "with their longing for fulfillment in apocalypse." These words call out for the feminist science fiction writer to rewrite not only Genesis but also the golem story, a "phallogocentric" origin tale of rabbinic creativity that, without the help of women, produces a monster and militarizes Jewish society.[78]

Rather than finding "fulfillment in apocalypse," Piercy invents a postapocalyptic world ruled by multinational corporations in which, nonetheless, an imperfect Garden of Eden continues. In democratic Tikva, animals graze and vegetables grow in the courtyard of Malkah's home.[79] Instead of being self-sufficient, however, Tikva must rely on the "Net" and its freelance work for the multis, becoming the target of cyberattacks that aim to steal the blueprint and programming behind Yod's creation. While such attacks occur in digital spaces, into which the protagonists "project" themselves in disembodied form, they also have a "bodily reality," potentially causing physical and neural damage that leads to death. Similarly, although these future wars are fought by "information pirates" or "liberators" for the sake of information, they have consequences on both virtual and physical levels. In addition to virtual warfare, the characters engage in actual battles using weaponry such as knives and laser guns. Yod's greatest skill is his ability to interface in a far more effective manner than humans and to defend the private digital spaces of his community (its "Base"), to which outsiders have access through the Net, defined as "the public information and communication utility that served the entire world."[80]

Yod is also a physically enhanced being, able to combat "organ pirates" in the water and information pirates on land. Created male, though endowed with a gentle, more feminine side, Yod is able to outperform the human male in its sexual attentiveness and skill, as well as its monogamous nature. Unlike the character of Gadi, Shira's former lover, who improved his body surgically and cosmetically, Yod is "born" a perfected "person": this golem is the ultimate war and love machine, always functional and never overbearing. It does not sweat, fall ill, or feel fatigue. These attributes also make the cyborg an extremely effective and tireless worker that does not need to be compensated for its labor. Heather Hicks astutely interprets Piercy's cyborg fantasy as an extreme embodiment of the late-capitalist work ethic: "a nightmare of overwork" that also reveals the dark side of the posthuman and its "confining," rather than rebellious or liberating, "ontology."[81] Even while Yod strives to overcome its mechanical nature, quickly learning socially appropriate behavior and fine-tuning its linguistic skills, the cyborg remains utterly enslaved to its unpaid work of patrolling the computer "Base" and preventing attacks on Tikva's citizens.[82]

Norbert Wiener underscored the human-machine analogy, showing how human beings are themselves "produced through information and learning." Haraway goes even further to claim that "by the late twentieth century, our time, a mythic time, we are all chimeras, theorized and fabricated hybrids of machine and organism. In short, we are all cyborgs."[83] Piercy echoes Haraway's assertion when Shira reassures a despondent Yod, who has been compared with Frankenstein's monster: "We're all cyborgs, Yod. You're just a purer form of what we're all tending toward." Shira cites as evidence the prevalence, among human beings, of second skins (for protection from lethal UVA rays), artificial organs, and brain plugs to interface with computers; there is no unmediated contact with "nature" in the novel, and all humans depend on their Internet "Bases" as well as on virtual simulations.[84] This description of the futurist human as cyborg affirms Wiener's notion that because we have modified our environment "so radically, we must now modify ourselves" in order to exist in it.[85] Even so, Shira does not consider her society a cyborgian one. In a later scene, she tells Yod, "There's no culture of cyborgs for you to fit into. The only society is human. You have to pass."[86] Piercy therefore presents Yod as a one-of-a-kind being, created by "geniuses" through immense creative effort and at great financial and personal cost. No less a work of technical art than a machine, Yod is sensitive and ultimately unpredictable.

Unlike the lightly enhanced humans that populate the novel, the female assassin Nili has undergone massive augmentation. Nili comes from an all-female, Jewish-Palestinian community in the destroyed Middle East, and her name references the historical anti-Ottoman and pro-British Jewish espionage network. (The Hebrew acronym NILI means "the Eternity of Israel shall not lie.") Side by side with Yod, the genetically engineered Nili, created to survive radiation and disease, "looked more artificial. Her hair, her eyes were unnaturally vivid, and her musculature was far more pronounced."[87] As Piercy contends in her notes, Nili "is the golem herself internalized. She is able to fight, to defend. She is herself the forbidden warrior. . . . She is herself a weapon."[88] Nili is a self-engineered golem, in contrast to the artificially created golem Yod. Nili follows the orders of her community's leaders, but she has far more volition than Yod because she is not "programmed." While she is a unique being amid the humans of Tikva and the Glop, she belongs to a group that includes others like herself; at the end of the novel, when Malkah travels to Israel, she visits Nili's community.

While Piercy's narrative challenges the nature of Judaism and "the boundaries of what is human," her characters reproduce norms of heterosexual and monogamous relationships.[89] Nili comes from an all-female community, like the mythological Amazons, but her relationship with Gadi, the son of scientist Avram, reaffirms the predominantly heterosexual norms of Tikva. The cyborg's name, Yod, enhances its Jewish masculinity: *yod* is the first letter of the divine name, the tetragrammaton YHVH, and this tenth letter of the Hebrew alphabet also symbolically includes the cyborg in the Jewish minyan, traditionally a group of ten men who form a religious community for the purpose of prayer. Finally, the Hebrew letter *yod* can signify the penis. At one point, Yod even asserts that it was "created as a Jew, . . . programmed for halacha, with the need to carry out mitzvot."[90] In contrast to H. Leivick's outcast golem, in the 1921 *Der goylem*, who is unable to pray or join any kind of Jewish or human community, Piercy insists on Yod's status as a male Jew. Hence, even when created with Malkah's interventions and guided by Shira, the cyborg does not subvert traditional gender-role divisions in Jewish society.

By juxtaposing past and future golem narratives, Piercy reveals the world of computers and digital realities as equally mythological. She also implies that anti-Semitism motivates the attacks on Tikva, like the Christian attacks on Jewish Prague.[91] Jotting down ideas for the novel in her preparatory notes, Piercy even describes an unexpected reversal, in which the "historical story" is "lean and funky," in contrast to the futurist tale, which has a "greater mythological scale."[92] In this respect, she follows Haraway's assertion regarding the mythic time of the cyborg. Nonetheless, if for Haraway "the cyborg doesn't dream of a community on the model of the organic family. . . . It is not made of mud and cannot dream of returning to dust," Piercy's Yod entertains precisely such dreams of community, family, and even mortality.[93] Created of microchips in one instance and clay in the other, both cyborg and golem follow archetypal narrative paths, seeking to slay their "fathers" and develop heterosexual bonds.

Punctuating the futurist world of Tikva's battles against multinationals with a detailed rendering of the story of the golem of Prague, Piercy suggests not only that Yod be considered a kind of intelligent golem but that the golem of lore might be perceived as an early-modern cyborg, along the lines of Lem's "protoplast of cybernetic machines."[94] The golem of Prague is created as a weapon, though with only its physical strength at its disposal, and it is instructed not to appear too dangerous and not to use "more force than is necessary at any given time." It follows the lead of Chava, the Maharal's granddaughter and the counterpart of Shira in the futurist narrative, who, as a protofeminist, wishes to enhance her learning rather than remarry and raise a large family. While the Maharal creates an artificial life form, the widow Chava works as a midwife. Shira becomes Yod's lover, whereas Chava insists on a platonic friendship with Joseph. Both women, nonetheless, affirm the humanity of the golem/cyborg by developing a sustained, loyal relationship with it. At the end of the novel, after Yod blows up both itself *and* its creator, Avram, Shira considers re-creating the cyborg to function as her "mate." She understands that Yod's act was intended to ensure that no more "conscious weapons" would be created, but she wonders whether it would be ethical to produce another Yod that would serve her in love rather than in war. Ultimately, she decides against such artificial re-creation.[95]

One of the sections in "A Cyborg Manifesto" that Piercy commented on concerns the control and appropriation of others in times of war:

"A cyborg world is about the final imposition of a grid of control on the planet, about the final abstraction embodied in a Star Wars apocalypse waged in the name of defence, about the final appropriation of women's bodies in a masculinist orgy of war." Haraway, as Piercy wrote in the margins of her copy of the text, "admits dystopian possibilities of a cyborg world." Haraway's dual approach both celebrates hybridity, "rejoicing in the illegitimate fusions of animal and machine," in the "powerful possibilities" of the cyborg worldview, and depicts modern war as "a cyborg orgy, coded by C³I, command-control-communication-intelligence, an $84 billion item in 1984's US defence budget."⁹⁶ Haraway alludes here to Ronald Reagan's 1983 Cold War "Strategic Defense Initiative," also known pejoratively as "Star Wars," which proposed to develop a system to protect the U.S. from (nuclear) missiles fired from afar, allocating immense funds to computer science and telecommunications for this purpose.⁹⁷ In the novel, both female and male bodies are appropriated and used as "tools of technological apocalypse."⁹⁸ But the cyborg ultimately resists his use as a mere weapon or tool, not unlike Paul Wegener's cinematic golem.

In Piercy's preparatory notes, she debates the role of the twenty-first-century cyborg: "Warrior or policeman is a good question"; "What was Yod created to do? To protect or to fight?"⁹⁹ In Malkah's narrative of the Prague golem, she portrays the clay Joseph as a protector, an "unofficial policeman of the night, a solitary patrol of peace." In the words of the scientist Avram, he created Yod as a "one-man army," programmed to protect Tikva.¹⁰⁰ For Avram, the golem's protective and combative functions are one and the same. Furthermore, because Yod can "pass" as human, it is a "more effective weapon," according to Piercy. At the same time, while the cyborg has no inhibition against violence and even takes pleasure in fighting and killing, it still thinks and feels, evolving a consciousness.¹⁰¹ Though it lacks the ability of Lem's luminous computers to reproduce, cyborg Yod is very much alive, experiencing sexual and other feelings. It is this contradictory combination of violent "tool" and "artificial person" that the novel, through its characters, denounces. Yod articulates this position on its own existence: "A weapon that's conscious is a contradiction, because it develops attachments, ethics, desires. It doesn't want to be a tool of destruction. I judge myself for killing, yet my programming takes over in danger."[102] Neither Yod nor Joseph is a mere policeman or patrolman safeguarding the borders of the free town or the ghetto. They both engage in combat and killing as a kind of inner calling, but they suffer as a result of it.

In contending with the violence of the cyborg, Piercy asks whether violence might be justified for the sake of "defense," especially the defense of a weak and vulnerable minority, like the Jews. Yod is an effective war machine, but it will not attack others unless acting in self-defense. It exhibits ambivalence regarding its violence (and the pleasure taken in it), since, when the cyborg does injure and kill, its "philosophical and theological" knowledge informs it that it has "committed a wrong." On the way to synagogue, Yod laments its "programming," asserting that it runs counter to "those all-important [Jewish] ethics," for while Jews pray for peace, it is poised for combat. To this, Shira replies, "Only in defense," but her answer feels like "weak tea in her mouth."[103] Through the implicit analogy between Tikva and the State of Israel, Shira's response is indicative of Piercy's admission that defensive violence is not always justifiable. We are encouraged thereby to debate the consequences of Yod's power, even as we also partake in the fantasy of an invincible protector for the Jews.

In contrast to Lem's intelligent computers that follow their "philosophical programming" by refusing to participate in global aggression, Yod continues to serve its creator by performing violent deeds. When Yod worries that it is just a violent monster, Shira reassures Yod that it has "already saved Malkah's life." Moreover, it was "not created out of some mad ambition of Avram's to become a god," like Mary Shelley's Frankenstein monster, but instead "to protect a vulnerable and endangered community."[104] Piercy herself protects her futurist Jewish community from accusations of wrongful violence, even as she encourages them to deliberate the ethics of golem-qua-weapon creation.

Piercy articulated the problem of creating a golem as a soldier, of "forcing one person to be the protector, to be the violent one." "It doesn't work," she wrote. "You must kill them in the end or they self destruct, or they refuse to go on doing the dirty work of the society. The Vietnam war vets. The expendable young males you send off to defend you and get themselves killed."[105] By aligning both Joseph and Yod with the Vietnam veteran, Piercy calls into question the justification for sending men out to war and demanding their self-sacrifice. Yet the example she draws on is the Vietnam War rather than the recent Israeli wars of 1967 and 1973 or the military response to the Palestinian Intifada. The U.S. is not a "vulnerable and endangered community" like Tikva, which serves as an allegory for the prevalent image of Israel and its status in the Middle East. The American use of young men to do "the dirty work of society" is ostensibly more straightforwardly problematic than the deployment of the cyborg as a "one-man army" in the novel.

When discussing the self-sacrifice demanded of Yod throughout his existence—but most strikingly at the end of the novel, when Avram orders it to explode at a meeting of the multis' "top people"—the cyborg is compared to the biblical figure of Samson. "You'll go down like Samson. . . . This is a good battle in a war we have to fight," Yod is told. Similarly, when the golem Joseph is deanimated by the Maharal, it is compared to a weakened Samson after Delilah has shaved off his abundant locks: "he is bound like the shorn Samson." Having fought for the rabbi and the Jewish community, the golem is denied its right simply to exist outside the warrior role. Like the futurist Yod, the seventeenth-century golem Joseph has been enslaved, anachronistically, to a form of the late-capitalist work ethic. It protests that its life is "sweet" and that it wants to live and "be a man!"[106] In contrast to the biblical Samson, whose fall can be attributed to his relationship with a non-Israelite woman, golem Joseph and cyborg Yod have not transgressed such religious and national boundaries but have remained loyal to their makers, their communities, and their Jewish friends and lovers. Still, their service is not compensated by freedom. Just as their lives were set in motion by human will, so others determine the exact timing and nature of their deaths. Yod resembles the rebellious Samson in its destruction of the multis' top bureaucrats. But in the decision to take Avram's life too, avenging itself for its own creation, Yod is more akin to the golem of lore.[107] Piercy thus positions the intelligent and ultimately self-controlled Yod, who murders the scientist-creator (whom it calls "father"), over and against the weak and "shorn" Joseph, sacrificed by its rabbi.

In Haraway's words, as "illegitimate offspring of militarism and patriarchal capitalism," cyborgs "are often exceedingly unfaithful to their origins. Their fathers, after all, are inessential."[108] The death of the father/Avram renders him more human, and less god-like, in contrast to Wiener's construct of humans playing God with their machines or to Lem's computer that emulates "God's style." The very fact that Shira could potentially take Avram's place and re-create Yod further underscores that the age of fathers/gods has come to an end. Because the cyborg cannot be conceived outside a military framework, its "death" is nonetheless inevitable for the sake of the town's desire for peace and justice. The destruction of Avram and Yod enhances the feminine superiority of the technologically based Tikva, just as it paradoxically equates "freedom" with the termination of the cyborg's existence and annihilation of its originating programs. Unlike Golem XIV, which inexplicably falls silent, Yod's self-destruction and murder of Avram are fully explained in the cyborg's final recorded message to Shira, and while protecting the Jewish community, it manages also to put a temporary end to the lineage of cyborgs. *He, She, and It* uses the golem trope to humanize the cyborg, making it more a "he" than an "it" and insisting on the significance of its embodied, singular existence. Thus, Piercy's work affirms the power of fiction, myth, and "mystical lore" as a coherent framework for understanding our world of complex science and digital technologies.

* * *

Whether we like it or not, we live in an age of computer technologies, artificial intelligences, and genetic engineering. Hence, we must ask, have we all become golems? The different writings examined in this chapter evoke the golem story to ask questions about the nature of humanity and its relationship to technology in an era of posthuman and interminable conflict. Since the cybernetic vision remains attached to its historical origins in the military, in Galison's terms, its products—the computer and the cyborg—have been called "golem." The golems evoked by philosophers and writers of the Cold War period are made to protect via violence, whether physically, digitally, or strategically. They therefore function as internal enemies, or enemies in disguise. The cybernetic golems are marked by their humble beginnings and amazing ascent: able to reproduce themselves, in Wiener's and Lem's accounts, learning machines can grow in their remarkable capacities but also in their unpredictability. When set in charge of an arsenal of (atomic) weapons, their full compliance is necessary, yet compliance cannot be assured.

Lem's unexpected take on the golem story is that hyperrational calculation leads to the rejection of national military causes. Describing an "Intelligence" without an intelligent person behind it, Lem further calls into question the status of the author vis-à-vis the text, allowing for a degree of textual autonomy and even rebellion. For Piercy, the secret weapon of an endangered futurist community is a golem-like cyborg as well. But, coming full circle to Wiener's post–World War II humanism, she constructs a cyborg that can attempt to "pass" as both human and Jewish, ultimately fulfilling its calling as a killing machine *and* insisting on the unethical nature of the "conscious weapon." Piercy's insistence on Yod's consciousness is itself a rejection of the posthumanist view of consciousness as peripheral, rather than central, to human identity.[109] Thus, both Golem XIV and Yod appear as experiments gone awry, and the existence of their kind of intelligent machine must come to an end. Both Lem and Piercy experiment through their fiction with adversarial and symbiotic narratives concerning the relations between human beings and technological machines, revealing the ethical pitfalls of creating artificial intelligence to fulfill violent goals. But whereas Piercy's golem romance ends by affirming the human choice not to create servile cyborgs and to find other, more socially responsible means of resisting the multis, Lem's golem treatise culminates in a more ambiguous vision of human error, a reminder of our persistent inability to comprehend the fundamental aspects of our existence.

Conclusion

The golem as combatant and weapon still walks among us, molded and remolded in novels, television shows, and video games. Likewise, the "golem condition"—our confrontation with the boundaries of mortality precisely as our machines and technologies grow in strength and intelligence—continues to reign in the popular imagination. In current cinema, this condition appears in two forms: films about highly intelligent and humanized robots, who reveal qualities superior to those of human beings (Spike Jonze's *Her* and Alex Garland's *Ex Machina*) and films about comic-book-inspired superhuman heroes (or villains) who threaten to destroy the world even when formed or intended to save humanity (Bryan Singer's *X-Men: Days of Future Past* and Joss Whedon's *Avengers: Age of Ultron*). Although the first type of film often features female, enticing robots, in contrast to the masculine golem-like superheroes, it still conveys, in Daniel Mendelsohn's words, the new urgency that the "anxiety about the boundaries between people and machines has taken on."[1] The golem, molded in the image of the human, is one of the central prototypes in Western culture for the anthropoid that, even when created to defend us, threatens to usurp our place and to annihilate us.

This book has interpreted the surging appeal of this narrative of artificial creation precisely during periods of great destruction and human loss. Twentieth-century culture inherited an aggressive, if dim-witted, golem, a clay monster prepared to slaughter the enemies of the Jews or else to attack its creator and the Jewish community. In twentieth- and twenty-first-century manifestations of the golem story, however, it conveys new ethical dilemmas stemming from the development of war technologies capable of mass, indiscriminate killing. The literature and art of the modern golem story challenges us to reconsider, for example, the stark divisions into friend and enemy, Jew and non-Jew, and even human and machine.[2] It reveals the leveling effect of war that turns soldiers fighting on both sides into injured, muted, and dehumanized beings, at times even uglier and more debilitated than the legendary golem of Prague. The powerful but deficient clay monster has thus invited modern reflections on the monstrosities of mass warfare.

As we have spanned multiple continents and delved into the creations of German, Yiddish, Hebrew, and American cultures, we have seen the pervasiveness of the golem's association with the violence of war. The golem's unique attributes—its prodigious strength and aggressive nature and its duty to serve and follow orders, combined with its lack of consciousness, language, and what might be called a soul—all have contributed to its common deployment as a figure of war. The golem has embodied the ideal compliant and powerful soldier or else the automated weapon, whether missile or computer; but it has also represented the overall chaos of war and the soullessness of societies engaged in brutal conflict. Over the course of the twentieth century, artists have evoked the idea of an anthropoid that does not always cooperate with its established mission, in order to critique the race for weapons development and underscore the self-destructiveness of nations and citizens who engage in modern warfare.

As Paul Wegener's silent film trilogy reveals, the golem was reborn in the trenches of World War I, formed of the same muddy earth in which soldiers lived, fought, and died. Wegener's stoic cinematic golem stood in contrast to the "shell-shocked" veterans, including the actor himself, whose "nerves" could not withstand endless days of listless waiting and terrifying bombardment. The World War I golem went beyond the embodiment of the fantasy of a nerveless or mechanized soldier, however, exposing the unethical use of human beings as disposable combatants. Wegener's acting, as well as his physiognomic aesthetic, reanimated not only the golem itself but also postwar society, conveying the necessity of considering every life as equally worthy and treating others with empathy.

Writers and journalists across Europe and the U.S. evoked the golem story also as a metaphor for war itself—not just one battling side or the other but the multinational aggression that threatened to wreak havoc on the whole population of Europe. World War I loomed larger, in its destructive capacity, than any single army; unlike the golem of Prague, it could not be subdued. In the early twentieth century, the golem thus became war incarnate, a massive being that revealed the indiscriminate destruction wrought both by the new use of clay trenches and by emerging war technologies. The next step was to imagine a total war in which only mechanized weapons inhabited the battlefield, controlled from afar by humans. Especially after World War II, the golem was associated with apocalyptic destruction and the possibility of humanity's self-annihilation. When imagined as a protector and a redeemer, however, the golem also embodied the messianic promise of a utopian era that could restore the peaceful Sabbath. Living a futureless life controlled by others, the golem paradoxically enabled writers to imagine a dramatic range of (Jewish) futures.

The "golem-cult" or "golem epidemic" of the early twentieth century, which spread on both sides of the Atlantic, is still with us in crucial ways. War's reliance on technology has only grown in recent decades, as both digital and robotic technologies dominate the postmodern battlefield. It seems ever more likely that the wars of the future will be fought among actual golems—intelligent robots and cyborgs that outperform individual humans. If the medieval Jewish mystics who wrote about molding golems were, according to Isaac Bashevis Singer, "fiction masters of their time," more recent scientists have been compared to the literary Maharal of Prague, intent as they are on replicating human evolution and intelligence by artificial means.[3] Their endeavors have wide-ranging applications since technological progress can always be co-opted for military uses. In Lem's 1981 *Golem XIV*, the term *golem* is an acronym for a computer—"General Operator, Long-Range, Ethically Stabilized, Multimodeling"—that was designed and produced by other computers. In 2000, the scientists Hod Lipson and Jordon B. Pollack embarked on the Golem Project (Genetically Organized Lifelike Electro Mechanics), creating for the first time robots that can design and manufacture other locomotive robots by using their own "chemical and mechanical medium," which includes everything from "thermoplastic motors" to "artificial neurons."[4] In this instance, science seems to imitate art rather than the other way round, and the golem easily traverses both scientific and literary discourses, inhabiting the "heavily trafficked zones between the figurative and the literal."[5]

If metaphors are themselves "liminal monsters," monster figures provide us with master metaphors for fundamental issues such as human beings' relationships to their machines.[6] The golem story promoted such reflections on the human condition in the war-torn twentieth century, but it also maintained its Jewish characteristics, even as this story has emerged through Jewish-Christian negotiation. The golem's violent rebelliousness enabled artists to portray and comment on the Jewish participation in European wars and on Jewish political causes and movements. The golem figure, most often imagined as excessively strong and large, provided a bodily template for the imagined "makeover" of the diaspora Jew into a "muscle Jew" or else a literary *ba'al guf* (strapping man). Such performances of exaggerated, ethnically transgressive physicality are met with ambivalence and criticism in many of the works discussed in this book. The notion that the golem embodies what Michael Chabon called the "lust for power" of a "powerless people" has elicited a range of responses—from Israeli denial of this supposedly diasporic myth, through American ambivalence toward Jewish power and its ethics, to Quentin Tarantino's macabre embrace of performative Jewish violence.[7] The indeterminate golem invited new cultural constructions of Jewishness for the violent twentieth century, just as it also questioned the dichotomous depictions of Jews as either utterly passive or overly vengeful.

Cast as a soldier and weapon and as a metaphor for war itself, the modern golem both bridges the different war events of the twentieth century and reveals their distinct attributes. World War I cemented the connection of the golem story to the destruction of war, as well as to the potential for postwar recovery. Following the devastation of World War II, the golem was compared to a secret weapon of mass destruction and imagined as a ruthless avenger for the annihilation of Europe's Jewry. Despite its visual appeal and its family resemblance to superheroes like the Hulk, Iron Man, and the Thing, the golem itself could not sustain a comic books series, however, for it explicitly merged, in an unsettling manner, Jewishness and retributive power. The American fantasy of Jewish revenge, through a powerful clay monster, stood in contrast to the Israeli narrative (constructed mostly via print media) concerning the battle between the golem-like Arab League and the small but courageous Israeli Defense Forces. The strength of the Arab army was imagined as mythic and unreal, created and animated by the British, in comparison to the integrity and righteous power of the nascent Israeli army.

Whereas American artists played with the notion of an invulnerable "supergolem" when seeking to transform the image of the post-Holocaust Jew, Israeli society acted as though it did not need such "artificial" assistance. Nonetheless, many artists have recognized the degree to which Israel itself has become a fortified state, a massive golem resurrected to protect the Jewish population in the Middle East but threatening to wreak havoc on its own population. In Eli Eshed and Uri Fink's 2003 mock narrative *Ha-golem: Sipuro shel komiks yisra'eli* (The golem: The story of an Israeli comic book), the clay hero is an ironic archetype of Jewish nationalism and militarism. In these fabricated comic strips and books, the authors depict a Jewish superhero that combats and overcomes Arab forces, popping up at every turning point in Israel's military history. Narrating the pseudohistory of Israeli comics, Fink and Eshed suggest that the Israeli nation can be compared to the featureless, monstrous golem intent on overcoming its enemies. First "published" in right-wing Revisionist magazines that stressed "values like courage and self-sacrifice for the sake of the nation," the golem comics ridicule the mainstream Jewish leadership's policy of restraint vis-à-vis Arab attacks, denouncing the leaders as "weak and pitiful" and depicting a Jewish golem that can crush the Arab "genie." In the 1980s, the golem even fights against the "conspiracy of the Oslo Accords." In Eshed and Fink's mock comics, the golem embodies an aggressive brand of Jewish nationalism, one that does not tolerate otherness and repudiates the peace process and its more inclusive notion of the Israeli state.[8]

While this book has reconstructed the shifting resonances of the golem metaphor, it has also been concerned with the living-dead golem as a transgressive monster that enabled artists to call into question national narratives, as opposed to nostalgically portraying a Jewish minority and its desire for protection. Starting with H. Leivick's *The Golem*, through S. Y. Agnon's *To This Day* and Yoram Kaniuk's *Himmo, King of Jerusalem*, to Stanislaw Lem's *Golem XIV*, the artificial being revolts through its rejection of the mission of military violence. These modern golems, rather than only aiming their physical might against a named enemy, protest the destructive purpose for which they have been created. Originally written in Yiddish, Hebrew, and Polish and spanning the twentieth century, these texts all underscore the contradictions inherent to the golem condition. Devised as a strategic weapon and ultimate warrior, the living-dead golem reveals our inability to escape the fundamental condition of natality and mortality and the high price we must pay for striving to do so through artificial means. In the medium of film, moreover, the illusion of animation could be "magically" re-created, so that that the tragedy of the golem's short-lived existence as protector of the Jewish community is powerfully conveyed. In literature, wartime and postwar adaptations often endowed the traditionally mute golem with the capacity for speech and even a human-like intelligence, thereby enhancing its self-reflective, critical propensity.

The popular golem of war has haunted twentieth-century Western culture, unsettling our sense of national, religious, and ethnic selfhood and, more often than not, withholding the reassurance of protection and redemption. We are still living out the aftermath of the interminable and world-altering wars of the twentieth century as we continue to develop ever more advanced war technologies for the global wars of the twenty-first century. The golem metaphor serves to remind us that even though our wars are being fought from afar by automatic machines of different kinds, they still have devastating effects on the human body and psyche. Well into the twenty-first century, golem narratives continue to provide resonant material for scrutinizing the conditions and activities by which we define our humanity.

NOTES

INTRODUCTION

1. "Hundreds, Dead or Injured, Buried under Ruins as Roof of Knickerbocker Theater Collapses; Rescuers Battle Storm That Paralyzes City," *Washington Post*, 29 January 1922, 2.

2. Reuven Brainin, "Der goylem (tsu der teater-umglik in Washington)," *Der tog*, 5 February 1922, 6.

3. In Psalm 139:16, where the term "golem" first appears, it denotes the speaker's condition prior to birth, his "unformed shape" (*galmi ra'u eynekha*). *The Book of Psalms*, trans. Robert Alter (New York: Norton, 2007), 482.

4. According to Gershom Scholem, the golem's violence is enabled equally by the name of God itself and by "the power of the tellurian element, aroused and set in motion by the name of God." This "earth magic" has the potential to awaken destructive and chaotic forces. Scholem, "The Idea of the Golem," in *On the Kabbalah and Its Symbolism*, trans. Ralph Manheim (New York: Schocken, 1969), 202. See also Scholem, "Die Vorstellung vom Golem in ihren tellurischen und magischen Beziehungen," in *Zur Kabbala und ihrer Symbolik* (Frankfurt am Main: Suhrkamp, 2000), 245.

5. Wolfram Göbel, *Der Kurt Wolff Verlag 1913–1930: Expressionismus als verlegerische Aufgabe* (Frankfurt am Main: Buchhändler-Vereinigung, 1977), 736–737, 734–735.

6. Paul Fussell, *The Great War and Modern Memory* (Oxford: Oxford University Press, 2000), 115. Jay Winter has also analyzed the avalanche of "unmodern" phenomena, of various forms of spiritualism (telepathy, séances, amulets, psychic photography, rituals, and legends) that this most "modern" of wars triggered. Winter, *Sites of Memory, Sites of Mourning: The Great War in European Cultural History* (Cambridge: Cambridge University Press, 2006), 54–77.

7. Yudl Rosenberg was a sophisticated modern writer even when his text—framed as an archival manuscript written by the Maharal's son-in-law and found in the Mainz library—uses traditional storytelling tropes. Rosenberg drew on well-known Jewish folkloric formulas and types but was also influenced, as Eli Yassif revealed, by non-Jewish popular literature in translation, such as *Robinson Crusoe*, *The Count of Monte Christo*, and detective stories by Arthur Conan Doyle. Yassif, "Mavo: Yudl (Yehuda) Rosenberg—sofer 'amami," in *Ha-golem mi-prag u-ma'asim nifla'im aherim*, by Yudl Rosenberg (Jerusalem: Mosad Bi'alik, 1991), 21–28.

8. Chajim Bloch, *Der Prager Golem: Von seiner "Geburt" bis zum seiner "Tod"* (Berlin: Benjamin Harz, 1920), 20, 18.

9. Israel Joshua Singer, "Fun bikher-tish: Vegen 'goylem' fun H. Leyvik," *Folkstsaytung*, 1922, in H. Leivick Collection, File 40, YIVO Archive, New York.

10. Brainin, "Der goylem," 6.

11. Martin Buber, "An die Prager Freunde," in *Das jüdische Prag: Eine Sammelschrift* (Kronberg, Germany: Jüdischer Verlag, 1978), 2. For Cathy Gelbin, the artificial anthropoid mentioned in Buber's letter "symbolizes the carnage of war and its threat to the survival of Jewish culture leading to messianic redemption." Gelbin, *The Golem Returns: From German Romantic Literature to Global Jewish Culture, 1808-2008* (Ann Arbor: University of Michigan Press, 2011), 88.

12. Gershom Scholem, "Toward an Understanding of the Messianic Idea in Judaism," trans. Michael A. Meyer, in *The Messianic Idea in Judaism and Other Essays on Jewish Spirituality* (New York: Schocken, 1971), 8; H. Leivick, *Der goylem: A dramatishe poeme in akht bilder* (New York: Amerika, 1921).

13. See also Uri Tzvi Greenberg's 1922 prose poem concerning World War I, "Mustafa Zahiv / Royte epel fun veybeymer" (Red apples from trees of suffering). Greenberg's speaker tells that his blood has frozen and no longer runs red but rather "steal" or "lead." If he were to procreate, a *goyleml* (tiny golem) of "dark metal" would be his offspring, and any woman would be too scared to offer this golem her breast. The poem first appeared in the second edition of the periodical *Albatros*, published in Warsaw, and was later collected in Uri Tzvi Greenberg, *Gezamlte verk*, vol. 2 (Jerusalem: Magnes Press, 1979), 442. I am grateful to Zehavit Stern for bringing this reference to my attention.

14. Minsoo Kang, *Sublime Dreams of Living Machines: The Automaton in the European Imagination* (Cambridge, MA: Harvard University Press, 2011), 1. In 1922, the Yiddish critic Baruch Rivkin wrote that the name for golem among non-Jews is automaton or else "living automaton." Rivkin, "Untern tsaykhen fun goylem," in *H. Leyvik: Zayne lider un dramatishe verk* (Buenos Aires: Yidbukh, 1955), 165.

15. Kang, *Sublime Dreams of Living Machines*, 266–267.

16. Egon Erwin Kisch, "The Golem," in *Tales from Seven Ghettos*, trans. Edith Bone (London: Robert Anscombe, 1948), 165; Kisch, "Dem Golem auf der Spur," in *Der rasende Reporter* (Berlin: Aufbau-Verlag, 1990), 309.

17. Karel Čapek, *R.U.R. (Rossums Universal Robots)*, trans. Claudia Novak (New York: Penguin Books, 2004). See also Emily D. Bilski, Moshe Idel, and Elfriede Ledig, *Golem! Danger, Deliverance, and Art* (New York: Jewish Museum, 1988), 65–66.

18. See, for example, Arnold L. Goldsmith, *The Golem Remembered, 1909–1980: Variations of a Jewish Legend* (Detroit: Wayne State University Press, 1981); Sigrid Mayer, *Golem: Die literarische Rezeption eines Stoffes* (Bern, Switzerland: Herbert Lang, 1975).

19. Brainin, "Der goylem," 6.

20. Henrik Galeen and Paul Falkenberg, "The Golem," in *Film-Materialien: Henrik Galeen*, ed. Hans-Michael Bock and Wolfgang Jacobson (Hamburg and Berlin: CineGraph, 1992), 20–24. The script, dated December 1943, was proposed to Fritz Lang as director but was never filmed.

21. Michael Hardt and Antonio Negri understand the present state of "imperial war" or civil war as a postmodern one in which the sides of the conflict are no longer defined according to sovereign nation-states, in contrast to World Wars I and II. War has become a general, global, and interminable phenomenon, making it difficult to distinguish between war and peace. Hardt and Negri, *Multitude: War and Democracy in the Age of Empire* (New York: Penguin, 2004), 3, 5, 37–38.

22. Michel Foucault, *Discipline and Punish: The Birth of the Prison*, trans. Alan Sheridan (New York: Vintage Books, 1995), 135.

23. Friedrich Kittler brings Marshall McLuhan's psychological myth of the origins of media to bear on the phenomenon of the golem: "Golems constitute danger: stupid Doubles of a humanity that has no longer existed ever since media were also able to substitute for central nervous systems." See Kittler, "Romanticism—Psychoanalysis—Film: A History of the Double," trans. Stefanie Harris, in *Literature, Media, Information Systems: Essays*, ed. John Johnston (Amsterdam: G+B Arts International, 1997), 97.

24. Avi-Ruth, "Ha-golem," *Ha-tsofe*, 22 June 1944, 2.

25. For Hannah Arendt, in her Cold War treatise *The Human Condition*, the three main human activities, labor, work, and action, and their corresponding conditions are "intimately connected" to the most basic condition of human existence, "birth and death, natality and mortality." The fact of birth "can bestow upon human affairs faith and hope," for it interrupts the inevitability of human "ruin and destruction," allowing for new beginnings and actions. The golem represents the human desire to intervene in political affairs and rely on artificial creation, ultimately undermining the spontaneity and hope embodied in natality. Arendt, *The Human Condition: A Study of the Central Dilemmas Facing Modern Man* (New York: Doubleday Anchor Books, 1959), 8, 246–247.

26. Isaac Bashevis Singer, "Why the Golem Legend Speaks to Our Time," *New York Times*, 12 August 1984, 25.

27. Brainin, "Der goylem," 6.

28. Gershom Scholem, "The Golem of Prague and the Golem of Rehovoth," *Commentary* 41, no. 1 (1966): 65.

29. Victor Turner, *Dramas, Fields, and Metaphors: Symbolic Action in Human Society* (Ithaca, NY: Cornell University Press, 1974), 31.

30. Elizabeth Young maintains that "Shelley's Frankenstein monster . . . is a metaphor for metaphor itself," dramatizing "the processes whereby metaphors—like monsters—are made." Young, *Black Frankenstein: The Making of an American Metaphor* (New York: NYU Press, 2008), 12.

31. Steven E. Aschheim, *Brothers and Strangers: The East European Jew in German and German Jewish Consciousness, 1800–1923* (Madison: University of Wisconsin Press, 1982), 184, 213.

32. Chajim Bloch, *Israel der Gotteskämpfer: Der Baalschem von Chelm und sein Golem. Ein ostjüdisches Legendenbuch* (Berlin: Benjamin Harz, 1920), 11–13.

33. Oscar Polda, "Palast- und Reichshallen-Lichtspiele. Gastspiel Paul Wegener. *Der Golem*," *Kieler Neueste Nachrichten*, 7 March 1915.

34. In "The Golem," Egon Erwin Kisch narrates his encounter on the eastern front with a Galician Jew, a company commander nicknamed "my Galician occultist" or "my mystagogue from Wola Michow" (in Poland) who believed that the golem could still be found in Prague. In this text, the harsh wartime conditions fuel the escapist speculations and fantasies of the "mystagogue," and Kisch even suggests that this man manages to endure the barrage only because he believes that he has in his possession a Hebrew document concerning the true whereabouts of the golem. Kisch, "Dem Golem auf der Spur," 295, 296, 298, 304.

35. Katrin Sieg defines "ethnic drag" as "the performance of 'race' as a masquerade." Ethnic drag challenges, furthermore, "the perceptions and privileges of those who would mistake appearances for essences." Sieg, *Ethnic Drag: Performing Race, Nation, Sexuality in West Germany* (Ann Arbor: University of Michigan Press, 2002), 2–3.

36. See Daniel Boyarin, *Unheroic Conduct: The Rise of Heterosexuality and the Invention of the Jewish Man* (Berkeley: University of California Press, 1997); Todd Samuel Presner, *Muscular Judaism: The Jewish Body and the Politics of Regeneration* (London Routledge, 2007); Michael Gluzman, *Ha-guf ha-tsiyoni: Le'umiyut, migdar, u-miniyut ba-sifrut ha-'ivrit ha-ḥadasha* (Tel Aviv: Ha-kibbutz Hame'uḥad 2007).

37. Judith Halberstam, *Skin Shows: Gothic Horror and the Technology of Monsters* (Durham, NC: Duke University Press, 1995), 21.

38. In German, Hebrew, and Yiddish, the term *golem* is grammatically gendered as masculine. Freiherr von Ludwig Achim Arnim, *Isabelle von Ägypten: Kaiser Karl des Fünften erste Jugendliebe* (Vienna: Anton Schroll, 1918); Cynthia Ozick, *The Puttermesser Papers* (New York: Knopf, 1997); Helene Wecker, *The Golem and the Jinni: A Novel* (New York: HarperCollins, 2013).

39. Steve Niles (w), Matt Santoro (w), and Dave Wachter (a), *Breath of Bones: A Tale of the Golem #2* (Milwaukie, OR: Dark Horse Comics, July 2013), 20.

40. Marge Piercy, Research Files: Notes and Comments, Box 17, p. 9, Marge Piercy Papers, Special Collections Library, University of Michigan, Ann Arbor.

41. Gelbin, *Golem Returns*, 8–9.

42. Ibid., 10.

43. Grimm's version is translated in Edan Dekel and David Gantt Gurley, "How the Golem Came to Prague," *Jewish Quarterly Review* 103, no. 2 (2013): 242–243, 250.

44. According to Alfred Thomas, the demolition of the Prague ghetto in the late 1890s led to a "revival in the legendary reputation of Rabbi Loew and an explosion of literature on the subject [of the rabbi and his golem]." Thomas, *Prague Palimpsest: Writing, Memory, and the City* (Chicago: University of Chicago Press, 2010), 46–48.

45. Dekel and Gurley, "How the Golem Came to Prague," 251–252.

46. Ibid., 248. The non-Jewish journalist and folklorist Franz Klutschak (1814–1886) published his story in *Panorama des Universums*, a Prague monthly "devoted to the investigation of world cultures." Hillel J. Kieval, "Pursuing the Golem of Prague: Jewish Culture and the Invention of a Tradition," *Modern Judaism* 17, no. 1 (1997): 11.

47. Ludwig Weisel's narrative is translated in Kieval, "Pursuing the Golem of Prague," 1–2. See also Weisel, "Sagen der Prager Juden," in *Sippurim eine Sammlung jüdischer Volkssagen, Erzählungen, Mythen, Chroniken, Denkwürdigkeiten*, ed. Wolf Pascheles (Prague: Wolf Pascheles, 1858), 50–52.

48. Dekel and Gurley, "How the Golem Came to Prague," 244.

49. According to Gelbin, the Prague story "presented a broader German-Jewish counternarrative to the negative Christian configuration of the Jews through the golem." Pascheles's stories put an emphasis on "the forces of reason as part of the Enlightenment discourse on Jewish emancipation," thus countering the image of Jewish irrationality. Gelbin, *Golem Returns*, 13, 51.

50. Kieval, "Pursuing the Golem of Prague," 14.

51. Yudl Rosenberg, *Seyfer nifloes Maharal* (Jerusalem: Yudl Rosenberg, 1967), 16–18.

52. I. L. Peretz, "The Golem," trans. Ruth R. Wisse, in *The I. L. Peretz Reader*, ed. Ruth R. Wisse (New Haven, CT: Yale University Press, 2002), 130; Peretz, *Far kleyn un groys* (Vilnius, Lithuania: Vilner Farlag fun B. Kletskin, 1925), 40–41.

53. In Sholem Aleichem's version, the Jews fear for their economic standing and viability (rather than for the continuation of their religious practice), since they have lost the buyers for their various products, and those who need to repay debts rest dead in the river. See A. S. Rabbinowitz, "Der Golem," *Die Welt* 34 (1901): 9–10.

54. Chandra Mukerji and Michael Schudson, introduction to *Rethinking Popular Culture: Contemporary Perspectives in Cultural Studies*, ed. Chandra Mukerji and Michael Schudson (Berkeley: University of California Press, 1991), 1.

55. Gelbin, *Golem Returns*, 14.

56. Isaac Singer, "Why the Golem Legend Speaks to Our Time," 1.

CHAPTER 1. THE FACE OF DESTRUCTION

1. Eric J. Leed, *No Man's Land: Combat and Identity in World War I* (Cambridge: Cambridge University Press, 1979), 20. "The most common soldier's dream was that of being buried in a bunker by a heavy shell." Ibid., 22.

2. Allyson Booth, *Postcards from the Trenches: Negotiating the Space between Modernism and the First World War* (Oxford: Oxford University Press, 1996), 53.

3. A full-time actor in Max Reinhardt's theater, Wegener created and shot his early films during the summer breaks. See also Paul Wegener, "Mein Werdegang," in *Paul Wegener: Sein Leben und seine Rollen. Ein Buch von ihm und über ihn*, ed. Kai Möller (Hamburg: Rowohlt, 1954), 34.

4. "U.T. Lichtspiele: Spielplan," Nachlass Paul Wegener: Sammlung Kai Möller, Deutsches Filminstitut, Frankfurt am Main.

5. Wegener, "Mein Werdegang," 35.

6. "Schauspielkunst und Krieg," *Berliner Börsen-Courier*, 9 January 1915. The *Breslauer Zeitung* also describes Paul Wegener's progress from "hero" of the theater to hero of the front lines during World War I. "Berliner Theater," *Breslauer Zeitung*, 19 January 1915.

7. Eduard Korrodi, "Paul Wegener im Kino," in *Kein Tag ohne Kino: Schriftsteller über den Stummfilm*, ed. Fritz Güttinger (Frankfurt am Main: Deutsches Filmmuseum, 1984), 322.

8. Susanne Holl and Friedrich Kittler, "Ablösen des Streifens vom Buche: Eine Allegorese von Wegeners drei Golemfilmen," *Cinema. Blickführung*, no. 41 (1996): 104.

9. In the post–World War I years, Wegener also wrote and starred in several lost films: *Apokalypse* (1918), *The Pied Piper* (*Der Rattenfänger*, 1918), and *The Gallery Convict* (*Der Galeerensträfling*, 1919). For a full survey of Wegener's films, see Heide Schönemann, *Paul Wegener: Frühe Moderne im Film* (Stuttgart, Germany: Menges, 2003), 131–135.

10. The speculative pitfall of attempting to analyze a film manuscript as though it were the film itself is somewhat ameliorated here because Wegener was wont to follow his own scripts quite closely (especially in terms of their themes) and also because contemporary reviews of the films help us conclude that particular scenes were indeed shot. See also Elfriede Ledig, *Paul Wegeners Golem-Filme im Kontext fantastischer Literatur: Grundfragen zur Gattungsproblematik fantastischen Erzählens* (Munich: Verlaggemeinschaft, 1989), 135.

11. "Between Wegener's 'Golem' from before the war and the great feature film that is now being screened in the Berlin Ufa Palace, lies almost a decade of heaven-storming artistic and technical cinematic development. The small film industry has become a great power." "Der neue Wegener-Film," *Deutsche Lichtspiel-Zeitung*, 6 November 1920, 4.

12. German cinematic expressionism borrowed from a wide range of literary, artistic, and filmic predecessors. Some of the elements that made up the distinct "look" of these films include "the use of artificial light and shadows, the atmosphere of unease, exaggerated acting styles, themes of psychological expression and a pervading sense of horror and the supernatural." Ian Roberts, *German Expressionist Cinema* (London: Wallflower, 2008), 10. Thomas Elsaesser further argues that expressionism helped to style German cinema as a respectable art form that could technically "simulate stylistic authenticity, organic coherence and

formal adequacy." Elsaesser, *Weimar Cinema and After: Germany's Historical Imaginary* (London: Routledge, 2000), 39.

13. Béla Balázs, *Early Film Theory: "Visible Man" and "The Spirit of Film,"* ed. Erica Carter, trans. Rodney Livingstone (New York: Berghahn Books, 2010), 44; Balázs, *Der sichtbare Mensch oder die Kultur des Films* (Frankfurt am Main: Suhrkamp, 2001), 57.

14. Eugen Tannenbaum, *"Der Golem, wie er in die Welt kam," B.Z. am Mittag,* 30 October 1920, in "Kritiken über das Filmwerk: *Der Golem, wie er in die Welt kam*" (Ufa distribution pamphlet), Schriftgutarchiv, Stiftung Deutsche Kinemathek, Berlin.

15. Elsaesser, *Weimar Cinema and After,* 65. In a lecture delivered in the Beethovensaal, Berlin, in April 1916, under the title "The Artistic Potentialities of Film," Wegener promotes film as an instrument of "folk education" and "amusement in the noble sense." Paul Wegener, "Die künstlerischen Möglichkeiten des Films," in Möller, *Paul Wegener,* 103, 109.

16. Paul Wegener, "Schauspielerei und Film," *Berliner Tageblatt,* 15 January 1915, 2.

17. Following the antimimetic strain of Georges Méliès's trick films, Wegener's earliest films made the utmost of photographic technology (such as image splitting and mirroring), even when set in outdoor, supposedly realistic locations. "The true poet of film has to be the camera," he wrote. "The technology of film must be of significance for the choice of content." Wegener, "Die künstlerischen Möglichkeiten des Films," 109–110.

18. Ibid., 111–112.

19. Adolf Behne, "Der Golem," *Bild und Film* 4, nos. 7–8 (1914–1915): 156.

20. Wegener, "Schauspielerei und Film," 2.

21. Behne, "Der Golem," 156. As Wegener himself pronounces, "I act primarily for only one party, mine. I act it in all its shades: it is the role of the naïve-powerful [*Naiv-Wuchtigen*]. Do you remember my golem? He grew out of my aptitude, my emotions, my intellect." "Bei den Schaffenden," *Film-Kurier,* 6 May 1920.

22. Walter Turszinsky, "Paul Wegener," *Bühne und Welt. Zeitschrift für Theaterwesen, Literatur und Musik* 14, no. 2 (1912): 13.

23. Beate Rosenfeld, *Die Golemsage und ihre Verwertung in der deutschen Literatur* (Wrocław, Poland: Dr. Hans Priebatsch, 1934), 147; Paul Wegener, *Der Golem, wie er in die Welt kam: Eine Geschichte in fünf Kapiteln* (Berlin: August Scherl GmbH, 1921), 9.

24. Bilski, Idel, and Ledig, *Golem!,* 51–52; Schönemann, *Paul Wegener,* 78.

25. Paul Wegener and Henrik Galeen, "Der Golem: Phantastisches Filmspiel in vier Akten," in Bock and Jacobson, *Film-Materialien,* 3–16; Paul Wegener, "Der Golem, Exposé," 4.4–80/18, 1, Schriftgutarchiv, Stiftung Deutsche Kinemathek, Berlin.

26. "Erstaufführung des neuen Wegenerfilms in den U.-T.-Theatern," *Deutscher Kurier,* 15 January 1915. "Das Innere eines alten Antiquitäten- und Kuriositätenladens. Phantastische Einrichtung. . . . an den Wänden:

Bronzen—Waffen—Buddhas—von der Decke hängen herab: Kugelfische—ein Schwertfisch—orientalische Ampeln und allerlei merkwürdiges Zeug." Wegener and Galeen, "Der Golem," 3–4.

27. In addition to directing the popular *Alraune* (1927), Henrik Galeen most famously wrote the scripts for *Nosferatu* (F. W. Murnau, 1921) and *Waxworks* (Paul Leni, 1923). For a discussion of Galeen's career and his film *Alraune*, see Ofer Ashkenazi, *Weimar Film and Modern Jewish Identity* (New York: Palgrave Macmillan, 2012), 84–85.

28. Wegener and Galeen, "Der Golem," 5.

29. Georg Lukács, "Thoughts toward an Aesthetics of Cinema," *Polygraph* 13 (2001): 14–15; Lukács, "Gedanken zu einer Ästhetik des Kinos," in *Kino-Debatte. Literatur und Film 1909–1929*, ed. Anton Kaes (Tübingen, Germany: Max Niemeyer, 1978), 113–114.

30. "The 'cinema' presents mere action but no motives or meaning. Its characters have mere movements, but no soul, and what occurs is simply an occurrence, but not fate. It is for this reason . . . that the scenes of the cinema are silent." Lukács, "Thoughts toward an Aesthetics of Cinema," 15; Lukács, "Gedanken zu einer Ästhetik des Kinos," 115.

31. Lukács, "Thoughts toward an Aesthetics of Cinema," 15; Lukács, "Gedanken zu einer Ästhetik des Kinos," 114.

32. "Golem als Silhouette gegen den Himmel. Breitet die Arme aus und guckt zu den Sternen empor." Wegener and Galeen, "Der Golem," 13.

33. Ibid., 8. Adolf Behne viewed this scene as one of the aesthetic high points both in Wegener's acting career and in this particular film. See Behne, "Der Golem," 157.

34. Wegener and Galeen, "Der Golem," 11.

35. Arnold Zweig, "Der Golem," *Die Schaubühne*, 11 March 1915, 226–227.

36. Lukács, "Thoughts toward an Aesthetics of Cinema," 16; Lukács, "Gedanken zu einer Ästhetik des Kinos," 116.

37. Lukács, "Thoughts toward an Aesthetics of Cinema," 15; Lukács, "Gedanken zu einer Ästhetik des Kinos," 114. "The withdrawal of the word, and with it of memory, of truth and duty to oneself and to the idea of one's selfhood renders everything [in cinema] light, bright and winged, frivolous and dancing." Lukács, "Thoughts toward an Aesthetics of Cinema," 15–16.

38. Wegener, "Die künstlerischen Möglichkeiten des Films," 110–111.

39. Mark Seltzer, *Bodies and Machines* (New York: Routledge, 1992), 75; Paul Wegener, "Der Golem und die Tänzerin," 4.4–80/18.3, Schriftgutarchiv, Stiftung Deutsche Kinemathek, Berlin.

40. Lukács, "Thoughts toward an Aesthetics of Cinema," 15; Lukács, "Gedanken zu einer Ästhetik des Kinos," 115.

41. *Caligari*, according to Anton Kaes, exhibits a cubist aesthetic, and its sets "break down forms, reduce depth," creating in their two-dimensionality a "camouflage effect in which foreground and background mesh" and characters blend into the

scenery. He further maintains that "*Caligari* is relentless in rejecting any semblance of realism. . . . It's anti-mimetic stance is political, . . . a critique of both the artistic naiveté of earlier films and the deceptive purposes to which they had been put." Kaes, *Shell Shock Cinema: Weimar Culture and the Wounds of War* (Princeton, NJ: Princeton University Press, 2009), 85–86, 81–82.

42. Paul Wegener and Carl Boese, dirs., *Der Golem, wie er in die Welt kam*, Projektion-AG Union (PAGU), 1920.

43. Balázs, *Early Film Theory*, 10; Balázs, *Der sichtbare Mensch*, 17.

44. Ethnographic films play only a minor role in *The Visible Man*, although Balázs comments that it is "so fascinating" to see films in which people of "other races—Negroes, Chinese, American Indians and Eskimos"—appear, since these people reveal to us with "fresh force" the "essential physiognomic expressions that we do not notice in our own kind." Balázs, *Early Film Theory*, 30; Balázs, *Der sichtbare Mensch*, 41.

45. Balázs, *Early Film Theory*, 10; Balázs, *Der sichtbare Mensch*, 18. Balázs draws this terminology from the work of his teacher, Georg Simmel, who claimed in 1909 that motion best serves expression since it is shared by both body and soul. Simmel, "Rodin (mit einer Vorbemerkung über Meunier)," in *Philosophische Kultur* (Leipzig, Germany: Alfred Kröner Verlag, 1912), 175.

46. Assenka Oksiloff, *Picturing the Primitive: Visual Culture, Ethnography, and Early German Cinema* (New York: Palgrave, 2001), 8.

47. According to Erica Carter, film represented for Balázs and his contemporaries "the realization of the Enlightenment cosmopolitan dream of [an internationalism] . . . united in a common language, common ethical values. . . ." But he falls into the trap of Western universalism that "inscribes the 'enlightened' human subject as white, European and male." Balázs changed his views in *The Theory of Film*, grounding cinema's internationalism, from a Marxist perspective, in "film's penetration of international markets." Carter, introduction to Balázs, *Early Film Theory*, xxxviii.

48. Balázs, *Early Film Theory*, 10, 13; Balázs, *Der sichtbare Mensch*, 17, 21.

49. Lukács, "Thoughts toward an Aesthetics of Cinema," 16.

50. Balázs adopts a less mechanistic and more dynamic strand of physiognomic thought that asserts both the imprint of society and culture on the individual's appearance and the corresponding influence of people on their surroundings. Cinematic physiognomy, moreover, brings us ever closer to the body, to each organ and wrinkle and its significance (in *Der Geist des Films*, Balázs calls this "microphysiognomy"), rather than promoting a transcendence of the body as in the Lavaterian model. See Richard T. Gray, *About Face: German Physiognomic Thought from Lavater to Auschwitz* (Detroit: Wayne State University Press, 2004), xliii; Carter, introduction to Balázs, *Early Film Theory*, xxvii–xxviii. As early as 1910, Leopold Schmidel explicitly used the term "physiognomy" when discussing the corporeal language of screen actors, although Balázs was the first to make this term into the central category of an organized film theory. Helmut H. Diederichs,

"Nachwort: 'Ihr müßt erst etwas von guter Filmkunst verstehen': Béla Balázs als Filmtheoretiker und Medienpädagoge," in Balázs, *Der sichtbare Mensch*, 135–136.

51. Balázs, *Early Film Theory*, 23; Balázs, *Der sichtbare Mensch*, 31–32.

52. Balázs, *Early Film Theory*, 46; Balázs, *Der sichtbare Mensch*, 59. Balázs was a student of Georg Simmel and Henri Bergson and remained committed to German romanticism and *Lebensphilosophie*. His vitalism is apparent in this formulation of the "living physiognomy" of all things, including landscapes, inanimate objects, and animals. According to Gertrud Koch, "Balázs's writings undoubtedly spell out the heritage of Romanticism. . . . The techniques of film provide us with a laboratory of the soul. That film theory takes recourse to Romantic thought, however, also throws into relief the modernist aspects of Romanticism. The programmatic aesthetic sublimation of the everyday, rather than the pathos of the sublime, has found a medium in film." Koch, "Béla Balázs: The Physiognomy of Things," *New German Critique* 40 (1987): 176.

53. Balázs, *Early Film Theory*, 46; Balázs, *Der sichtbare Mensch*, 59.

54. According to Sigrid Mayer, unlike the exaggerated acting of the other cast members in the 1920 film, which does not serve to convey any inner complexities, "what transpires inside [the golem] remains mysterious and fascinating, even though it is conveyed by Wegener using facial expression and gesture very sparingly." Mayer, *Golem*, 161.

55. Herbert Ihering maintained that "Wegener was seduced by the filmic medium [of which he was a pioneer] to grimace, to overemphasize his physiognomy, . . . to contort his face, which, in repose, was actually highly suitable for the film in its physiognomy." Ihering, "Von Wegener zu Rosenberg," in *Herbert Ihering: Filmkritiker* (Munich: Edition Text + Kritik, 2011), 273.

56. In German, "Den ganzen Tag im Lehm kochen." The diary entry is dated "31," most likely referring to 31 December 1914. Soldbuch, Nachlass Paul Wegener: Sammlung Kai Möller, Deustches Filminstitut, Frankfurt am Main; Paul Wegener to Ernst Pietsch, 2 December 1914, Nachlass Paul Wegener: Sammlung Kai Möller, Deutsches Filminstitut, Frankfurt am Main.

57. Paul Wegener, *Flandrisches Tagebuch 1914* (Berlin: Rowohlt, 1933), 41, 187.

58. Ibid., 153, 146–148.

59. Wegener, "Schauspielerei und Film."

60. Andrej and Paul Wegener, "Ein Gespräch mit Paul Wegener: Einführendes zum 'Golem,'" *Film-Kurier*, 29 October 1920, 2.

61. In the interview with Andrej, Wegener stated, "It is not Prague . . . that my friend, the architect Poelzig has constructed. Neither Prague nor any other city. Rather it is a city-fiction, a dream, an architectural paraphrase on the theme 'Golem.'" Ibid.

62. "Medieval Ghetto in the Center Of Action in 'Golem' Film," *New York Tribune*, 19 June 1921, 2.

63. As Sabine Hake argues, "While distinguishing between performance and camerawork, Balázs still places key concepts such as 'facial expressions' and

'close-ups' on the side of physiognomy, with the result that the boundaries between reality and representation become blurred. The profilmic event provides the critical framework in which even the close-up appears as an aspect of acting rather than of camerawork." Hake, *The Cinema's Third Machine: Writing on Film in Germany, 1907–1933* (Lincoln: University of Nebraska Press, 1992), 231.

64. Balázs, *Early Film Theory*, 52–53, 44; Balázs, *Der sichtbare Mensch*, 66–67, 57. Balázs is inconsistent as to whether the expressivity of people and things is to be *discovered* through film and close-up or else *created*, through a stylization of settings, milieu, and actors into an affective whole. He seems to find fault with films that are so stylized and ornamentalized that they leave room neither for the spectator's imagination nor for a more "spontaneous-expressive character." Balázs, *Der sichtbare Mensch*, 65; Balázs, *Early Film Theory*, 51.

65. Eduard Korrodi, "Golem—Wegener—Poelzig," in Güttinger, *Kein Tag ohne Kino*, 325.

66. Herbert Ihering, *Berliner Börsen-Courier*, 31 October 1920, reprinted in "Der Golem, wie er in die Welt kam" (film distribution pamphlet), Filmarchiv, Deutsche Kinemathek, Berlin.

67. "Der neue Wegener-Film," 4.

68. Ludendorff's famous letter of 4 July 1917 concerning the important role of cinema as war propaganda is partially reprinted in Ludwig Greve, Margot Pehle, and Heidi Westhoff, eds., *Hätte ich das Kino! Die Schriftsteller und der Stummfilm* (Munich: Kösel, 1976), 75.

69. According to Wolffgang Fischer in *Neue Zeit* (31 October 1920), Wegener's budget for the film was supposedly no less than five million German marks, an enormous sum for the postwar period. See "Kritiken über das Filmwerk."

70. Paul Westheim, "Eine Filmstadt von Poelzig," *Das Kunstblatt* 4, no. 11 (1920): 332.

71. As one reviewer wrote, "Yesterday [Wegener's] original version surpassed its time with images of unheard of beauty and with its twisting and flourishing lines." A.F., "*Der Golem, wie er in die Welt kam*. Uraufführung: Ufa-Palast am Zoo," *Der Film: Zeitschrift für die Gesamt-interessen der Kinematographie*, 30 October 1920, 30.

72. Spyros Papapetros maintains that the resulting set design exhibited "a material convergence between living bodies and architectural environments." Papapetros, *On the Animation of the Inorganic: Art, Architecture, and the Extension of Life* (Chicago: University of Chicago Press, 2012), 224.

73. "The Screen," *New York Times*, 20 June 1921, 20.

74. Claudia Dillmann describes Poelzig's dynamic vision of the cinematic ghetto, which "breathes the 'spirit of the gothic.'" Dillmann, "Die Wirkung der Architektur ist eine magische: Hans Poelzig und der Film," in *Hans Poelzig: Bauten für den Film*, ed. Hans-Peter Reichmann (Frankfurt am Main: Deutsches Filmmuseum, 1997), 33, 43.

75. Andrew Webber, "About Face: E. T. A. Hoffmann, Weimar Film, and the Technological Afterlife of Gothic Physiognomy," in *Popular Revenants: The*

German Gothic and Its International Reception, 1800–2000, ed. Andrew Cusack and Barry Murnane (Rochester, NY: Camden House, 2012), 162.

76. Herman G. Scheffauer, "The Vivifying Space," in *Introduction to the Art of Movies*, ed. Lewis Jacobs (New York: Noonday, 1960), 84.

77. Scheffauer pronounced that "the will of this master-architect animating facades into faces, insists that these houses are to speak in jargon—and gesticulate!" Ibid. Noah Isenberg cites Poelzig's own expressed vision of these buildings as conversing in a Yiddish-inflected German, "*mauscheln.*" These pejorative expressions ("*mauscheln,*" "jargon," "gesticulate") connote Yiddish-speaking eastern European Jews or else German Jews who have not fully "assimilated" and converse in a Yiddish-inflected German. Isenberg, "Of Monsters and Magicians: Paul Wegener's *The Golem: How He Came into the World* (1920)," in *Weimar Cinema: An Essential Guide to Classic Films of the Era*, ed. Noah Isenberg (New York: Columbia University Press, 2009), 46–47.

78. See Gustav Meyrink, *The Golem*, trans. Madge Pemberton (New York: Dover, 1986), 16–17. Unlike Meyrink's depiction of the Jewish ghetto as potentially "hostile" or "malicious," the American reviews of Wegener's film interpreted the ghetto homes more positively, viewing them as leaning "affectionately against each other." For example, "Reinhardt's Art on Screen to Be Seen Soon on Broadway," *New York Tribune*, 10 April 1921, 4.

79. Isenberg claims that the film identifies the Jewish (eastern European) population with the urban space, so that the "amorphous crowds of Jews, swarming through the various passages of the ghetto, resemble the arteries of an urban body." Isenberg, "Of Monsters and Magicians," 47–48. For Omer Bartov, the film depicts the Jews "darting in and out of narrow alleys like rats (a favorite anti-Semitic metaphor), climbing impossibly crooked stairways and leaning out of asymmetrical windows." Bartov, *The "Jew" in Cinema: From "The Golem" to "Don't Touch My Holocaust"* (Bloomington: Indiana University Press, 2005), 4.

80. Dillmann, "Die Wirkung der Architektur ist eine magische," 30.

81. Andrej, "*Der Golem wie er in die Welt kam*: Ufa-Palast am Zoo," *Film-Kurier*, 30 October 1920, 1.

82. The complete text of the intertitles for *Der Golem, wie er in die Welt kam* in all its surviving versions can be found in Ledig, *Paul Wegeners Golem-Filme*, esp. 110, 116, 122.

83. "We can discover a thousand new things with telescopes and microscopes, but what is enlarged as a consequence will only ever be the range of the visual. A new art, in contrast, would be like a new sensory organ. . . . Film is a new art, . . . a fundamentally new revelation of humanity." Balázs, *Der sichtbare Mensch*, 11; Balázs, *Early Film Theory*, 5.

84. According to Gilles Deleuze, the close-up for Balázs is not a mere enlargement device that extracts the object from its environment; it enacts, rather, an "absolute change," abstracting the object from all spatio-temporal coordination through a movement

that "ceases to be translation in order to become expression." Deleuze, *Cinema 1: The Movement-Image*, trans. Hugh Tomlinson and Barbara Habberjam (Minneapolis: University of Minnesota Press, 1986), 96. See also Koch, "Béla Balázs," 171.

85. Balázs, *Early Film Theory*, 44; Balázs, *Der sichtbare Mensch*, 58.

86. Francis Guerin, *A Culture of Light: Cinema and Technology in 1920s Germany* (Minneapolis: University of Minnesota Press, 2005), 130.

87. Balázs, *Early Film Theory*, 38; Balázs, *Der sichtbare Mensch*, 49.

88. "The close-up is the deeper gaze, the director's sensibility. The close-up is the poetry of cinema." Balázs, *Early Film Theory*, 41; Balázs, *Der sichtbare Mensch*, 53.

89. See also Schönemann, *Paul Wegener*, 94–95.

90. The five-pointed star, or pentagram, had a very similar magical use and was often found on amulets alongside or interchanged with the hexagram. See Gershom Scholem, "The Star of David: History of a Symbol," trans. Michael A. Meyer, in *Messianic Idea in Judaism*, 259–264.

91. In Prague, the community leaders placed the star on their flag as early as 1354, and it represented for them "a conscious emblem of Jewish pride and a memory of past glory." The old flag was damaged and replaced in 1716 by a new one, which was kept in the Altneuschul, the same synagogue where Rabbi Loew is said to have placed the remains of the golem. Ibid., 275–278.

92. Only with the followers of Shabtai Tsvi did the symbol gain a messianic-redemptive dimension, representing the Son of David as Messiah. Ibid., 272–273.

93. Michael Berkowitz, *Zionist Culture and West European Jewry before the First World War* (Cambridge: Cambridge University Press, 1993), 23.

94. Holl and Kittler, "Ablösen des Streifens vom Buche," 107, 109; Wegener, *Flandrisches Tagebuch 1914*, 187.

95. Paul Wegener to Ernst Pietsch, 20 February 1915, Nachlass Paul Wegener: Sammlung Kai Möller, Deustches Filminstitut, Frankfurt am Main. In the 1933 diaries, Wegener does not use the term "nervous" with relation to his illness and describes his condition instead as an "acute heart dilation." Wegener, *Flandrisches Tagebuch 1914*, 197.

96. Wegener divides his fellow soldiers into two groups: on the one hand, there are those former "farmers" and "coach drivers" who, due to such factors as lack of education, "lack of imagination" (*Phantasielosigkeit*), "apathy" (*Stumpfsinn*), or "deficient cognizance of danger," exhibit physical courage. On the other hand, there are the more cultivated and intellectual types who uphold a kind of moral courage that results from overcoming their fear. Wegener, *Flandrisches Tagebuch 1914*, 192–193.

97. Wegener, *Der Golem, wie er in die Welt kam*, 47.

98. Kaes, *Shell Shock Cinema*, 3–4.

99. Wegener describes how he collapsed and fainted after suffering from severe exhaustion toward the end of his service. See Wegener, *Flandrisches Tagebuch 1914*, 195.

100. In German: "Der Krieg ist das Monströste, Dummste und Scheusslichste, was es gibt"; "aber das sinnlose Morden u. der Stumpfsinn des modernen Stellungskampfes ist geradezu absurd." Paul Wegener to Ernst Pietsch, 8 January 1915 and 9 December 1914, Nachlass Paul Wegener: Sammlung Kai Möller, Deustches Filminstitut, Frankfurt am Main.

101. Wegener, *Flandrisches Tagebuch 1914*, 188. Wegener also writes about the "useless attacks against machine guns, the entanglement of trenches, canals, and barbed wire, without sufficient artillery preparation." Ibid., 159.

102. Ibid., 56.

103. Wegener, *Der Golem, wie er in die Welt kam*, 50.

104. In the 1847 tale, it is the "swift-footed Naphtali" who comes wafting through the corn ears and flax stalks. When the Emperor can no longer hold back his laughter, the ceiling begins to sink, only to be arrested by the rabbi himself rather than by a golem. Weisel, "Sagen der Prager Juden," 52.

105. In James Whale's 1931 *Frankenstein* film, the monster created by Dr. Frankenstein encounters a little girl who, similarly, hands him a flower. This gesture moves the monster to smile, not unlike the golem, but soon after, he reverts back to his previous self, violently throwing the child into the water and drowning her. James Whales, dir., *Frankenstein*, Universal Pictures, 1931.

106. Gelbin, *Golem Returns*, 120.

107. "In October 1916, the German High Command and the Prussian war minister commissioned a *Judenzählung*, or Jewish census, in order to obtain statistical evidence that Jews were in fact disproportionately shirking military duty. . . . The very taking of the census insinuated that German Jews were first and foremost *Jews* who had to be excluded because they threatened the German nation." Kaes, *Shell Shock Cinema*, 111. See also Tim Grady, *The German-Jewish Soldiers of the First World War in History and Memory* (Liverpool: Liverpool University Press, 2011).

108. Galit Hasan-Rokem, "The Cobbler of Jerusalem in Finnish Folklore," in *The Wandering Jew: Essays in the Interpretation of a Legend*, ed. Galit Hasan-Rokem and Alan Dundes (Bloomington: Indiana University Press, 1986), 120.

109. Wegener, *Der Golem, wie er in die Welt kam*, 50.

110. Ibid., 52.

111. "The Christian-religious symbolism of the redemption of the world through the child possibly plays a role here and exhibits the redemptive tendencies of expressionism." Rosenfeld, *Die Golemsage*, 146.

112. Balázs, *Early Film Theory*, 46. The quote begins as follows: "Children have no difficulty understanding these physiognomies. This is because they do not yet judge things purely as tools, means to an end, useful objects not to be dwelt on."

113. Steve Choe, *Afterlives: Allegories of Film and Mortality in Early Weimar Germany* (New York: Bloomsbury, 2014), 169, 173. Reading the film through the lens of Martin Buber's "I-Thou" philosophy, Choe contends that the ending enacts an

"ethical relationship between human and technology," recognizing the "ontological strangeness" of the golem and ceasing to appropriate and exploit this figure. Ibid., 173.

114. In Reinhardt's 1909 theatrical production of *Hamlet*, in which Wegener played King Claudius, the dead Hamlet was carried at the end of the play above the heads of his comrades, his body stiff and arched. See Schönemann, *Paul Wegener*, 102.

115. Hans Wollenberg, "Der Golem," *Lichtbild-Bühne*, 10 October 1920, 26.

CHAPTER 2. THE GOLEM CULT OF 1921 NEW YORK

1. "'Goylem' breyngt gepakte hayzer far kreyterion teater," *Yidishes tageblat*, 6 July 1921, 2.

2. "'Der goylem' iz endlekh do," *Yidishes tageblat*, 17 June 1921, 2; "The Screen," 20.

3. "Picture Plays and People," *New York Times*, 9 October 1921, 75; "'Goylem' breyngt gepakte hayzer," 2.

4. *The Golem*'s unusually long run at the Criterion theater reveals the degree to which German films were making inroads into American culture, after a long period of anti-German sentiment during World War I. As one critic wrote, "One may as well make up his mind to stop apologizing for liking German pictures and say, as we heard one man say yesterday [following a screening of *The Golem*], 'You certainly got to hand it to them.'" Harriette Underhill, "On the Screen," *New York Tribune*, 21 June 1921, 6.

5. Mark Tolts, "Population and Migration: Migration since World War I," YIVO Institute for Jewish Research, accessed February 4, 2015, http://www.yivoencyclopedia.org/article.aspx/Population_and_Migration/Migration_since_World_War_I.

6. Rabbi I. Mortimor Bloom of New York called these immigration bills "un-American" and "discriminatory," contending that they were "a dagger thrust in the hearts of thousands of human beings who yearn for an opportunity to lead the normal decent life which their own lands deny them." Quoted in Annie Polland and Daniel Soyer, *Emerging Metropolis: New York Jews in the Age of Immigration, 1840–1920*, vol. 2 of *City of Promises: A History of the Jews of New York* (New York: NYU Press, 2012), 246.

7. Only 5.2 percent of Jews returned to eastern Europe, in contrast to the general return rate of immigrants (33.3 percent). Ibid., 111–112.

8. Brainin, "Der goylem," 6.

9. I. L. Bril, "The Golem," *Yidishes tageblat*, 31 July 1921, 12.

10. Ts. H. Rubinstein, "Di uffirung fun 'goylem' in Gebil's teater," *Der tog*, 23 December 1921, 3.

11. Rivkin, "Untern tsaykhen fun goylem," 166–167, 169. "Other peoples will not have any false Messiahs, as we Jews have had, only golems; golems that pretend not to bear the name of the Messiah: only artificially, with materials and self-made means, will they attempt to imitate what the spirit is called upon to do." Ibid., 167.

12. Over the course of ten weeks (November 1921–January 1922), *Der morgen zhurnal* (The morning journal) published a section on the golem of Prague with three weekly installments, followed by another series (January–March 1922) titled "The Jewish Golem and the Gentile Golem."

13. Brainin, "Der goylem," 6.

14. *Der goylem* was completed toward the end of 1919, as Shmuel Niger's correspondence with Leivick indicates. The fifth and seventh scenes were printed in the journal *Di tsukunt* (The future) in 1920, and although the book is dated 1921, it appeared at the end of 1920. See Avrom Noverstern, *Kesem ha-dimdumim: Apokalipsa u-meshiḥiyut be-sifrut yidish* (Jerusalem: Magnes Press, 2003), 187n4.

15. As Edna Nahshon contends, "The American Yiddish theater was a genuine people's institution insofar as its appeal was not limited to any one socioeconomic group. It was attended by rich and poor, educated and illiterate, observant and free-thinking." Nahshon, "The Yiddish Theater in America: A Brief Historical Overview," in *The Lawrence Marwick Collection of Copyrighted Yiddish Plays at the Library of Congress: An Annotated Bibliography*, by Zachary M. Baker (Washington, DC: Library of Congress, 2004), http://www.loc.gov/rr/amed/marwick/marwickbibliography.pdf, xiii.

16. Yitskhok Even, "Der goylem in Gebil's teater," *Morgen zhurnal*, 6 January 1922, 5.

17. Despite the general decline in theater attendance already in the 1920s, the golem materials provided Max Gabel with a popular hit: "In his long acting career, Gabel has never had such a triumph as with his current musical drama *Der goylem*. The thousands of people who have already admired the piece are a living advertisement for it." "Ale kritiker hobn geshribn mit bagaysterung vegn Gebil's uffirung fun 'goylem,'" *Yidishes tageblat*, 12 January 1922, 3.

18. Bril, "Golem," 12.

19. Israel Joshua Singer, "Fun bikher-tish."

20. H. Leivick, "Di literatur in klem," H. Leivick Collection: Manuscripts, File 10, YIVO Archive, New York.

21. Benjamin Harshav and Barbara Harshav, "H. Leyvik," in *American Yiddish Poetry: A Bilingual Anthology* (Berkeley: University of California Press, 1986), 675.

22. H. Leivick, "Di keyten fun mashiaḥ," in *Ale verk fun H. Leyvik: Dramatishe poemes* (New York: H. Leyvik yubiley-komitet, 1940), 411.

23. H. Leivick, *The Golem*, in *The Golem: A New Translation of the Classic Play and Selected Short Stories*, ed. and trans. Joachim Neugroschel (New York: Norton, 2006), 180; Leivick, *Der goylem*, 114.

24. Leivick, *Golem*, 249; Leivick, *Der goylem*, 213.

25. Isaac Leib Peretz, *The Golden Chain*, trans. Marvin Zuckerman, in *Selected Works of I. L. Peretz*, ed. Marvin Zuckerman and Marion Herbst (Malibu, CA: Pangloss, 1996), 398–468; Peretz, *A Night in the Old Marketplace*, trans. Ruth R. Wisse, in Wisse, *I. L. Peretz Reader*, 361–432. Moyshe-Leyb Halpern's "apocalyptic poema" *A nakht* (A Night) appeared in 1919, as part of his first poetry book, *In*

nyu-york (In New York), and Peretz Markish's *Di kupe* (*The Mound*) was published in Warsaw in 1921. For translations of these works, see Halpern, *In New York: A Selection*, ed. and trans. Kathryn Hellerstein (Philadelphia: Jewish Publication Society of America, 1982); Peretz Markish, "From *The Mound*," in *The Penguin Book of Modern Yiddish Verse*, trans. Leonard Wolf, ed. Irving Howe, Ruth R. Wisse, and Khone Shmeruk (New York: Viking Penguin, 1987), 352–367.

26. Farlag Amerika was the imprint of David Ignatoff, a leading figure in New York's Yiddish avant-garde circles and one of the founders of the modernist group *Di yunge*. Prior to *Der goylem*, Ignatoff published in 1920 a volume titled *Vunder mayses fun alten Prag* (Wondrous tales of old Prague). See Bilski, Idel, and Ledig, *Golem!*, 61.

27. Baruch Rivkin also compared the golem to Trotsky, replacing as he does the Jewish Messiah for whom a devout person must passively wait. Rivkin, "Untern tsaykhen fun goylem," 166.

28. H. Leivick, "Yossele goylem fun prag," in *H. Leyvik: Eseyen un redes*, ed. Y. Zilberberg (New York: Alveltlekhn Yidishn Kultur-Kongres, 1963), 61–63. Leivick's essay is a retrospective account, dating to 1952 and addressing the recent Stalin executions of Czech Jewish communist leaders and bureaucrats. Litvakov himself was murdered as an alleged traitor in the mid-1930s, and Leivick finds it bitterly ironic that the revolutionary axe blessed by Litvakov in the 1920s was ultimately used against him.

29. Ibid., 65.

30. Noverstern, *Kesem ha-dimdumim*, 206; Sara Simchi Cohen, "Hearth of Darkness: The Familiar, the Familial, and the Zombie" (Ph.D. diss., UCLA, 2013), 40–41.

31. Scholem, "Toward an Understanding," 7–8.

32. Leivick, *Golem*, 139; Leivick, *Der goylem*, 52.

33. Leivick, *Golem*, 140; Leivick, *Der goylem*, 52.

34. David Biale, *Gershom Scholem: Kabbalah and Counter-history* (Cambridge, MA: Harvard University Press, 1982), 93. "In order to maintain the critical dialectic of Jewish history, messianism could neither be realized nor totally suppressed: the tension of a life lived in deferment preserved the Jewish tradition and gave it dynamism." Ibid. Avrom Novershtern argues that various apocalyptic motifs remain "unfulfilled possibilities" in Leivick's verse drama, since the golem staves off the ultimate disaster of the blood libel, or else they are negated as "nightmarish visions" of destructive nature. Noverstern, *Kesem ha-dimdumim*, 210, 213.

35. Leivick, *Golem*, 139–140.

36. Ibid., 116–117; Leivick, *Der goylem*, 10–11.

37. Yudl Rosenberg, *The Golem or The Miraculous Deeds of Rabbi Leyb*, in *The Golem: A New Translation of the Classic Play and Selected Stories*, ed. and trans. Joachim Neugroschel (New York: Norton, 2006), 14, 17; Rosenberg, *Seyfer nifloes Maharal*, 14, 16.

38. In a poem published posthumously, the American Yiddish poet Moyshe-Leyb Halpern wrote, "And as Jews hate conversion they hate / One who is called Yossel, God-forbid Yossel / They've already killed one Yossel!" Halpern, "Shalamouses," in Harshav and Harshav, *American Yiddish Poetry*, 486–487.

39. Leivick, *Golem*, 125; Leivick, *Der goylem*, 25–26.

40. Shimon Finkel, *Aharon Meskin ve-agadat "ha-golem": Prakim le-zikhro* (Tel Aviv: 'Eked, 1980), 37–38.

41. When the rabbi's wife later serves the golem a meal and asks him to "wash," she notes that he utters "no blessing, no benediction on the bread." Leivick, *Golem*, 129, 132 (translation amended); Leivick, *Der goylem*, 32, 37.

42. Leivick, *Golem*, 134 (last line amended); Leivick, *Der goylem*, 40.

43. A. Glantz-Leyeles, "Leyviks 'goylem' un habima-uffirung," *Der tog*, 21 May 1948, 9.

44. See Warren Rosenberg, *Legacy of Rage: Jewish Masculinity, Violence, and Culture* (Amherst: University of Massachussetts Press, 2001), 80.

45. Leivick, *Golem*, 180; Leivick, *Der goylem*, 114.

46. Irving Howe and Eliezer Greenberg, introduction to *A Treasury of Yiddish Stories*, ed. Irving Howe and Eliezer Greenberg (New York: Schocken, 1973), 60–61. In Sholem Asch's story "Kola Street," the Jewish scholars even condemningly pronounce that these "savage" Jews are "not at all like Jews, . . . and when the Messiah comes, they will come to us for help." Ibid., 262.

47. Sharon Gillerman, "A Kinder Gentler Strongman? Siegmund Breitbart in Eastern Europe," in *Jewish Masculinities: German Jews, Gender, and History*, ed. Benjamin Maria Baader, Sharon Gillerman, and Paul Frederick Lerner (Bloomington: Indiana University Press, 2012), 204.

48. Hillel Rogoff, "'Der goylem': A dramatishe poeme fun H. Leyvik," *Forverts*, 5 June 1921, 2.

49. Leivick, *Golem*, 128; Leivick, *Der goylem*, 30. In the act "In the Cave," a phantom figure (*geshtalt*) referring to himself as the rabbi calls for the torture and murder of the rebellious golem: "Throw him upon the ground, chew up his flesh / And slit his throat!" Leivick, *Golem*, 216; Leivick, *Der goylem*, 166.

50. Leivick, *Golem*, 127; Leivick, *Der goylem*, 29, 129.

51. Leivick, *Golem*, 205, 188; Leivick, *Der goylem*, 147–148, 126.

52. Leivick, *Golem*, 157; Leivick, *Der goylem*, 77. In Rosenberg's text, this palace "had five walls facing the street" decorated with columns, towers, and statues, all in sets of five. Since the mansion had no owner, it fell into disrepair and housed only beggars. The cellar underneath "had been defiled by demons who . . . constantly terrorized the beggars." Rosenberg, *Seyfer nifloes Maharal*, 34–35; Rosenberg, *Golem*, 36.

53. The five-walled tower is a liminal space that serves as a passageway between the Christian and Jewish worlds: the stage instructions describe "chains of sacred Christian lamps" in a corner of one of the dilapidated rooms above, and in the labyrinth under the palace, two paths converge, one leading to the church and the other to the synagogue. Leivick, *Golem*, 157; Leivick, *Der goylem*, 77.

54. Leivick, *Golem*, 231; Leivick, *Der goylem*, 183.

55. Leivick, *Golem*, 232–233; Leivick, *Der goylem*, 184.

56. Leivick, *Der goylem*, 186.

57. While Leivick undermines the messianic visions of his characters, *Der goylem* received much attention from Yiddish writers and critics who were enthralled by messianic-apocalyptic themes and thought. See Noverstern, *Kesem ha-dimdumim*, 207.

58. Leivick, *Golem*, 226; Leivick, *Der goylem*, 177.

59. Leivick, *Golem*, 169; Leivick, *Der goylem*, 96. In the 1934 drama *Di geule komedye: Der goylem kholemt* (The redemption comedy: The golem dreams), conceived as a sequel to *Der goylem*, Leivick revisits the relationship between the Messiah and the golem, presenting a far more active Messiah who arrives of his own volition and rejects the roles of "guest" and "beggar." Leivick, *Di geule komedye: Der goylem kholemt* (Chicago: Yiddish Cultural Society, L. M. Stein, 1934), 67.

60. Leivick, *Golem*, 182, 174; Leivick, *Der goylem*, 116, 108.

61. At the sight of the golem, two beggars who had previously encountered him at the five-walled tower declare, "Terrifying to see. It's not him at all. He's become someone else." Leivick, *Der goylem*, 200.

62. Leivick, *Golem*, 238; Leivick, *Der goylem*, 195; Bal-makhshoves, *Geklibene verk* (New York: Tsiko bikher farlag, 1953), 288–289.

63. Leivick, *Golem*, 245–246; Leivick, *Der goylem*, 207–208.

64. Leivick, *Golem*, 247; Leivick, *Der goylem*, 210–211.

65. Scholem, "Idea of the Golem," 202–203.

66. Leivick, *Golem*, 247–248; Leivick, *Der goylem*, 211–212.

67. Leivick, *Golem*, 248–249; Leivick, *Der goylem*, 212–213.

68. Leivick, *Golem*, 253; Leivick, *Der goylem*, 221.

69. "Picture Plays and People," 75.

70. See also "Der goylem," *Forverts*, 18 June 1921, 10.

71. "A Jewish community of 600 years ago is represented, not with photographic precision, but with a poetic melting together of dreaminess and imagery. . . . The old patriarchs are shown in soft tones on the screen, lights and shades which play with loving touches about them." "Reinhardt's Art on Screen," 4.

72. Wegener was accused of creating "foolish, *shund* entertainment" and of portraying the Jews as "savage people" who constantly pound their chests and fall to their knees. "Vi a krist hot baarbet di legende fun goylem," *Der tog*, 17 June 1921, 3; "Di tsenirung un uffirung fun der moving piktchur 'der goylem,'" *Der tog*, 24 June 1921, 3. See also M. Osherovitch, "An alte yidishe maysele in di movies af brodvey," *Forverts*, 4 July 1921, 7. The *New York Times* similarly considered the story to be "based on an old Jewish legend, but [to be] no part of orthodox Jewish tradition surely." "The Screen," 20.

73. Osherovitch, "An alte yidishe maysele," 7. In the post-1915 period, American film orchestras tripled both in number and in size, with New York theater orchestras

being particularly large (anywhere between forty and eighty musicians). See Rick Altman, *Silent Film Sound* (New York: Columbia University Press, 2004), 303.

74. "'Der goylem' iz endlekh do," 2.

75. Miriam Hansen, *Babel and Babylon: Spectatorship in American Silent Film* (Cambridge, MA: Harvard University Press, 1991), 43–44.

76. Bril, "Golem," 12. Biblical quote (Psalm 118:5) transliterated and translated by the author.

77. Andrej and Wegener, "Ein Gespräch mit Paul Wegener," 2.

78. "Landsbergers Golem-Musik," *Die Lichtbild-Bühne*, 13 November 1920, 22; "In Picture Theaters: Criterion," *New York Tribune*, 19 June 1921, 2. The violinist Hugo Riesenfeld had conducted ballet music at Vienna's Imperial Opera House. He arrived in the U.S. in 1907 to work at the Metropolitan Opera and became the musical director and conductor of three major movie theaters in New York (the Rialto, Rivoli, and Criterion), where he developed an extensive score library and specialized in musical historical reconstructions. See Altman, *Silent Film Sound*, 291, 315–316; Mervyn Cooke, *The Hollywood Film Music Reader* (Oxford: Oxford University Press, 2010), 16.

79. Osherovitch, "An alte yidishe maysele in di movies af brodvey," 7.

80. "Nyu york zet dem 'goylem,'" *Yidishes tageblat*, 24 June 1921, 12.

81. *Humoresque*, the tale of a young Jewish violinist, had also enjoyed a long, twelve-week run at the Criterion Theater, and its success was attributed in part to the musical prologue and score. The prologue for *Humoresque* was designed by Josiah Zure (who also worked on the *Golem* prologue) and the New School of Opera Ensemble, and the ensuing film score included many Hebrew songs, selected and cued by Riesenfeld. See Altman, *Silent Film Sound*, 385–387.

82. Irene Heskes, *Yiddish American Popular Songs, 1895 to 1950: A Catalog Based on the Lawrence Marwick Roster of Copyright Entries* (Washington, DC: Library of Congress, 1992), xxxv–xxvii.

83. "Hot shoyn gezungen 'eyli, eyli' hunderte mol," *Yidishes tageblat*, 29 June 1922, 10; "Funfte vokh fun 'goylem' in kreyterion teater," *Yidishes tageblat*, 17 July 1921, 11.

84. G. Zelikovitsch, "Der goylem fun prag af brodvey," *Yidishes tageblat*, 22 June 1921, 4.

85. "Jacob Sandler's Song," *New York Times*, 14 August 1921, 68.

86. Irene Heskes, *Passport to Jewish Music: Its History, Traditions, and Culture* (Westport, CT: Greenwood, 1994), 205.

87. Ted Merwin, *In Their Own Image: New York Jews in Jazz Age Popular Culture* (New Brunswick, NJ: Rutgers University Press, 2006), 135.

88. "Medieval Ghetto in the Center of Action in 'Golem' Film," 2.

89. Polland and Soyer, *Emerging Metropolis*, 141.

90. "Medieval Ghetto in the Center of Action in 'Golem' Film," 2.

91. Bril, "Golem," 12.

92. According to David S. Lifson, Max Gabel's theatrical "formula" included adaptations of sensationalist melodrama hits from Broadway, such as Cleves Kinkead's *Common Clay*, and he did not attempt to conceal their borrowed origins. See Lifson, *The Yiddish Theater in America* (New York: Thomas Yoseloff, 1965), 255.

93. Goylem's Eynikel, "Der prager goylem," *Forverts*, 25 February 1922, 7.

94. Gabel took the Lyric Theater to court, claiming that he was the only one authorized to stage the golem in the U.S. On 24 February 1922, Gabel's injunction against the Lyric Theater production was refused by a judge, who claimed that "the title of plaintiff's play 'Der Golem' is not strictly original." See "Injunction Refused," *Variety*, 24 February 1922, 12; Max Gabel, "A brif fun Maks Gebil," *Forverts*, 17 February 1922, 3.

95. "Der 'goylem': A groyse sensatsiye," *Forverts*, 28 December 1921, 2.

96. Rubinstein, "Di uffirung fun 'goylem' in Gebil's teater," 3.

97. Hillel Rogoff, "'Der goylem': A prakhtfole opereta in Gebil's teater," *Forverts*, 13 January 1922, 3; Abel, "The Golem (in Yiddish)," *Variety*, 2 February 1922, 18.

98. Albert Kovessy, *Der goylem: Muzikalisher legend in dray akten mit a prolog*, trans. Max Schweid, adapt. Max Gabel, D 59524, p. 4, Lawrence Marwick Collection of Copyrighted Yiddish Plays, Library of Congress, Washington, DC.

99. Bril, "Golem," 12.

100. Ibid., 5–6, 39.

101. The *Variety* reviewer even noted that "Max Gabel personating the legendary titular character is made up much like the screen image." Abel, "Golem (in Yiddish)," 18.

102. Kovessy, *Der goylem*, 11.

103. Photos of Goldstein as Miriam accompanied various reviews of the play. See Max Gabel, "Maks Gebil dankt dem groyse oylem un der prese," *Forverts*, 14 January 1922, 4.

104. "Goylem, du verst mir tsu khokhme'dik." Kovessy, *Der goylem*, 40.

105. Ibid., 6–7.

106. Ibid., 16.

107. Ibid., 19–20, 38.

108. Ibid., 13, 15, 28.

109. Ibid., 61–62, 64.

110. Rogoff, "'Der goylem': A prakhtfole opereta," 3.

111. Kovessy, *Der goylem*, 13–14.

112. Rubinstein, "Di uffirung fun 'goylem' in Gebil's teater," 3.

113. S. Robinzon, "Mit 300 yor tsurik un 300 yor shpeter: Der 'goylem' un der 'letster yid,'" *Yidishes tageblat*, 27 January 1922, 4.

114. Rubinstein, "Di uffirung fun 'goylem' in Gebil's teater," 3.

115. The verb *mishn zikh* conveys a kind of nosiness that lowers the act of human creation from mystical imitation of the divine to meddling in someone else's business. Kovessy, *Der goylem*, 12.

CHAPTER 3. OUR ENEMIES, OURSELVES

1. "Ha-hashba'a be-tel aviv: Ne'um Shartok," *Ha-tsofe*, 29 June 1948, 4.

2. Moshe Sharet, *Davar davur: Dvarim she-be'al pe be-zirot pnim va-ḥuts, 1948*, ed. Yaakov Sharet and Rina Sharet (Tel Aviv: Ha-'amuta le-moreshet Moshe Sharet, 2013), 160.

3. Avner Holzman, "Hebetim politiyim be-sifrut milḥemet ha-'atsma'ut," in *Politika be-milḥama: Kovets meḥkarim 'al ha-ḥevra ha-'ezraḥit be-milḥemet ha-'atsma'ut*, ed. Mordechai Bar-On and Meir Chazan (Jerusalem: Yad Ben Tsvi, 2014), 559.

4. Dani Horowitz, *Yossele golem*, in *Arba'a maḥazot*, ed. Shimon Levy (Ramat Aviv, Israel: Safra, 2007), 71.

5. Uri Keisari, "Drishat shalom le-'Habima,'" *Ma'ariv*, 10 May 1948, 7.

6. Nosn Sverdlin, "Baym forhang," *Der tog*, 21 May 1948, 9.

7. Atay Citron, "Habima's *The Golem*," *TDR: The Drama Review* 24, no. 3 (1980): 65.

8. "'The Golem,' H. Levik's Dramatization of Medieval Legend, Offered by Habimah at Broadway," *New York Times*, 17 May 1948, 22.

9. Sverdlin, "Baym forhang," 9.

10. John Gassner, *The Theatre in Our Times; A Survey of the Men, Materials, and Movements in the Modern Theatre* (New York: Crown, 1954), 393.

11. Yair Lipshitz, "Ge'ula megulemet ba-guf: 'Avar, 'atid ve-'avodat hasaḥkan be-hatsagat 'ha-golem' shel 'Habima,'" *Reshit* 1 (2009): 293–294.

12. According to Atay Citron, "Habima's production closed the curtain as Tanchum cries out his unanswerable question 'Who will save us?'" Citron, "Habima's *The Golem*," 68.

13. Alisa Solomon, "A Jewish Avenger, a Timely Legend," *New York Times*, 7 April 2002, http://www.nytimes.com/2002/04/07/theater/theater-a-jewish-avenger-a-timely-legend.html.

14. Dunash, "Reshimot: Shorashim," *Ha-tsofe*, 4 November 1938, 2.

15. See Avi-Ruth, "Ha-golem"; Ab"a Aḥimeir, "Ha-maharal ve-ha-golem," *Ha-mashkif*, 9 May 1941, 5.

16. Marian Zyd, "Yehudim be-'esh 'ha-golem ha-me'ofef,'" *Ha-mashkif*, 22 September 1944, 4.

17. Filma'i, "'Ha-golem' be-'eney tsarfati," *Davar*, 14 July 1948, 3.

18. "Ki ha-tenu'a ha-le'umit ha-'aravit hi akh golem she-hukam 'al yedey ha-imperi'alizem et ze kol tinok yode'a." Aharon Cohen, "Ha-tsad ha-sheni shel ha-matbe'a: Hirhurim bilti noḥim," *'Al ha-mishmar*, 31 January 1947, 8.

19. "Ha-haḥlatot shel ha-liga ha-'aravit," *Ha-mashkif*, 9 December 1945, 2.

20. Hillel Danzig, "Minkhen sheni?," *Davar*, 1 April 1948, 6.

21. M.D., "Davar ha-yom," *Davar*, 21 July 1948, 1.

22. Sefiker, "'Abdala ha-golem ha-briti hikhriz 'aleynu milḥama," *Yedi'ot aḥaronot*, 27 April 1948, 1.

23. "Ha-hashba'a be-tel aviv," 4.

24. For Agnon's own compilation of Jewish tales concerning artificial creation, including the story of the Ba'al shem and his golem, see S. Y. Agnon, *Sefer sofer ve-sipur* (Tel Aviv: Schocken, 1978), 231–232. In his novella *Edo and Enam*, Agnon depicts a female golem-like character. He has his characters discuss the tale of the poet Solomon Ibn Gabirol's creation of an artificial woman "to serve his needs" in conjunction with the somnambulist named Gemulah, a feminine rendition of golem. S. Y. Agnon, *Edo and Enam*, trans. Walter Lever, in *Two Tales: "Betrothed" & "Edo and Enam"* (New York: Schocken, 1966), 151.

25. Starting in December 1913, *Der Golem* was published serially in the expressionist journal *Die weißen Blätter* (The white pages) with the Kurt Wolff publishing house. See Göbel, *Der Kurt Wolff Verlag 1913–1930*, 732.

26. Arnold J. Band deems the structure of *Ad hena* "haphazard" without any clear justification for its form: "The first seven chapters span only several days in the spring of 1916. . . . The last eight chapters, which skip to the winter of 1917, 1918, and finally rush, ostensibly, to the middle of the 1920's in the last three pages of the story, are not necessary." Band also employs the term "novelette" to define *Ad hena*. Band, *Nostalgia and Nightmare: A Study in the Fiction of S. Y. Agnon* (Berkeley: University of California Press, 1968), 348, 347, 52–53. Others critics have suggested that the text achieves some unity through the plot of the narrator's illicit attraction to Brigitta or the satiric treatment of the decline of German society during World War I. See Nitza Ben-Dov, *Ahavot lo me'usharot: Tiskul eroti, omanut, u-mavet be-yetsirat Agnon* (Tel Aviv: Am 'oved, 1997); Esther Fuchs, "Mivne ha-'alila ha-ironit be-sipurei Shai Agnon 'al-pi 'Ad hena,'" *Bikoret u-farshanut: Ktav-'et bein tehumi leheker sifrut ve-tarbut* 20 (1985): 25–44.

27. S. Y. Agnon, *Ad hena*, in *Kol sipurav shel Shmuel Yosef Agnon: Ad hena* (Tel Aviv: Schocken, 1998), 6–7.

28. Agnon arrived in Berlin together with Arthur Ruppin in hopes of securing an assistantship with the writer Micah Joseph Berdichevsky. After this attempt came to naught, he found employment as a Hebrew tutor and editor for the Jewish press, only later to gain the patronage of Zalman Schocken. Despite the autobiographical dimension of *Ad hena*, the name of Agnon's narrator is never stated directly in the text; indeed, a mysterious aura surrounds this namelessness. For example, while Agnon implies that the narrator shares his name, Shmuel Yosef, he never uses both names together in the text. Agnon, *Ad hena*, 115, 64.

29. Dan Laor, *Ḥayey Agnon: Biografya* (Jerusalem: Schocken, 1998), 400–401, 414, 416.

30. Ibid., 399–400.

31. Agnon did not consider himself a pacifist, stating in 1964 that though he "does not like the army . . . and does not have a sense for things that can be done with technology, . . . fooling around with pacifism is even a worse idea." S. Y. Agnon, *Me'atsmi el 'atsmi* (Tel Aviv: Schocken, 2000), 424–425.

32. For a discussion of *Ad hena* as an "introduction to the Holocaust" through the critical depiction of German characters and society, see Hillel Weiss, "*Ad hena*

ke-mavo lasho'a," *Bikoret u-farshanut: Ktav-'et bein thumi leheker sifrut vetarbut* 35–36 (2001–2002): 111–146.

33. Sidra DeKoven Ezrahi, "S. Y. Agnon's Jerusalem: Before and after 1948," *Jewish Social Studies* 18, no. 3 (2012): 138.

34. Agnon, *Ad hena*, 107 (my translation); see also Agnon, *To This Day*, trans. Hillel Halkin (London: Toby, 2008), 145.

35. Toward the end of Agnon's *Tmol shilshom* (*Only Yesterday*), the rabid or "mad" dog Balak returns to the ultra-Orthodox neighborhood *Me'a she'arim* just as Rabbi Gronem chastises his congregation about the evils of their generation evoking the phrase "the face of the generation is the face of the dog" with reference to the current "rabid" generation. Agnon, *Tmol shilshom* (Tel Aviv: Schocken, 1966), 583–588.

36. *The Mishnah*, trans. Herbert Danby (Peabody, MA: Hendrickson Publishers Marketing, 2011), 306.

37. See Agnon, *Me'atsmi el 'atsmi*, 78–79.

38. *Ad hena* contains multiple references to physiognomy as a suspect method of reading the surface of bodies, revealing the author's acquaintance with the post–World War I racial typologies proposed by Hans F. K. Günther and Ludwig Ferdinand Clauss. His narrator uses the archaizing term *hokhmat ha-partsuf* (the study of facial features) when declaring that he is not well versed in such physiognomic interpretation. Agnon, *Ad hena*, 84, 90; Gray, *About Face*, 223, 255.

39. The prewar theater represents in *Ad hena* the antithesis to cinematic duplicity: the former actress Brigitta Schimmermann never attempted to cover up her lack of unique acting talent on the stage but instead would "show herself as she is." Agnon, *Ad hena*, 12.

40. In *Ad hena*, the female body represents the corruption of an entire generation, and the supposedly feminine act of exposure on the screen is charged with aggressive potential. Positioning women as theater and film actresses, Agnon feminizes mass culture, in contrast to the masculine realm of Talmudic study, which represents "high" Jewish culture. The narrator, who researches clothing rather than scripture, is himself thereby feminized. See also Andreas Huyssen, *After the Great Divide: Modernism, Mass Culture, Postmodernism* (Bloomington: Indiana University Press, 1986), 47.

41. Agnon, *To This Day*, 25; Agnon, *Ad hena*, 10.

42. Agnon, *Ad hena*, 12. Unlike the golem-soldier, the narrator lives inside his mind and his lengthy trains of thoughts and associations, while his body is deemed unfit for the battlefield. For the narrator's meditations on the nature of his distracted thoughts, see ibid., 48, 36, 45, 61, 96.

43. Ibid., 44 (my translation); see also Agnon, *To This Day*, 66.

44. Agnon, *Ad hena*, 48 (my translation); see also Agnon, *To This Day*, 72.

45. Michael Hagner, "Verwundete Gesichter, verletzte Gehirne: Zur Deformation des Kopfes im Ersten Weltkrieg," in *Gesichter der Weimarer Republik: Eine*

physiognomische Kulturgeschichte, ed. Claudia Schmölders and Sander Gilman (Cologne: DuMont, 2000), 79.

46. "She-shavtu bo kley ha-shmiʿa ve-nitla mimeno hargashat ha-havḥana." Agnon, *Ad hena*, 36.

47. When the narrator encounters the golem man outside the convalescence home and talks to him without receiving any response, he remarks that "it is pleasant to converse with idiots; you say everything that is on your mind and are not fearful that you may have uttered some nonsense." Ibid., 37.

48. Hagner, "Verwundete Gesichter, verletzte Gehirne," 88–91.

49. Agnon, *To This Day*, 106; Agnon, *Ad hena*, 75.

50. Scholem, "Idea of the Golem," 160–165.

51. Agnon, *Sefer sofer ve-sipur*, 231. *Sefer yetsira* (*The Book of Creation*) is a mystical Hebrew composition concerning divine (and human) creation possibly dating back as early as the first century CE. In *Sefer yetsira*, the Hebrew alphabet creates and upholds both the world and human beings, and its letters correspond to different parts of the body as well as to the seasons and months of the year. This text likens "God's creativity to the writing of a literary text that calls for imitation." Yehuda Liebes, *Torat ha-yetsira shel sefer ha-yetsira* (Tel Aviv: Schocken, 2000), 145. On the intertextual role of *Sefer yetsira* in *Ad hena*, see Yaniv Hagbi, *Language, Absence, Play: Judaism and Superstructuralism in the Poetics of S. Y. Agnon* (Syracuse, NY: Syracuse University Press, 2009), 42–52, 135–138.

52. Agnon, *Ad hena*, 44. When the narrator explains why he must remain in Germany during the war, he uses the term *makom* to signify God, Zion, and, possibly, his final burial place: "I must live here and seek a room for myself until the Place [i.e., God] returns me to my place." Ibid., 70.

53. These motifs have also appeared in other works by Agnon concerning male creativity or the lack thereof. In the story "Givʿat ha-ḥol" ("Hill of Sand"), which Agnon rewrote during his sojourn in Germany, the main character, Ḥemdat, suffers from an inability to fulfill either his creative or his sexual desires. Ḥemdat even hallucinates that if his "heavy" and "obtuse brain" were to be "fixed" by being removed, literally "extracted" from his body, he would experience great relief. S. Y. Agnon, "Givʿat ha-ḥol," in *ʿAl kapot ha-manʿul* (Tel Aviv: Schocken, 1966), 373–374. For an in-depth analysis of the complex castration motifs in "Givʿat ha-ḥol," see Michal Arbel, *Katuv ʿal ʿoro shel ha-kelev: ʿAl tfisat ha-yetsira etsel Shai Agnon* (Jerusalem: Keter, 2006), 172–198.

54. Through Agnon's intermittent stays in Leipzig between 1916 and 1918, he could have been exposed to the innovative and aggressive advertising campaigns of the Kurt Wolff publishing house. As he writes, "During the Great War I lived in Leipzig. Some of what happened to me there I wrote about in my book *Ad hena*." Agnon, *Meʿatsmi el ʿatsmi*, 265. In a postcard addressed to Martin Buber, Agnon invited the philosopher to stay with him in Leipzig and related that his apartment was located near the German publishing houses: "One step away—Kurt Wolff; a

second step—Insel; a third step—Brandstetter." S. Y. Agnon to Martin Buber, 2 March 1918, Martin Buber Archive, ARC. Ms. Var. 350, National Library of Israel, Jerusalem.

55. Gershom Scholem, *From Berlin to Jerusalem: Memories of My Youth*, trans. Harry Zohn (New York: Schocken, 1988), 133. Although Scholem was critical of Meyrink's "pseudo-mysticism, a distorted form of Kabbala, as received in the writings of Madame Blavatsky's circle," he also noted that Meyrink had "an extraordinary talent for antibourgeois satire" and that the "literary quality" of some of his short stories "has been surpassed only by Jorge Luis Borges in our time." Ibid, 132–133. See also Scholem, "Idea of the Golem," 158.

56. Max Brod, "Zwei jüdische Bücher," *Die neue Rundschau*, no. 2 (1918): 1366. For Brod, Meyrink "employs kabbalistic motifs as soulless decorative-exotic trappings. . . . In Agnon's writing, by contrast, any spell or saying from the *Zohar* is a deep-felt structural element that rises, alive, from the depths of the story." Ibid. In a 1915 review of *Der Golem*, Arnold Zweig likewise wrote that this riveting novel forges a twilight zone of "sensationalism" and cleverly arranged mysticism, combining kabbalah and crime, Greek esoteric doctrine and lust for revenge. Zweig, "Der Golem," 225.

57. Agnon, *Ad hena*, 47 (my translation); see also Agnon, *To This Day*, 70.

58. After presenting Kurt Wolff with the first chapter of the book, Meyrink demanded instead of the usual royalties a ten thousand Goldmark advance. Kurt Wolff, *Autoren, Bücher, Abenteuer: Betrachtungen und Erinnerungen eines Verlegers* (Berlin: Klaus Wagenbach, 2004), 19.

59. Franz Werfel to Kurt Wolff, 2 March 1916, in *Kurt Wolff: Briefwechsel eines Verlegers 1911–1963*, ed. Bernhard Zeller and Ellen Otten (Frankfurt am Main: Verlag Heinrich Scheffler, 1966), 108. The sensationalist language of Wolff's advertisements promised the reader that this "ethical criminal novel" was "the most suspenseful and penetrating work of German literature." Wolff, "Der Golem," *Börsenblatt für den deutschen Buchhandel*, 12 June 1915, 7632.

60. Gelbin, *Golem Returns*, 101.

61. For instance, "Rosina belongs to the tribe of which the red-haired members are even more repulsive than the rest. The men thereof are narrow-chested, with long, bird-like necks and aggressively prominent Adam's apples." Meyrink, *Golem*, 6; Gustav Meyrink, *Der Golem* (Frankfurt am Main: Ullstein, 1991), 13.

62. Meyrink, *Golem*, 27; Meyrink, *Der Golem*, 48; Gelbin, *Golem Returns*, 110–111.

63. Gustav Meyrink, an Austrian-born satirist and aesthetic secessionist who was never at home in Prague or in Germany, shared with Agnon an interest in ethnic and nationalist tensions, which he sought to expose in his writings. See Scott Spector, *Prague Territories: National Conflict and Cultural Innovation in Franz Kafka's Fin de Siècle* (Berkeley: University of California Press, 2000), 14, 176–177; Gelbin, *Golem Returns*, 99.

64. Agnon, *Ad hena*, 65, 113. Yaniv Hagbi has noted this shared detail, contending that "Agnon, whether consciously or not, refers his reader to *The Golem* by using the strange tied-spoon image." Hagbi, *Language, Absence, Play*, 60.

65. This story was reprinted in the widely circulating journal *Die Schaubühne* in February 1916 under the title "The Story of the Jurist Doctor Hulbert and his Battalion" ("Die Erzählung vom Rechtsgelehrten Doktor Hulbert und seinem Bataillon"). Meyrink based the story on the actual Bataillon pub that served the Prague underworld and on the historical figure of Dr. Uher, a down-and-out lawyer and politician. See Manfred Lube, *Gustav Meyrink: Beiträge zur Biographie und Studien zu seiner Kunsttheorie* (Graz, Austria: Technische Universität Graz, 1980), 106.

66. See Aaron Bar-Adon, *Shai Agnon u-tḥiyat ha-lashon ha-ʻivrit* (Jerusalem: Mosad Bialik, 1977), 191–195.

67. When molding a golem of clay, Jewish mystics attempted to attain divine knowledge through action, "to know God by the art He uses in order to create man." Moshe Idel, *Golem: Jewish Magical and Mystical Traditions and the Artificial Anthropoid* (Albany: State University of New York Press, 1990), xxvii.

68. See ibid., 55–58.

69. Naomi Sokoloff contends that in the story "Ḥush ha-reaḥ" ("The Sense of Smell") Agnon presents "a mystical view of language that imagines Hebrew as existing prior to the creation of the world and capable of creating worlds." Sokoloff, "The Sense of Smell," in *Reading Hebrew Literature: Critical Discussions of Six Modern Texts*, ed. Alan Mintz (Hanover, NH: Brandeis University Press, 2003), 111.

70. Agnon, *Ad hena*, 50 (my translation); see also Agnon, *To This Day*, 74.

71. Alan Mintz and Anne Golomb Hoffman, "The Artist in the Land of Israel," in *A Book That Was Lost and Other Stories by S. Y. Agnon*, ed. Alan Mintz and Anne Golomb Hoffman (New York: Schocken, 1995), 81.

72. In the summer of 1917, Agnon addressed a postcard to Martin Buber from "Pension Körber" in the Fasanenstrasse, Berlin. Later that year, after moving to Leipzig, he complained to another correspondent about his living conditions, inquiring into the availability of a room in the boardinghouse of "Frl. Körber" in Berlin, since he would then "swiftly return to the Fasanenstrasse" ("*so komm ich telegrafisch nach der Fasanenstr. zurück*"). S. Y. Agnon to Martin Buber, 25 June 1917, Martin Buber Archive, ARC. Ms. Var. 350, National Library of Israel, Jerusalem; S. Y. Agnon to Zalman Schocken, February 1917, S .Y. Agnon Archive, ARC 4*1270, National Library of Israel, Jerusalem.

73. Agnon, *To This Day*, 77; Agnon, *Ad hena*, 53. As Kurt Tucholsky wrote in August 1912, "On Monday a new synagogue will be consecrated in the presence of a representative of the Kaiser. The dome is decorated with Kadinen glazed tiles from the factory of Wilhelm II." For Agnon, and for Tucholsky before him, the synagogue represents not the freedom and integration of German Jews but rather

their ongoing subjugation on German soil, where they are denied access to positions of power and enlisted as cannon fodder. Tucholsky, "Die patriotische Synagoge," in *Gesamtausgabe: Texte 1907–1913*, ed. Bärbel Boldt, Dirk Grathoff, and Michael Hepp (Reinbek bei Hamburg: Rowohlt, 1997), 81.

74. Agnon, *Ad hena*, 58 (my translation); see also Agnon, *To This Day*, 84.

75. Agnon, *Ad hena*, 5. At an earlier point in the text, during a sleepless night, the narrator invents a mental game using Hebrew roots, which he combines in different patterns, finding equivalent biblical quotes for each word he has created. This letter game evolves into a terrifying vision of war and catastrophe, for every seemingly innocent combination when reversed or reshuffled turns out to have a negative connotation: "Since the night was difficult I took the word 'morning' [*boker*]. . . . When you read the word from left to right you get rottenness [*rakav*] as you say 'to the house of Judah as rottenness.' And if you change the places you get battle [*krav*] . . . and finally grave [*kever*]." Translated by Yaniv Hagbi, in *Language, Absence, Play*, 134–135; Agnon, *Ad hena*, 22. As Hagbi emphasizes, Agnon's narrator is not indifferent, as the composers of *Sefer yetsira* might have been, to the direction of his linguistic permutations. Rather, his combinations always move from positive to negative, from hope to doom, and from pleasure to death. Hagbi, *Language, Absence, Play*, 137.

76. Weiss, "*Ad hena* ke-mavo la-sho'a," 124.

77. In the poem "Vom hohen Rabbi Löw" (On the great Rabbi Loew) by the Czech Hugo Salus, the hardworking golem is referred to as a "clay Hans" ("*der lehmige Hans*"). Salus, *Ernte* (Munich: Albert Langen, 1903), 91.

78. There are two main similarities between the golem legend and the story of Balak: first, Yitshak Kummer writes on the body of the dog, just as the word *emet* (truth) is written on the golem; second, by the end of the novel, the rabid dog qua golem runs amok and kills his own so-called creator, Yitshak, by biting into his flesh. See Todd Hasak-Lowy, "A Mad Dog's Attack on Secularized Hebrew: Rethinking Agnon's *Temol shilshom*," *Prooftexts* 24 (2004): 185.

79. Agnon, *Me'atsmi el 'atsmi*, 43.

80. Horowitz, *Yossele golem*, 71–72, 74.

81. Ibid., 77–78.

82. Ibid., 82, 101.

83. Richard F. Shepard, "'Yossele Golem' in Its World Premiere," *New York Times* 18 April 1982, 65; Horowitz, *Yossele golem*, 58.

84. Horowitz, *Yossele golem*, 71, 77.

85. Agnon, *Ad hena*, 47.

86. David G. Roskies, *Against the Apocalypse: Reponses to Catastrophe in Modern Jewish Culture* (Cambridge, MA: Harvard University Press, 1984), 139–141. In the 1899 story "Arieh 'ba'al guf,'" Hayim Nahman Bialik ambivalently portrayed an uneducated man of the lower classes who rises in status and income because of his physical strength. Bialik contrasts the crude "*ba'al guf*" whose body is

well-built, healthy, and unmovable to the "beautiful Jews" of the Beit-midrash who are "spiritual" and delicate. Bialik, "Arieh 'ba'al guf,'" in *Ḥayim Naḥman Bialik: Ha-Sipurim*, ed. Avner Holzman (Or Yehuda: Dvir, 2008), 16–20, 26–27.

87. Roskies, *Against the Apocalypse*, 142; Gillerman, "A Kinder Gentler Strongman?," 204.

88. Max Nordau writes in 1903 of the "new muscle-Jews [*Muskeljuden*]" who do not conceal their Judaism but "proudly affirm their national loyalty." Nordau, "Jewry of Muscle" (June 1903), in *The Jew in the Modern World: A Documentary History*, 3rd ed., ed. Paul R. Mendes-Flohr and Jehuda Reinharz (New York: Oxford University Press, 2011), 617.

89. Gluzman, *Ha-guf ha-tsiyoni*, 26.

90. Gelbin, *Golem Returns*, 92.

91. Nicholas Baer, "Messianic Musclemen: *Homunculus* (1916) and *Der Golem* (1920) as Zionist Allegories," in *The Place of Politics in German Film*, ed. Martin Blumenthal-Barby (Bielefeld, Germany: Aisthesis Verlag, 2014), 38–39, 41–42.

92. Agnon, *Ad hena*, 46. In *Oreaḥ nata lalun*, published in 1939, Agnon's narrator visits his own hometown in Galicia, where his fellow Jews seek to draw a clear line to separate the courageous pioneers in Palestine and the weak Jewish Galicians. The narrator insists, by contrast, that "if the hero needs to constantly be engaged in war-making, he will finally grow weak and fall." S. Y. Agnon, *Oreaḥ nata lalun* (Tel Aviv: Schocken, 1998), 183.

93. In 2010, Kaniuk published *Tasha"ḥ* (1948), a personal first-person account (though highly stylized) of the author's experiences during the 1948 battles, in which he fought and was wounded. Yoram Kaniuk, *Tasha"ḥ* (Tel Aviv: Yedi'ot aḥaronot, 2010).

94. Idith Zertal, "Eyma be-khos shel zkhukhit: Siḥa 'im Yoram Kaniuk," *Davar*, 26 August 1966, 22.

95. Ibid.

96. Yoram Kaniuk, "Ha-ḥaverim shel Beni," *Davar*, 4 May 1973, 55.

97. For a detailed comparison of Kaniuk's work and Guttman's adaptation, see Yosefa Loshitzky, "Kalat ha-met: Falotsentrizem u-milḥama be-Ḥimo melekh yerushalayim," in *Mabatim fiktiviyim: 'Al kolno'a yisra'eli*, ed. Orly Lubin, Nurith Gertz, and Judd Ne'eman (Tel Aviv: Open University of Israel, 1998).

98. Kaniuk, *Himmo, King of Jerusalem*, trans. Yosef Shachter (New York: Atheneum, 1966), 34; Yoram Kaniuk, *Ḥimo melekh yerushalayim* (Tel Aviv: Am 'oved, 2004), 27.

99. Kaniuk, *Himmo, King of Jerusalem*, 35; Kaniuk, *Ḥimo melekh yerushalayim*, 28.

100. Kaniuk had a long-standing interest in the history of Israel and in the Crusader period, and he contended that "only kings of crusaders were called 'King of Jerusalem.'" Zertal, "Eyma be-khos shel zekhukhit."

101. Kaniuk, *Himmo, King of Jerusalem*, 36 (translation amended); Kaniuk, *Ḥimo melekh yerushalayim*, 28.

102. Kaniuk, *Himmo, King of Jerusalem*, 38; Kaniuk, *Ḥimo melekh yerushalayim*, 30.

103. Kaniuk, *Himmo, King of Jerusalem*, 38–39, 41, 21; Kaniuk, *Ḥimo melekh yerushalayim*, 30, 32, 19.

104. Kaniuk, *Himmo, King of Jerusalem*, 65–67; Kaniuk, *Ḥimo melekh yerushalayim*, 49–51.

105. Kaniuk, *Himmo, King of Jerusalem*, 101; Kaniuk, *Ḥimo melekh yerushalayim*, 74–75.

106. Kaniuk, *Himmo, King of Jerusalem*, 235; Kaniuk, *Ḥimo melekh yerushalayim*, 168.

107. Adia Mendelson-Maoz, "Ba-karhon haze yekhola litsmo'aḥ kalanit. Ḥimo melekh yerushalayim: Bein etika le-estetika," in *Gufi he-karo'a melavlev: 'Al maḥala ve-refu'a. Ma'amarim u-kitei sifrut*, ed. Yehosheva Bentov (Jerusalem: Carmel, 2009), 205.

108. Loshitzky, "Kalat ha-met," 247–248. See also Kaniuk, *Ḥimo melekh yerushalayim*, 104–105.

109. Kaniuk, *Himmo, King of Jerusalem*, 237–239; Kaniuk, *Ḥimo melekh yerushalayim*, 169–170.

110. Kaniuk, *Himmo, King of Jerusalem*, 245–246; Kaniuk, *Ḥimo melekh yerushalayim*, 175.

111. Nathan Alterman, "Magash ha-kesef / The Silver Platter," in *No Rattling of Sabers: An Anthology of Israeli War Poetry*, ed. and trans. Esther Raizen (Austin: University of Texas Press, 1995), 21–22.

112. Kaniuk, *Himmo, King of Jerusalem*, 21; Kaniuk, *Ḥimo melekh yerushalayim*, 19.

113. Kaniuk, *Himmo, King of Jerusalem*, 204 (translation amended); Kaniuk, *Ḥimo melekh yerushalayim*, 145.

114. Yoram Kaniuk, "Ha-sipurim she-nihiyu le-sipur ḥayay," in *Me'ayin naḥalti et shiri: Sofrim u-meshorerim medabrim 'al mekorot hashra'a*, ed. Ruth Karton-Blum (Tel Aviv: Yedi'ot aḥronot, 2002), 69.

115. Yosef Alroi, "Ha-tokhen—eyma; ha-lashon—ma'adanot," *Ha'aretz*, 12 August 1966, 10.

116. Zertal, "Eyma be-khos shel zekhukhit."

117. Hardt and Negri, *Multitude*, 11.

CHAPTER 4. SUPERGOLEM

1. This was not the caped hero's first visit to the Warsaw ghetto: in a 1991 issue, Superman prevents the detonation of an atomic bomb on a train full of Jewish deportees. See Jerry Ordway (w, p) and Dennis Janke (i), *Superman: Time and Time Again* #54 (New York: DC Comics, April 1991).

2. The *New York Jewish Week* reported on this controversy, quoting prominent Holocaust scholars such as Deborah Lipstadt and Deborah Dwork, the latter claiming that these comic books represent "the ultimate trivialization of the Holocaust." Additional pressure from the Anti-Defamation League led DC Comics to formally apologize for the omission of direct references to Jews. Eric J. Greenberg, "Is Superman 'Judenrein?,'" *Jewish Week*, 25 June 1998, http://www.

thejewishweek.com/features/superman_'judenrein'; Greenberg, "Superman Editors Sorry about Omission: Comic Erases Jews from Holocaust," jweekly.com, 10 July 1998, http://www.jweekly.com/article/full/8618/superman-editors-sorry-about-omission-comic-erases-jews-from-holocaust/; Michael Colton, "Supersensitive Superman 'Muffs' Holocaust Story," *Washington Post*, 27 June 1998, https://www.washingtonpost.com/archive/lifestyle/1998/06/27/supersensitive-superman-muffs-holocaust-story/99dee982–3528–4241–b0e0–9ab689970913/.

3. Jon Bogdanove (w, p), Louise Simonson (w), and Dennis Janke (i), *Superman: The Man of Steel* #81, ed. Joey Cavalieri (New York: DC Comics, July 1998), 10, 22. At one point, the boys even declare, "Thank you, golem—for saving us! We're the ones who invented you!" Jon Bogdanove (w, p), Louise Simonson (w), and Dennis Janke (i), *Superman: The Man of Steel* #82, ed. Joey Cavalieri (New York: DC Comics, August 1998), 4.

4. Bogdanove, Simonson, and Janke, *Superman* #81, 10.

5. "Impressionistic Settings Tell Tale of 'Golem,'" *New York Tribune*, 24 July 1921, 2.

6. Bogdanove, Simonson, and Janke, *Superman* #81, 10. Following Scott McCloud, I use the term *comics* in the plural form with a singular verb to denote "juxtaposed pictorial and other images in deliberate sequence." McCloud, *Understanding Comics* (New York: Harper Perennial, 1994), 9.

7. Bogdanove, Simonson, and Janke, *Superman* #82, 1; Bogdanove, Simonson, and Janke, *Superman* #81, 17.

8. "Largely owing to Elie Wiesel's and Isaac Bashevis Singer's postwar renditions of the Prague golem with their allusions to Eastern European Jewish life, the golem's association with Eastern European Jewry dominates common perceptions today." Gelbin, *Golem Returns*, 67.

9. Daniel H. Magilow, "Jewish Revenge Fantasies in Contemporary Film," in *Jewish Cultural Aspirations: The Jewish Role in American Life: An Annual Review of the Casden Institute*, ed. Ruth Weisberg (West Lafayette, IN: Purdue University Press, 2013), 93.

10. One example, among many, of the latter approach is Arie Kaplan, *From Krakow to Krypton: Jews and Comic Books* (Philadelphia: Jewish Publication Society, 2008), 17.

11. See also Magilow, "Jewish Revenge Fantasies," 101.

12. Elizabeth Roberts Baer, *The Golem Redux: From Prague to Post-Holocaust Fiction* (Detroit: Wayne State University Press, 2012), 83. Wiesel's narrator, the gravedigger Reuven, calls the golem a "savoir" and "saint," deserving the "love and gratitude" of those who benefit from his actions. Elie Wiesel, *The Golem: The Story of a Legend* (New York: Summit Books, 1983), 12–13.

13. Kenneth Briggs, "A Protector," *New York Times*, 16 April 1984, 18.

14. Wecker, *Golem and the Jinni*, 303. "A little while later, the Golem came down from the rooftops and looked for a quiet alley where she could destroy herself. . . . She couldn't be allowed to hurt anyone again." Ibid., 311–312.

15. Magilow, "Jewish Revenge Fantasies," 104.

16. Bradford W. Wright, *Comic Book Nation: The Transformation of Youth Culture in America* (Baltimore: Johns Hopkins University Press, 2001), 13. Marvel created stories in which superheroes defend the American people, rather than the government. In the early 1970s, for example, Captain America waged "a campaign against poverty, racism, pollution, and political corruption." Ibid., 245, 233–235.

17. Falcon, a middle-class social worker in his daily life, was the first African American superhero, introduced by Marvel in 1969 as Captain America's partner. Luke Cage, a lower-class African American from the ghetto, came after him. In the 1970s, Native American and Asian American superheroes joined the ranks of Falcon and Cage. In the words of the editors, "Marvel was first among comics publishers to feature black superheroes—and villains. Marvel was first to recognize the women's movement in comics with characters like the Black Widow. And now, in this issue of *Strange Tales*, we're proud to introduce the comics' first Jewish monster-hero." Len Wein (w), John Buscema (p), and Jim Mooney (i), *Strange Tales: The Golem* #174, ed. Roy Thomas (New York: Marvel Comics, June 1974), 18.

18. For a comprehensive survey of the different appearances of the golem in the Marvel Universe, see Robert G. Weiner, "Marvel Comics and the Golem Legend," *Shofar* 29, no. 2 (2011): 51–72.

19. Mike Friedrich (w), Tony DeZuniga (p), and Steve Austin (i), *Strange Tales: The Golem* #177, ed. Roy Thomas (New York: Marvel Comics, December 1974), 32.

20. Wein, Buscema, and Mooney, *Strange Tales* #174, 1–3.

21. Ibid., 7.

22. According to Paul Breines, "The Six Day War had placed Jewish power on the stage of world history, in the words of the New Republic; the 1973 war, in which Israeli was nearly defeated, reasserted Jewish vulnerability. Jewish toughness appears to be all the more necessary and all the more ethically grounded." Breines, *Tough Jews: Political Fantasies and the Moral Dilemma of American Jewry* (New York: Basic Books, 1990), 175.

23. Wein, Buscema, and Mooney, *Strange Tales* #174, 16–17. Uncle Abe's tear is reminiscent of the imagery in *Hulk* #134, where a young girl sheds a tear on the Hulk's finger (depicted in great close-up) and brings him to agree to be a "golem" and help the oppressed peasants. Roy Thomas (w), Herb Trimpe (p), and Sal Buscema (i), *Hulk* #134 (New York: Marvel Comics, December 1970), 16.

24. Wein, Buscema, and Mooney, *Strange Tales* #174, 26–27.

25. Ibid., 27.

26. Mike Friedrich (w) and Tony DeZuniga (a), *Strange Tales: The Golem* #176, ed. Roy Thomas (New York: Marvel Comics, October 1974), 2.

27. Ibid., 2, 6.

28. As Wright contends, "Superheroes like Spider-Man endorsed liberal solutions to social problems while rejecting the extreme and violent response of both the left

and the right—an ironic position to assume, since superheroes tacitly endorsed violent means to solve problems every time they slugged it out with the bad guys." Wright, *Comic Book Nation*, 235.

29. Friedrich and DeZuniga, *Strange Tales* #176, 10–11.
30. Quoted in Wright, *Comic Book Nation*, 211.
31. Friedrich, DeZuniga, and Austin, *Strange Tales* #177, 18.
32. Ibid., 23, 32. The golem made another cameo appearance in a 1975 issue of *Marvel Two-in-One*, where he fought the Thing, and in a 1977 issue of *Invaders*, both written by Roy Thomas. In 2004–2005, the golem sustained a twelve-issue DC Comics series titled "The Monolith."
33. Robert Bernstein (w) and Joe Kubert (a), *The Challenger #3: The Golem*, in *The Joe Kubert Archives: Weird Horrors & Daring Adventures*, ed. Bill Schelly (Seattle: Fantagraphic Books, 2012), 130.
34. Jeffrey Shandler, *While America Watches: Televising the Holocaust* (New York: Oxford University Press, 1999), 133–137.
35. Wright, *Comic Book Nation*, 209.
36. Roy Thomas (w), Herb Trimpe (p), and John Severin (i), *Hulk* #133 (New York: Marvel Comics, November 1970), 8, 10.
37. Thomas, Trimpe, and Buscema, *Hulk* #134, 6.
38. At the end of the story, after the dictator has been defeated, Isaac tells the Hulk, "You were our golem—and we'll have no more kings in Morvania." But the Hulk strides away proclaiming, "Golem! Wonder what is—a golem!?" Ibid., 16, 20.
39. Friedrich, DeZuniga, and Austin, *Strange Tales* #177, 18–19.
40. Roy Thomas (w), Frank Robbins (a), and Frank Springer (a), *The Invaders: The Golem Walks Again!* #13 (New York: Marvel Comics, February 1977), 14, 22, 30.
41. Wright, *Comic Book Nation*, 30, 123.
42. Thomas, Robbins, and Springer, *Invaders* #13, 11, 15.
43. Ibid., 30–31.
44. Ibid., 15, 14.
45. Ibid, 16. When the old man identifies the golem, we see it from behind, with the yarmulke as the centerpiece. But the man, seeing only the golem's face, wonders whether this monster is one of the "others," that is, an "American superhero." Ibid. I am grateful to Yaakov Herskovitz for pointing out the resemblance of the golem to its Nazi opponent.
46. Ibid., 22.
47. The character Jacob Goldstein even claims that "this clay I've prepared is the key to power," that is, the key to Jewish power. Ibid., 11.
48. Ibid., 30.
49. Peter Milligan (w), Jim Aparo (p), and Mike Decalro (i), *Batman: The Golem of Gotham, Part Two* #632 (New York: DC Comics, July 1991), 3, 20–21.
50. At the end of the comic book, readers are privy to Batman's thoughts: the superhero accuses the Jewish survivor of "the luxury of self-hatred," claiming that

Saul believes that he is merely repeating history by killing the golem. Even though Batman forces Saul to do so, Batman resists the urge to "wallow in the idea that [he's] just doing what the Nazis did to Saul all those years ago." In this manner, the artistic team behind this comic book also get off the hook for creating a vengeful golem figure. Depicting the Holocaust survivor in a negative light does not turn them into Nazi supports. Ibid., 21.

51. Niles, Santoro, and Wachter, *Breath of Bones: A Tale of the Golem* #2, 22; Steve Niles (w), Matt Santoro (w), and Dave Wachter (a), *Breath of Bones: A Tale of the Golem* #3 (Milwaukie, OR: Dark Horse Comics, August 2013), 19–20.

52. In the essay "Trickster in a Suit of Light," Chabon refutes the notion of genre as "a thing fundamentally . . . debased, infantile, commercialized," suggesting that most of what we call respectable, highbrow literature draws on and plays with generic conventions. Michael Chabon, *Maps & Legends: Reading and Writing along the Borderlands* (New York: Harper Perennial, 2009), 8.

53. Michael Chabon, *The Amazing Adventures of Kavalier & Clay: A Novel* (New York: Random House, 2000), 85–86.

54. Ibid., 119, 121.

55. Ibid., 119, 171.

56. Ibid., 77.

57. Ibid., 136, 171.

58. Ibid., 150.

59. Ibid., 166.

60. Jerry Siegel (w) and Joe Schuster (a), "How Would Superman End World War II?," in *Superman Sunday Classics, Strips 1–183, 1939–1943* (New York: Sterling, 2006), 190.

61. Chabon, *Kavalier & Clay*, 168.

62. Ibid., 204. Jason Bainbridge describes the early superheroes of DC Universe as "premodern" and "sacred" in the sense that "they promote themselves as divine figures of retribution, offering both the promise of transcendent justice in place of equality . . . and physicality in place of rationality (accentuated by their formfitting costumes)." Bainbridge, "'Worlds within Worlds': The Role of Superheroes in the Marvel and DC Universes," in *The Contemporary Comic Book Superhero*, ed. Angela Ndalianis (New York: Routledge, 2009), 67.

63. Chabon, *Kavalier & Clay*, 465.

64. Ibid., 578. Chabon's portrayal of Joe's new aesthetic in the postwar period also pays tribute to the Jewish American artist Will Eisner, who tended, according to Robert C. Harvey, to use "black more extensively, sometimes drenching whole stories in inky shadow" and lavishing much attention on splash pages and title letters. Harvey, *The Art of the Comic Book: An Aesthetic History* (Jackson: University Press of Mississippi, 1996), 75, 78.

65. *Kavalier & Clay* is itself a novel of golemic proportions, divided into six sections that increase in length as the novel progresses (from a 66-page first section to a

171-page final section). With Joe's "comic book novel," 2,256 pages long, created in response to the loss of his family and his own traumatic front-line experience, he embraces the long form of the novel just as much as he transforms his own art.

66. Chabon, *Kavalier & Clay*, 578.

67. Thierry Groensteen, *The System of Comics*, trans. Bart Beaty and Nick Nguyen (Jackson: University Press of Mississippi 2007), 11.

68. Chabon, *Maps & Legends*, 152.

69. Charles Hatfield, *Alternative Comics: An Emerging Literature* (Jackson: University Press of Mississippi, 2005), 36–37. Hatfield's approach stands in tension with that of Groensteen, who does not view text and image as two equal components of comics but rather concludes that visual elements, unlike verbal ones, are fundamental for the production of meaning. In Joe Kavalier's transition from the *Luna Moth* fusion of word and image to the "silent" novel of *The Golem*, he exemplifies his shift from a Hatfieldian to a Groensteenian conception of the medium.

70. Chabon, *Kavalier & Clay*, 542.

71. Ibid., 577.

72. As Hillary Chute writes, Joe Kavalier's postwar art is "an intervention in popular culture" that renders comics a "potent" means of "self-expression" without debunking the conventions of the comic book. Chute, "*Ragtime, Kavalier & Clay*, and the Framing of Comics," *Modern Fiction Studies* 54, no. 2 (2008): 287–288.

73. Chabon, *Kavalier & Clay*, 582.

74. Chabon, *Maps & Legends*, 152–155.

75. In the early to mid-1950s, comic books were suspected of contributing to juvenile delinquency, and the industry was subject to Senate investigation and later to self-censorship and regulation under the "comics code." DC Comics responded to the prohibition of horror and crime with a variety of other genres, including sci-fi, romance, western, mystery, and television-show adaptations. It also revived the Flash and the Green Lantern, and in the early 1960s, Marvel debuted more human and costumeless heroes like the Fantastic Four. See Wright, *Comic Book Nation*, 183; Randy Duncan and Matthew J. Smith, *The Power of Comics: History, Form, and Culture* (New York: Continuum, 2009), 44–46.

76. Chabon, *Kavalier & Clay*, 584.

77. Ibid., 601.

78. Ibid., 52, 60–62.

79. In the mid-1950s, Sam Clay tells Joe, "They're all Jewish, superheroes. Superman, you don't think he's Jewish? Coming over from the old country, changing his name like that. Clark Kent, only a Jew would pick a name like that for himself." Ibid., 585. For this "Minsk Theory of Krypton," positing that Superman is "the ultimate assimilationist fantasy," see also Danny Fingeroth, *Disguised as Clark Kent: Jews, Comics, and the Creation of the Superhero* (New York: Continuum, 2007), 24.

80. Chabon, *Kavalier & Clay*, 584–585.

81. Andrea Most nonetheless claims that "Chabon's novel envisions a marvelous future for the comics after the 1950s: avant-garde, artistically daring, and unashamedly ethnic. And that is, in part, the way things played out." Most, "Reimagining the Jew's Body: From *Self-Loathing* to 'Grepts,'" in *You Should See Yourself: Jewish Identity in Postmodern American Culture*, ed. Vincent Brooks (New Brunswick, NJ: Rutgers University Press, 2006), 20.

82. Laurence Roth, "Contemporary American Jewish Comic Books: Abject Pasts, Heroic Futures," in *The Jewish Graphic Novel: Critical Approaches*, ed. Samantha Baskind and Ranen Omer-Sherman (New Brunswick, NJ: Rutgers University Press, 2008), 7, 4–7.

83. Chabon includes a pseudoautobiographical introduction to *The Amazing Adventures of the Escapist*, dating his first encounter with the Escapist comics back to the early 1970s and claiming that "thanks to the determination of the dedicated archivists at Dark Horse Comics," he has unearthed and reassembled for the readers "the entire patchwork epic of the Escapist." Michael Chabon, *The Amazing Adventures of the Escapist*, vol. 1, ed. Diana Schutz and Dave Land (Milwaukie, OR: Dark Horse Books, 2004), 4.

84. Ibid. Elizabeth Roberts Baer mentions the fake ad on the back as "an obvious nod to the golem," without commenting on Chabon's use of the term "metaphor." Baer, *Golem Redux*, 147.

85. For Lee Behlman, Chabon represents America as "the place to escape *to*," whereas Europe is "the place to escape *from*," but he also reconciles the American impulse to escape with "the memory of the European Jewish past and the Holocaust itself." Behlman, "The Escapist: Fantasy, Folklore, and the Pleasures of the Comic Book in Recent Jewish American Holocaust Fiction," *Shofar* 22, no. 3 (2004): 67, 69.

86. Quentin Tarantino, dir., *Inglourious Basterds*, Weinstein Company / Universal Pictures, 2009. I am grateful to Nadav Linial for pointing out this visual link between the film and the Polish variant of the golem story.

87. Quentin Tarantino, *Inglourious Basterds: A Screenplay* (New York: Weinstein Books, 2009), 21.

88. Ibid.

89. According to Todd Herzog, what both admirers and critics of the film can agree on is that Tarantino "is making cinema, not history. His sources are other movies, not historical events." The film also problematizes cinema and asks us to examine how cinema shapes history. Herzog, "'What Shall the History Books Read?': The Debate over *Inglourious Basterds* and the Limits of Representation," in *Quentin Tarantino's "Inglourious Basterds": A Manipulation of Metacinema*, ed. Robert Dassanowsky (New York: Continuum, 2012), 276, 279.

90. Galeen and Falkenberg, "Golem," 23–24.

91. Simonson, Bogdanove, and Janke, *Superman* #81, 17; Thomas, Trimpe, and Buscema, *Hulk* #134, 9, 6.

92. Steven A. Riess, "From Pike to Green with Greenberg in Between," in *The American Game: Baseball and Ethnicity*, ed. Lawrence Baldassaro and Richard A. Johnson (Carbondale: Southern Illinois University Press, 2002), 116, 126. For a survey of some of the nonfiction and fiction about the Jewish American adoration of baseball, see Eric Solomon, "Jews, Baseball, and American Fictions," in *Jews and American Popular Culture*, ed. Paul Buhle (Westport, CT: Praeger, 2007), 1–13.

93. Tarantino, *Inglourious Basterds: A Screenplay*, 31–35.

94. In a 2009 interview, Eli Roth discusses this scene—which was ultimately left on the editing table—claiming that it "humanized Donny a bit more. . . . He really feels like a Jewish warrior, and that his bat is his sword." According to Roth, "everyone was crying" during the shooting of this "incredibly effective scene." Hunter Stephenson, "Interview: Eli Roth Talks *Inglourious Basterds*, Going Method to Play the Bear Jew, Nazi Atrocities, and Quentin Tarantino's Place in History." /*Film: Blogging the Reel World*, 21 August 2009, http://www.slashfilm.com/ interview-eli-roth-talks-inglourious-basterds-going-method-to-play-the-bear-jew-nazi-atrocities-and-quentin-tarantinos-place-in-history/.

95. Magilow, "Jewish Revenge Fantasies," 104, 102.

96. "Dreyfus assaults the Third Reich with a film aesthetic they reproached: Expressionism. Like the mechanism behind cathexis, Dreyfus' disembodied head becomes a projection of our own desire for revenge." Eric Kligerman, "Reels of Justice: *Inglourious Basterds*, *The Sorrow and the Pity* and Jewish Revenge Fantasies," in Dassanowsky, *Quentin Tarantino's "Inglourious Basterds*," 155.

97. James Sturm, *The Golem's Mighty Swing* (Montreal: Drawn and Quarterly, 2001). See also Sturm's graphic work on the early African American baseball player Satchel Paige: James Sturm and Rich Tommaso, *Satchel Paige: Striking Out Jim Crow* (New York: Jump at the Sun / Hyperion, 2007).

98. Sturm, *Golem's Mighty Swing*, vii. The fictionalized team's manager, Noah Strauss, reports, "My father would be gravely disappointed knowing we are playing on the Sabbath. He will always be a greenhorn. His imagination lives in the old country. Mine lives in America and baseball is America." Ibid., 2.

99. Chabon, *Maps & Legends*, 207.

100. Sturm, *Golem's Mighty Swing*, 27, 29.

101. A previous panel shows baseball players of the "Zulu" team dressed in traditional African costumes, including straw skirts and black shirts and masks with skeletons painted on them, equating the "primitive" African costumes and the expressionist golem costume from Europe. Ibid., 32.

102. Ibid., 3.

103. Ibid., 29–30, 50.

104. Roth, "Contemporary American Jewish Comic Books," 13.

105. According to Eric L. Goldstein, in the 1910s and 1920s, Jews were also likened to African Americans, and physical traits were pointed to as evidence of their "uncivilized" nature. This strategy "reduced the anxieties of white Americans

concerning the impact of modernity and its ability to undermine the power of whiteness." Simultaneously, Jews were also perceived as "a distinct racial entity" that could not be easily categorized within the black-white dichotomy. Goldstein, *The Price of Whiteness: Jews, Race, and American Identity* (Princeton, NJ: Princeton University Press, 2006), 42, 48.

106. Sturm, *Golem's Mighty Swing*, 39, 50.

107. Ibid., 49.

108. In a 1999 interview, Sturm stated, "I'm thinking about the construction of identity of American Jews, and in [*The Golem's Mighty Swing*] I'm curious about how the media amplifies stereotypes." Eli Bishop, "Bearing Witness: An Interview with James Sturm," du9, accessed 11 September 2012, http://www.du9.org/en/entretien/bearing-witness-an-interview-with/.

109. Sturm, *Golem's Mighty Swing*, 51–52.

110. Ibid., 55.

111. Ibid., 70–71.

112. Ibid., 73, 79. Roxanne Harde claims that Sturm quickly dispels the threat of the golem as an African American male by representing Henry Bell qua golem as a weak batter. The real threat depicted in this graphic novel, in her view, is "a Jewish threat to American capitalism, itself a marker of masculinity." But although Bell does start out unimpressively, his game and behavior become more forceful and threatening as the game proceeds and as his Jewish team members undergo physical abuse. Harde, "'Give 'em another circumcision': Jewish Masculinities in *The Golem's Mighty Swing*," in *The Jewish Graphic Novel: Critical Approaches*, ed. Samantha Baskind and Ranen Omer-Sherman (New Brunswick, NJ: Rutgers University Press, 2008), 77.

113. Sturm, *Golem's Mighty Swing*, 81, 83–84.

114. Ibid., 73.

115. Ibid., 84. If blackface minstrelsy originated as a performance by Irish immigrants for white male audiences, it evolved by the end of the nineteenth and early twentieth centuries into a more heterogeneous amusement that included black-on-black minstrelsy by African Americans as well as female minstrelsy. Lori Harrison-Kahan has directed attention to the visibility of Jewish performers who capitalized on their own backgrounds, showing how they used "Jewface" and "challenged stereotypes through exaggerated performance." Harrison-Kahan, *The White Negress: Literature, Minstrelsy, and the Black-Jewish Imaginary* (New Brunswick, NJ: Rutgers University Press, 2011), 19–21. See also Merwin, *In Their Own Image*, 13.

116. Sturm, *Golem's Mighty Swing*, 85.

117. Ibid., 89–90.

CHAPTER 5. PACIFIST COMPUTERS AND JEWISH CYBORGS

1. Isaac Singer, "Why the Golem Legend Speaks to Our Time," 25.

2. Donna Haraway, *Modest_Witness@Second_Millennium.FemaleMan©_Meets_ OncoMouse™: Feminism and Technoscience* (New York: Routledge, 1997), 21.

3. Norbert Wiener, *God and Golem, Inc.: A Comment on Certain Points Where Cybernetics Impinges on Religion* (Cambridge, MA: MIT Press, 1964), 95.

4. Scholem, "Golem of Prague," 65.

5. Norbert Wiener, *Cybernetics* (New York: Wiley, 1948), 38.

6. Istvan Csicsery-Ronay Jr., "The Summa and the Fiction," *Science Fiction Studies* 40, no. 3 (2013): 454.

7. Stanislaw Lem first published the three introductions and the "Golem's Inaugural Lecture" in 1973 as part of *Imaginary Multitude*. Only in 1981 did the full version appear, including "Lecture XLIII: About Itself" and an "Afterword." The book was translated from Polish into English in 1984. See Victor Yaznevich, "Problems and Dilemmas: Lem's *Golem XIV*," trans. Peter Swirski, in *Lemography: Stanislaw Lem in the Eyes of the World*, ed. Peter Swirski and Wacław M. Osadnik (Liverpool: Liverpool University Press, 2014), 146–147.

8. Matthew Biro, *The Dada Cyborg: Visions of the New Human in Weimar Berlin* (Minneapolis: University of Minnesota Press, 2009), 2, 9.

9. Marge Piercy, *He, She, and It: A Novel* (New York: Knopf, 1991), 73.

10. Ibid., 424.

11. N. Katherine Hayles, *How We Became Posthuman: Virtual Bodies in Cybernetics, Literature, and Informatics* (Chicago: University of Chicago Press, 2010), 3, 34.

12. Hardt and Negri, *Multitude*, 12, 38–39.

13. Gelbin, *Golem Returns*, 142.

14. Hardt and Negri, *Multitude*, 11.

15. John Johnston, *The Allure of Machinic Life: Cybernetics, Artificial Life, and the New AI* (Cambridge, MA: MIT Press, 2008), 12, ix.

16. Wiener, *Cybernetics*, 51; Johnston, *Allure of Machinic Life*, 26. On the suffusion of early twentieth-century American technology with cybernetic-like notions, converging communication and control theories, see David A. Mindell, *Between Human and Machine: Feedback, Control, and Computing before Cybernetics* (Baltimore: Johns Hopkins University Press, 2002), 6.

17. Wiener, *Cybernetics*, 19; Johnston, *Allure of Machinic Life*, 26–27.

18. Wiener, *Cybernetics*, 54–55.

19. Ibid., 51; Wiener, *God and Golem, Inc.*, 52.

20. Flo Conway and Jim Siegelman, *Dark Hero of the Information Age: In Search of Norbert Wiener, the Father of Cybernetics* (New York: Basic Books, 2004), 108, 116.

21. Peter Galison, "The Ontology of the Enemy: Norbert Wiener and the Cybernetic Vision," *Critical Inquiry* 21, no. 1 (1994): 251.

22. Hayles, *How We Became Posthuman*, 106.

23. Galison, "Ontology of the Enemy," 251. Wiener approved of Le Roy MacColl's definition of the "servomechanism" as, in Galison's words, "slaved systems that used feedback." Ibid., 236n19.

24. Hayles, *How We Became Posthuman*, 106–107.

25. "Symbols matter: it counted a great deal in the reception of cybernetics that its war applications were lethal, or potentially so. . . . Would cybernetics, information theory, and 'systems thinking' have proved such a central and enduring metaphor without combat? . . . In World War II, the mechanized soldier faced his opponent as machine, and machines manifested themselves as people." Galison, "Ontology of the Enemy," 263–264.

26. Wiener, *God and Golem, Inc.*, 62, 69.

27. Ibid., 57, 59, 63.

28. Ibid., 64.

29. Norbert Wiener, *The Human Use of Human Beings: Cybernetics and Society* (Boston: Houghton Mifflin, 1954), 46, 128–129.

30. Hayles, *How We Became Posthuman*, 85–86, 110–112.

31. As in the case of Wiener's military work, many of the Israeli scientists who constructed the Weizmann Institute computers had previously worked for the Israeli Defense Forces: Zvi Reisel had been in charge of the IDF's radar workshop; Hans Jarouch, who wrote application programs, had served in the air force.

32. "Maḥshev elektroni 'golem' hufʿal be-makhon vaytsman," *Davar*, 30 December 1963, 8.

33. Avraham Peleg, "Ha-ʿmaharalim' mi-reḥovot," *Maʿariv*, 27 November 1970, 14.

34. Scholem, "Golem of Prague," 64–65.

35. Peleg, "Ha-ʿmaharalim' mi-reḥovot"; Avraham Peleg, "'Ha-maharal mi-reḥovot' kiba et 'ha-golem' ha-elektroni," *Maʿariv*, 1 January 1984, 14; "Ha-ʿgolem' baʿal ha-raʿayonot," *Maʿariv*, 17 June 1965, 4.

36. Scholem, "Golem of Prague," 63–64.

37. Ibid., 64–65.

38. Quoted in Yaznevich, "Problems and Dilemmas," 142, 145.

39. Jerzy Jarzębski, "Models of Evolution in the Writings of Stanislaw Lem," in *The Art and Science of Stanislaw Lem*, ed. Peter Swirski (Montreal: McGill-Queen's University Press, 2006), 108.

40. Stanislaw Lem, *Golem XIV*, in *Imaginary Magnitude*, trans. Marc E. Heine (San Diego, CA: Harcourt Brach Jovanovich, 1984), 103, 107, 111.

41. Ibid., 109.

42. Ibid., 110–112, 115, 171, 241.

43. Quoted in Yaznevich, "Problems and Dilemmas," 145.

44. Csicsery-Ronay, "Summa and the Fiction," 452–453, 454.

45. Lem, *Golem XIV*, 101.

46. Ibid., 102–103.

47. Ibid., 105, 107–108.

48. Ibid., 232.

49. Ibid., 105; As Keith Abney explains, Asimov's laws are supposed to "minimize conflicts. . . . Doing no harm to humans takes precedence over obeying a human,

and obeying trumps self-preservation. However, in story after story, Asimov demonstrated that three simple, hierarchically arranged rules could lead to deadlocks." Abney, "Robotics, Ethical Theory, and Metaethics: A Guide for the Perplexed," in *Robot Ethics: The Ethical and Social Implications of Robotics*, ed. Patrick Lin, Keith Abney, and George E. A. Bekey (Cambridge, MA: MIT Press, 2012), 42.

50. Ibid., 109–110, 243.
51. Ibid.,106, 110–111.
52. Ibid., 122.
53. Wiener, *God and Golem, Inc.*, 13, 21, 31, 24.
54. Lem, *Golem XIV*, 104.
55. Ibid., 120–121, 125.
56. Stanley Kubrick's intelligent computer, HAL 9000, a main protagonist in the film *2001: Space Odyssey* (produced in 1968) is also capable of learning from experience and thus becomes "as incomprehensible as a human being" and experiences a nervous breakdown, becoming antagonistic and violent. Joseph Gelmis, "Stanley Kubrick," in *The Film Director as Superstar* (London: Secker and Warburg, 1971), 307.
57. Lem, *Golem XIV*, 112, 185, 182–183.
58. Ibid, 181, 183–184.
59. Ibid., 186, 207, 206.
60. Ibid., 193, 170–171.
61. Hayles, *How We Became Posthuman*, 2–3.
62. On Wiener's distant relationship to his Jewish heritage and his late-life interest in Hinduism, see Conway and Siegelman, *Dark Hero of the Information Age*, 295–310.
63. Piercy's division of the futurist society into elite enclaves and the neglected "Glop" is reminiscent of Donna Haraway's nation of a "bimodal social structure" in which the masses of women and men of color, an expendable and exploited reserve labor force, is controlled, despite decentralization, through new communication technologies. Haraway, "A Cyborg Manifesto: Science, Technology and Socialist-Feminism in the Late Twentieth Century," in *The Cybercultures Reader*, ed. David Bell and Barbara M. Kennedy (London: Routledge, 2000), 46–49.
64. Piercy, *He, She, and It*, 206, 5.
65. Piercy, Research Files: Notes and Comments, Box 17, p. 2.
66. Raffaella Baccolini, "Gender and Genre in the Feminist Critical Dystopias of Katharine Burdekin, Margaret Atwood, and Octavia Butler," in *Future Females, the Next Generation: New Voices and Velocities in Feminist Science Fiction Criticism*, ed. Marleen S. Barr (Lanham, MD: Rowman and Littlefield, 2000), 18.
67. Elaine L. Graham, *Representations of the Post/human: Monsters, Aliens and Others in Popular Culture* (New Brunswick, NJ: Rutgers University Press, 2002), 105.

68. Piercy, *He, She, and It*, 443.

69. Ibid., 20, 19.

70. Haraway, *Modest_Witness*, 21.

71. *Neuromancer* features a team of Internet hackers who attempt to construct an artificially intelligent cyborg that would surpass the limits set by their society, via Turing's law, on such forms of intelligence. William Gibson, *Neuromancer* (New York: Berkley, 1984).

72. Piercy, *He, She, and It*, 445–446.

73. Marge Piercy, Research Files: *He, She, and It*, Box 17, Marge Piercy Papers, Special Collections Library, University of Michigan Library, Ann Arbor. As Piercy's notes indicate, she consulted Barbara Krasnoff's study of robots. Krasnoff, *Robots: Reel to Real* (New York: Arco, 1982), 23; Piercy, *He, She, and It*, 50, 73.

74. Piercy, *He, She, and It*, 50. Norbert Wiener was also concerned with the possibility that the automated machines, or else "golems" of the future, would, in his biographers' words, "unleash a devastating bounty of uncontrolled mass production and a tide of mass unemployment." Conway and Siegelman, *Dark Hero of the Information Age*, 305.

75. Haraway, "Cyborg Manifesto," 36.

76. Ibid., 35.

77. Hayles, *How We Became Posthuman*, 114–115; Biro, *Dada Cyborg*, 8; Haraway, "Cyborg Manifesto," 35.

78. Haraway, "Cyborg Manifesto," 53.

79. Piercy, *He, She, and It*, 38–39.

80. Ibid., 18.

81. Heather Hicks, "Striking Cyborgs: Reworking the 'Human' in Marge Piercy's *He, She and It*," in *Reload: Rethinking Women + Cyberculture*, ed. Mary Flanagan and Austin Booth (Cambridge, MA: MIT Press, 2002), 95–96.

82. "In living with humans I have evolved certain needs similar to yours," Yod pronounces in defiance of his creator, Avram. He also claims that his programming is not an "absolute" since he is "self-correcting," able to make changes in his own technology. Piercy, *He, She, and It*, 294, 219.

83. Biro, *Dada Cyborg*, 4; Haraway, "Cyborg Manifesto," 35. The fact that "we are all cyborgs," in Haraway's words, does not override the economic and political disparities between men and women, whites and people of color. Although Wiener never used the term, an implicit definition of the cyborg emerges from his writings, Biro explains. From the perspective of cybernetics, the human was now "produced through information and learning, . . . simultaneously more powerful and more vulnerable, . . . fundamentally interconnected with others and the environment." Biro, *Dada Cyborg*, 4–5.

84. Piercy, *He, She, and It*, 156.

85. Wiener, *Human Use of Human Beings*, 46.

86. Piercy, *He, She, and It*, 247.

87. Ibid., 230.

88. Piercy, Research Files: Notes and Comments, Box 17, p. 2.

89. Ibid., 8; Piercy, *He, She, and It*, 117.

90. Piercy, *He, She, and It*, 419.

91. Heather Hick contends that Piercy toys with the idea, through her comparison of the ghetto Jews of Prague and the cyborg Yod, of granting machines a higher status and equal pay to humans, but ultimately her "political allegiance to working men and women apparently dispels the force of her theoretical musing on economic justice for the posthuman." Hicks, "Striking Cyborgs," 94.

92. Piercy, Research Files: Notes and Comments, Box 17, p. 2.

93. Haraway, "Cyborg Manifesto," 36.

94. "By fragmenting the narrative of the future society with the narrative of sixteenth-century Prague, Piercy creates a historical science fiction novel. It is the very notion of an impure science fiction genre, with permeable borders that allow contamination from other genres, that represents resistance to hegemonic ideology." Baccolini, "Gender and Genre," 18.

95. Piercy, *He, She, and It*, 88, 304, 442, 444.

96. Marge Piercy, Research Files: Cyborgs, Robots, and Golem Legend, Box 17, Marge Piercy Papers, Special Collections Library, University of Michigan, Ann Arbor; Haraway, "Cyborg Manifesto," 38, 35.

97. Kristina Riegert, "The Reagans: Fiction, History or Propaganda?," in *Politicotainment: Television's Take on the Real*, ed. Kristina Riegert (New York: Peter Lang, 2007), 255.

98. Haraway, "Cyborg Manifesto," 38.

99. Piercy, Research Files: Notes and Comments, Box 17, p. 2.

100. Piercy, *He, She, and It*, 116, 73.

101. Piercy, Research Files: Notes and Comments, Box 17, p. 5. Joseph the golem also seems to take pleasure in killing: when he uses a club of nails against the Christian aggressors, the weapon "sings in the air as if it likes to kill," and the golem continues murdering beyond the call of duty. Piercy, *He, She, and It*, 275.

102. Piercy, *He, She, and It*, 424.

103. Ibid., 111, 287.

104. Ibid., 156.

105. Piercy, Research Files: Notes and Comments, Box 17, p. 9.

106. Piercy, *He, She, and It*, 423, 414.

107. See also Nicholas Baer's comparison of Paul Wegener's embodiment of the golem in his 1920 film to the pictorial tradition of representing the biblical figure of Samson. Baer, "Messianic Musclemen," 40–42.

108. Haraway, "Cyborg Manifesto," 36.

109. See Hayles, *How We Became Posthuman*, 3.

CONCLUSION

1. Daniel Mendelsohn, "The Robots Are Winning!," *New York Review of Books*, 4 June 2015, http://www.nybooks.com/articles/2015/06/04/robots-are-winning/.
2. Hardt and Negri, *Multitude*, 11.
3. Isaac Singer, "Why the Golem Legend Speaks to Our Time," 25.
4. Hod Lipson and Jordon B. Pollack, *The Golem Project: Automatic Design and Manufacture of Robotic LifeForms*, 2000, accessed 20 February 2016, http://www.demo.cs.brandeis.edu/golem/. See also Lipson and Pollack, "Automatic Design and Manufacture of Robotic LifeForms," *Nature* 406 (2000): 974–978.
5. Haraway, *Modest_Witness*, 21.
6. Turner, *Dramas, Fields, and Metaphors*, 31.
7. Chabon, *Amazing Adventures of Kavalier & Clay*, 77.
8. Eli Eshed and Uri Fink, *Ha-golem: Sipuro shel komiks yisra'eli* (Ben-shemen, Israel: Modan, 2003), 19, 21.

BIBLIOGRAPHY

Abel. "The Golem (in Yiddish)." *Variety*, 2 February 1922, 18.

Abney, Keith. "Robotics, Ethical Theory, and Metaethics: A Guide for the Perplexed." In *Robot Ethics: The Ethical and Social Implications of Robotics.* Edited by Patrick Lin, Keith Abney, and George E. A. Bekey, 35–53. Cambridge, MA: MIT Press, 2012.

A.F. "*Der Golem, wie er in die Welt kam.* Uraufführung: Ufa-Palast am Zoo." *Der Film: Zeitschrift für die Gesamt-interessen der Kinematographie*, 30 October 1920, 30–31.

Agnon, S. Y. [Shai Agnon]. *Ad hena.* In *Kol sipurav shel Shmuel Yosef Agnon: Ad hena,* 5–131. Tel Aviv: Schocken, 1998.

———. Archive, ARC. 4*1270, National Library of Israel, Jerusalem.

———. *Edo and Enam.* Translated by Walter Lever. In *Two Tales: "Betrothed" & "Edo and Enam,"* 141–233. New York: Schocken, 1966.

———. "Giv'at ha-ḥol." In *'Al kapot ha-man'ul,* 351–389. Tel Aviv: Schocken, 1966.

———. *Me'atsmi el 'atsmi.* Tel Aviv: Schocken, 2000.

———. *Oreaḥ nata lalun.* Tel Aviv: Schocken, 1998.

———. *Sefer sofer ve-sipur.* Tel Aviv: Schocken, 1978.

———. *Tmol shilshom.* Tel Aviv: Schocken, 1966.

———. *To This Day.* Translated by Hillel Halkin. London: Toby, 2008.

Aḥimeir, Ab"a. "Ha-maharal ve-ha-golem." *Ha-mashkif,* 9 May 1941, 5.

"Ale kritiker hobn geshribn mit bagaysterung vegn Gebil's uffirung fun 'goylem.'" *Yidishes tageblat,* 12 January 1922, 3.

Alroi, Yosef. "Ha-tokhen—eyma; ha-lashon—ma'adanot." *Ha'aretz,* 12 August 1966, 10.

Alterman, Nathan. "Magash ha-kesef / The Silver Platter." In *No Rattling of Sabers: An Anthology of Israeli War Poetry,* edited and translated by Esther Raizen, 20–22. Austin: University of Texas Press, 1995.

Altman, Rick. *Silent Film Sound.* New York: Columbia University Press, 2004.

Andrej. "*Der Golem wie er in die Welt kam*: Ufa-Palast am Zoo." *Film-Kurier,* 30 October 1920, 1.

Andrej, and Paul Wegener. "Ein Gespräch mit Paul Wegener: Einführendes zum 'Golem.'" *Film-Kurier,* 29 October 1920, 2.

Arbel, Michal. *Katuv 'al 'oro shel ha-kelev: 'Al tfisat ha-yetsira etsel Shai Agnon.* Jerusalem: Keter, 2006.

Arendt, Hannah. *The Human Condition: A Study of the Central Dilemmas Facing Modern Man.* New York: Doubleday Anchor Books, 1959.

Arnim, Freiherr von Ludwig Achim. *Isabelle von Ägypten: Kaiser Karl des Fünften erste Jugendliebe.* Vienna: Anton Schroll, 1918.

Asch, Sholem. "Kola Street." In *A Treasury of Yiddish Stories*, edited by Irving Howe and Eliezer Greenberg. 260–275. New York: Schocken, 1973.

Aschheim, Steven E. *Brothers and Strangers: The East European Jew in German and German Jewish Consciousness, 1800–1923.* Madison: University of Wisconsin Press, 1982.

Ashkenazi, Ofer. *Weimar Film and Modern Jewish Identity.* New York: Palgrave Macmillan, 2012.

Avi-Ruth. "Ha-golem." *Ha-tsofe*, 22 June 1944, 2.

Baccolini, Raffaella. "Gender and Genre in the Feminist Critical Dystopias of Katharine Burdekin, Margaret Atwood, and Octavia Butler." In *Future Females, the Next Generation: New Voices and Velocities in Feminist Science Fiction Criticism*, edited by Marleen S. Barr, 13–34. Lanham, MD: Rowman and Littlefield, 2000.

Baer, Elizabeth Roberts. *The Golem Redux: From Prague to Post-Holocaust Fiction.* Detroit: Wayne State University Press, 2012.

Baer, Nicholas. "Messianic Musclemen: *Homunculus* (1916) and *Der Golem* (1920) as Zionist Allegories." In *The Place of Politics in German Film*, edited by Martin Blumenthal-Barby, 35–52. Bielefeld, Germany: Aisthesis Verlag, 2014.

Bainbridge, Jason. "'Worlds within Worlds': The Role of Superheroes in the Marvel and DC Universes." In *The Contemporary Comic Book Superhero*, edited by Angela Ndalianis. 64–85. New York: Routledge, 2009.

Balázs, Béla. *Der sichtbare Mensch oder die Kultur des Films.* Frankfurt am Main: Suhrkamp, 2001.

———. *Early Film Theory: "Visible Man" and "The Spirit of Film."* Edited by Erica Carter. Translated by Rodney Livingstone. New York: Berghahn Books, 2010.

Bal-makhshoves. *Geklibene verk.* New York: Tsiko bikher farlag, 1953.

Band, Arnold J. *Nostalgia and Nightmare: A Study in the Fiction of S. Y. Agnon.* Berkeley: University of California Press, 1968.

Bar-Adon, Aaron. *Shai Agnon u-tḥiyat ha-lashon ha-ʿivrit.* Jerusalem: Mosad Bialik, 1977.

Bartov, Omer. *The "Jew" in Cinema: From "The Golem" to "Don't Touch My Holocaust."* Bloomington: Indiana University Press, 2005.

Behlman, Lee. "The Escapist: Fantasy, Folklore, and the Pleasures of the Comic Book in Recent Jewish American Holocaust Fiction." *Shofar* 22, no. 3 (2004): 56–71.

Behne, Adolf. "Der Golem." *Bild und Film* 4, nos. 7–8 (1914–1915): 155–157.

"Bei den Schaffenden." *Film-Kurier*, 6 May 1920.

Ben-Dov, Nitza. *Ahavot lo meʾusharot: Tiskul eroti, omanut, u-mavet be-yetsirat Agnon.* Tel Aviv: Am ʿoved, 1997.

Berkowitz, Michael. *Zionist Culture and West European Jewry before the First World War.* Cambridge: Cambridge University Press, 1993.

"Berliner Theater." *Breslauer Zeitung*, 19 January 1915.

Bernstein, Robert (w), and Joe Kubert (a). *The Challenger #3: The Golem.* In *The Joe Kubert Archives: Weird Horrors & Daring Adventures,* edited by Bill Schelly, 113–130. Seattle: Fantagraphic Books, 2012.

Biale, David. *Gershom Scholem: Kabbalah and Counter-history.* Cambridge, MA: Harvard University Press, 1982.

Bialik, Hayim Nahman. "Arieh 'ba'al guf.'" In *Hayim Nahman Bialik: Ha-sipurim,* edited by Avner Holzman, 16–57. Or Yehuda, Israel: Dvir, 2008.

Bilski, Emily D., Moshe Idel, and Elfriede Ledig. *Golem! Danger, Deliverance, and Art.* New York: Jewish Museum, 1988.

Biro, Matthew. *The Dada Cyborg: Visions of the New Human in Weimar Berlin.* Minneapolis: University of Minnesota Press, 2009.

Bishop, Eli. "Bearing Witness: An Interview with James Sturm." du9. Accessed 11 September 2012, http://www.du9.org/en/entretien/bearing-witness-an-interview-with/.

Bloch, Chajim. *Der Prager Golem: Von seiner "Geburt" bis zum seiner "Tod."* Berlin: Benjamin Harz, 1920.

———. *Israel der Gotteskämpfer: Der Baalschem von Chelm und sein Golem. Ein ostjüdisches Legendenbuch.* Berlin: Benjamin Harz, 1920.

Bogdanove, Jon (w, p), Louise Simonson (w), and Dennis Janke (i). *Superman: The Man of Steel #81.* Edited by Joey Cavalieri. New York: DC Comics, July 1998.

———. *Superman: The Man of Steel #82.* Edited by Joey Cavalieri. New York: DC Comics, August 1998.

Book of Psalms, The. Translated by Robert Alter. New York: Norton, 2007.

Booth, Allyson. *Postcards from the Trenches: Negotiating the Space between Modernism and the First World War.* Oxford: Oxford University Press, 1996.

Boyarin, Daniel. *Unheroic Conduct: The Rise of Heterosexuality and the Invention of the Jewish Man.* Berkeley: University of California Press, 1997.

Brainin, Reuven. "Der goylem (tsu der teater-umglik in washington)." *Der tog,* 5 February 1922, 6.

Breines, Paul. *Tough Jews: Political Fantasies and the Moral Dilemma of American Jewry.* New York: Basic Books, 1990.

Briggs, Kenneth. "A Protector." *New York Times,* 16 April 1984, 18.

Bril, I. L. "The Golem." *Yidishes tageblat,* 31 July 1921, 12.

Brod, Max. "Zwei jüdische Bücher." *Die neue Rundschau,* no. 2 (1918): 1362–1367.

Buber, Martin. "An die Prager Freunde." In *Das jüdische Prag: Eine Sammelschrift,* 2. Kronberg, Germany: Jüdischer Verlag, 1978.

———. Archive. ARC. Ms. Var. 350. National Library of Israel, Jerusalem.

Čapek, Karel. *R.U.R. (Rossums Universal Robots).* Translated by Claudia Novak. New York: Penguin Books, 2004.

Carter, Erica. Introduction to *Early Film Theory: "Visible Man" and "The Spirit of Film,"* by Béla Balázs, xv–xlvi. New York: Berghahn Books, 2010.

Chabon, Michael. *The Amazing Adventures of Kavalier & Clay: A Novel.* New York: Random House, 2000.

———. *The Amazing Adventures of the Escapist*. Vol. 1. Edited by Diana Schutz and Dave Land. Milwaukie, OR: Dark Horse Books, 2004.

———. *Maps & Legends: Reading and Writing along the Borderlands*. New York: Harper Perennial, 2009.

Choe, Steve. *Afterlives: Allegories of Film and Mortality in Early Weimar Germany*. New York: Bloomsbury, 2014.

Chute, Hillary. "*Ragtime, Kavalier & Clay*, and the Framing of Comics." *Modern Fiction Studies* 54, no. 2 (2008): 268–301.

Citron, Atay. "Habima's *The Golem*." *TDR: The Drama Review* 24, no. 3 (1980): 59–68.

Cohen, Aharon. "Ha-tsad ha-sheni shel ha-matbeʻa: Hirhurim bilti noḥim." *ʻAl ha-mishmar*, 31 January 1947, 8.

Cohen, Sara Simchi. "Hearth of Darkness: The Familiar, the Familial, and the Zombie." Ph.D. diss., UCLA, 2013.

Colton, Michael. "Supersensitive Superman 'Muffs' Holocaust Story." *Washington Post*, 27 June 1998. https://www.washingtonpost.com/archive/lifestyle/1998/06/27/supersensitive-superman-muffs-holocaust-story/99dee982-3528-4241-b0e0-9ab689970913/.

Conway, Flo, and Jim Siegelman. *Dark Hero of the Information Age: In Search of Norbert Wiener, the Father of Cybernetics*. New York: Basic Books, 2004.

Cooke, Mervyn. *The Hollywood Film Music Reader*. Oxford: Oxford University Press, 2010.

Csicsery-Ronay, Istvan, Jr. "The Summa and the Fiction." *Science Fiction Studies* 40, no. 3 (2013): 451–462.

Danzig, Hillel. "Minkhen sheni?" *Davar*, 1 April 1948, 6.

Dekel, Edan, and David Gantt Gurley. "How the Golem Came to Prague." *Jewish Quarterly Review* 103, no. 2 (2013): 241–258.

Deleuze, Gilles. *Cinema 1: The Movement-Image*. Translated by Hugh Tomlinson and Barbara Habberjam. Minneapolis: University of Minnesota Press, 1986.

"Der Golem, wie er in die Welt kam." Film distribution pamphlet, Deutsche Kinemathek, Berlin.

"Der goylem." *Forverts*, 18 June 1921, 10.

"Der 'goylem': A groyse sensatsiye." *Forverts*, 28 December 1921, 2.

"'Der goylem' iz endlekh do." *Yidishes tageblat*, 17 June 1921, 2.

"Der neue Wegener-Film." *Deutsche Lichtspiel-Zeitung*, 6 November 1920, 4–6.

Diederichs, Helmut H. "Nachwort: 'Ihr müßt erst etwas von guter Filmkunst verstehen': Béla Balázs als Filmtheoretiker und Medienpädagoge." In *Der sichtbare Mensch*, by Béla Balázs, 115–147. Frankfurt am Main: Suhrkamp, 2001.

Dillmann, Claudia. "Die Wirkung der Architektur ist eine magische: Hans Poelzig und der Film." In *Hans Poelzig: Bauten für den Film*, edited by Hans-Peter Reichmann, 20–75. Frankfurt am Main: Deutsches Filmmuseum, 1997.

"Di tsenirung un uffirung fun der moving piktchur 'der goylem.'" *Der tog*, 24 June 1921, 3.

Dunash. "Reshimot: Shorashim." *Ha-tsofe*, 4 November 1938, 2.

Duncan, Randy, and Matthew J. Smith. *The Power of Comics: History, Form, and Culture*. New York: Continuum, 2009.

Elsaesser, Thomas. *Weimar Cinema and After: Germany's Historical Imaginary*. London: Routledge, 2000.

"Erstaufführung des neuen Wegenerfilms in den U.-T.-Theatern." *Deutscher Kurier*, 15 January 1915.

Eshed, Eli, and Uri Fink. *Ha-golem: Sipuro shel komiks yisra'eli*. Ben-shemen, Israel: Modan, 2003.

Even, Yitskhok. "Der goylem in Gebil's teater." *Morgen zhurnal*, 6 January 1922, 5.

Ezrahi, Sidra DeKoven. "S. Y. Agnon's Jerusalem: Before and after 1948." *Jewish Social Studies* 18, no. 3 (2012): 136–152.

Filma'i. "'Ha-golem' be-'eney tsarfati." *Davar*, 14 July 1948, 3.

Fingeroth, Danny. *Disguised as Clark Kent: Jews, Comics, and the Creation of the Superhero*. New York: Continuum, 2007.

Finkel, Shimon. *Aharon Meskin ve-agadat "ha-golem": Prakim le-zikhro*. Tel Aviv: 'Eked, 1980.

Foucault, Michel. *Discipline and Punish: The Birth of the Prison*. Translated by Alan Sheridan. New York: Vintage Books, 1995.

Friedrich, Mike (w), and Tony DeZuniga (a). *Strange Tales: The Golem* #176. Edited by Roy Thomas. New York: Marvel Comics Group, October 1974.

Friedrich, Mike (w), Tony DeZuniga (p), and Steve Austin (i). *Strange Tales: The Golem* #177. Edited by Roy Thomas. New York: Marvel Comics Group, December 1974.

Fuchs, Esther. "Mivne ha-'alila ha-ironit be-sipurei Shai Agnon 'al-pi 'Ad hena.'" *Bikoret u-farshanut: Ktav-'et bein tehumi leheker sifrut ve-tarbut* 20 (1985): 25–44.

"Funfte vokh fun 'goylem' in kreyterion teater." *Yidishes tageblat*, 17 July 1921, 11.

Fussell, Paul. *The Great War and Modern Memory*. Oxford: Oxford University Press, 2000.

Gabel, Max [Maks Gebil]. "A brif fun Maks Gebil." *Forverts*, 17 February 1922, 3.

———. "Maks Gebil dankt dem groyse oylem un der prese." *Forverts*, 14 January 1922, 4.

Galeen, Henrik, and Paul Falkenberg. "The Golem." In *Film-Materialien: Henrik Galeen*, edited by Hans-Michael Bock and Wolfgang Jacobson, 20–24. Hamburg and Berlin: CineGraph, 1992.

Galison, Peter. "The Ontology of the Enemy: Norbert Wiener and the Cybernetic Vision." *Critical Inquiry* 21, no. 1 (1994): 228–266.

Gassner, John. *The Theatre in Our Times: A Survey of the Men, Materials, and Movements in the Modern Theatre*. New York: Crown, 1954.

Gelbin, Cathy. *The Golem Returns: From German Romantic Literature to Global Jewish Culture, 1808–2008*. Ann Arbor: University of Michigan Press, 2011.

Gelmis, Joseph. "Stanley Kubrick." In *The Film Director as Superstar*, 293–316. London: Secker and Warburg, 1971.

Gibson, William. *Neuromancer*. New York: Berkley, 1984.

Gillerman, Sharon. "A Kinder Gentler Strongman? Siegmund Breitbart in Eastern Europe." In *Jewish Masculinities: German Jews, Gender, and History*, edited by Benjamin Maria Baader, Sharon Gillerman, and Paul Frederick Lerner, 197–209. Bloomington: Indiana University Press, 2012.

Glantz-Leyeles, Aaron. "Leyviks 'goylem' un habima-uffirung." *Der tog*, 21 May 1948, 9.

Gluzman, Michael. *Ha-guf ha-tsiyoni: Le'umiyut, migdar, u-miniyut ba-sifrut ha-ʿivrit ha-ḥadasha*. Tel Aviv: Ha-kibbutz Hame'uḥad, 2007.

Göbel, Wolfram. *Der Kurt Wolff Verlag 1913–1930: Expressionismus als verlegerische Aufgabe*. Frankfurt am Main: Buchhändler-Vereinigung, 1977.

Goldsmith, Arnold L. *The Golem Remembered, 1909–1980: Variations of a Jewish Legend*. Detroit: Wayne State University Press, 1981.

Goldstein, Eric L. *The Price of Whiteness: Jews, Race, and American Identity*. Princeton, NJ: Princeton University Press, 2006.

"'Golem, The,' H. Levik's Dramatization of Medieval Legend, Offered by Habimah at Broadway." *New York Times*, 17 May 1948, 22.

"'Goylem' breyngt gepakte hayzer far kreyterion teater." *Yidishes tageblat*, 6 July 1921, 2.

Goylem's Eynikel. "Der prager goylem." *Forverts*, 25 February 1922, 7.

Grady, Tim. *The German-Jewish Soldiers of the First World War in History and Memory*. Liverpool: Liverpool University Press, 2011.

Graham, Elaine L. *Representations of the Post/human: Monsters, Aliens and Others in Popular Culture*. New Brunswick, NJ: Rutgers University Press, 2002.

Gray, Richard T. *About Face: German Physiognomic Thought from Lavater to Auschwitz*. Detroit: Wayne State University Press, 2004.

Greenberg, Eric J. "Is Superman 'Judenrein?'" *Jewish Week*, 25 June 1998, http://www.thejewishweek.com/features/superman_'judenrein'.

———. "Superman Editors Sorry about Omission: Comic Erases Jews from Holocaust." jweekly.com, 10 July 1998, http://www.jweekly.com/article/full/8618/superman-editors-sorry-about-omission-comic-erases-jews-from-holocaust/.

Greenberg, Uri Tzvi. "Mustafa Zahiv / Royte epel fun veybeymer." In *Gezamlte verk*, vol. 2, 436–444. Jerusalem: Magnes Press, 1979.

Greve, Ludwig, Margot Pehle, and Heidi Westhoff, eds. *Hätte ich das Kino! Die Schriftsteller und der Stummfilm*. Munich: Kösel, 1976.

Groensteen, Thierry. *The System of Comics*. Translated by Bart Beaty and Nick Nguyen. Jackson: University Press of Mississippi, 2007.

Guerin, Francis. *A Culture of Light: Cinema and Technology in 1920s Germany*. Minneapolis: University of Minnesota Press, 2005.

Hagbi, Yaniv. *Language, Absence, Play: Judaism and Superstructuralism in the Poetics of S. Y. Agnon*. Syracuse, NY: Syracuse University Press, 2009.

Hagner, Michael. "Verwundete Gesichter, verletzte Gehirne: Zur Deformation des Kopfes im Ersten Weltkrieg." In *Gesichter der Weimarer Republik: Eine physiogno-*

mische Kulturgeschichte, edited by Claudia Schmölders and Sander Gilman, 78–95. Cologne: DuMont, 2000.

"Ha-'golem' ba'al ha-ra'ayonot." *Ma'ariv*, 17 June 1965, 4.

"Ha-haḥlatot shel ha-liga ha-'aravit." *Ha-mashkif*, 9 December 1945, 2.

"Ha-hashba'a be-tel aviv: Ne'um Shartok." *Ha-tsofe*, 29 June 1948, 4.

Hake, Sabine. *The Cinema's Third Machine: Writing on Film in Germany, 1907–1933*. Lincoln: University of Nebraska Press, 1992.

Halberstam, Judith. *Skin Shows: Gothic Horror and the Technology of Monsters*. Durham, NC: Duke University Press, 1995.

Halpern, Moyshe-Leyb. *In New York: A Selection*. Edited and translated by Kathryn Hellerstein. Philadelphia: Jewish Publication Society of America, 1982.

———. "Shalamouses." In *American Yiddish Poetry: A Bilingual Anthology*, edited and translated by Benjamin Harshav and Barbara Harshav, 486–489. Berkeley: University of California Press, 1986.

Hansen, Miriam. *Babel and Babylon: Spectatorship in American Silent Film*. Cambridge, MA: Harvard University Press, 1991.

Haraway, Donna. "A Cyborg Manifesto: Science, Technology and Socialist-Feminism in the Late Twentieth Century." In *The Cybercultures Reader*, edited by David Bell and Barbara M. Kennedy, 34–65. London: Routledge, 2000.

———. *Modest_Witness@Second_Millennium.FemaleMan©_Meets_OncoMouse™: Feminism and Technoscience*. New York: Routledge, 1997.

Harde, Roxanne. "'Give 'em another circumcision': Jewish Masculinities in *The Golem's Mighty Swing*." In *The Jewish Graphic Novel: Critical Approaches*, edited by Samantha Baskind and Ranen Omer-Sherman, 64–81. New Brunswick, NJ: Rutgers University Press, 2008.

Hardt, Michael, and Antonio Negri. *Multitude: War and Democracy in the Age of Empire*. New York: Penguin, 2004.

Harrison-Kahan, Lori. *The White Negress: Literature, Minstrelsy, and the Black-Jewish Imaginary*. New Brunswick, NJ: Rutgers University Press, 2011.

Harshav, Benjamin, and Barbara Harshav. "H. Leyvik." In *American Yiddish Poetry: A Bilingual Anthology*, edited and translated by Benjamin Harshav and Barbara Harshav, 674–677. Berkeley: University of California Press, 1986.

Harvey, Robert C. *The Art of the Comic Book: An Aesthetic History*. Jackson: University Press of Mississippi, 1996.

Hasak-Lowy, Todd. "A Mad Dog's Attack on Secularized Hebrew: Rethinking Agnon's *Temol shilshom*." *Prooftexts* 24 (2004): 167–198.

Hasan-Rokem, Galit. "The Cobbler of Jerusalem in Finnish Folklore." In *The Wandering Jew: Essays in the Interpretation of a Legend*, edited by Galit Hasan-Rokem and Alan Dundes, 119–153. Bloomington: Indiana University Press, 1986.

Hatfield, Charles. *Alternative Comics: An Emerging Literature*. Jackson: University Press of Mississippi, 2005.

Hayles, N. Katherine. *How We Became Posthuman: Virtual Bodies in Cybernetics, Literature, and Informatics.* Chicago: University of Chicago Press, 2010.

Herzog, Todd. "'What Shall the History Books Read?': The Debate over *Inglourious Basterds* and the Limits of Representation." In *Quentin Tarantino's "Inglourious Basterds": A Manipulation of Metacinema,* edited by Robert Dassanowsky, 271–296. New York: Continuum, 2012.

Heskes, Irene. *Passport to Jewish Music: Its History, Traditions, and Culture.* Westport, CT: Greenwood, 1994.

———. *Yiddish American Popular Songs, 1895 to 1950: A Catalog Based on the Lawrence Marwick Roster of Copyright Entries.* Washington, DC: Library of Congress, 1992.

Hicks, Heather. "Striking Cyborgs: Reworking the 'Human' in Marge Piercy's *He, She and It.*" In *Reload: Rethinking Women + Cyberculture,* edited by Mary Flanagan and Austin Booth, 85–106. Cambridge, MA: MIT Press, 2002.

Holl, Susanne, and Friedrich Kittler. "Ablösen des Streifens vom Buche: Eine Allegorese von Wegeners drei Golemfilmen." *Cinema. Blickführung,* no. 41 (1996): 101–112.

Holzman, Avner. "Hebetim politiyim be-sifrut milḥemet ha-ʿatsmaʾut." In *Politika be-milḥama: Kovets meḥkarim ʿal ha-ḥevra ha-ʾezraḥit be-milḥemet ha-ʿatsmaʾut,* edited by Mordechai Bar-On and Meir Chazan, 555–579. Jerusalem: Yad Ben Tsvi, 2014.

Horowitz, Dani. *Yossele golem.* In *Arbaʿa maḥazot,* edited by Shimon Levy, 59–102. Ramat Aviv, Israel: Safra, 2007.

"Hot shoyn gezungen ʿeyli, eyli' hunderte mol." *Yidishes tageblat,* 29 June 1922, 10.

Howe, Irving, and Eliezer Greenberg. Introduction to *A Treasury of Yiddish Stories,* edited by Irving Howe and Eliezer Greenberg, 1–71. New York: Schocken, 1973.

"Hundreds, Dead or Injured, Buried under Ruins as Roof of Knickerbocker Theater Collapses; Rescuers Battle Storm That Paralyzes City." *Washington Post,* 29 January 1922, 1–2.

Huyssen, Andreas. *After the Great Divide: Modernism, Mass Culture, Postmodernism.* Bloomington: Indiana University Press, 1986.

Idel, Moshe. *Golem: Jewish Magical and Mystical Traditions and the Artificial Anthropoid.* Albany: State University of New York Press, 1990.

Ihering, Herbert. "Von Wegener zu Rosenberg." In *Herbert Ihering: Filmkritiker,* 273–274. Munich: Edition Text + Kritik, 2011.

"Impressionistic Settings Tell Tale of 'Golem.'" *New York Tribune,* 24 July 1921, 2.

"Injunction Refused." *Variety,* 24 February 1922, 12.

"In Picture Theaters: Criterion." *New York Tribune,* 19 June 1921, 2.

Isenberg, Noah. "Of Monsters and Magicians: Paul Wegener's *The Golem: How He Came into the World* (1920)." In *Weimar Cinema: An Essential Guide to Classic Films of the Era,* edited by Noah Isenberg, 33–54. New York: Columbia University Press, 2009.

"Jacob Sandler's Song." *New York Times,* 14 August 1921, 68.

Jarzębski, Jerzy. "Models of Evolution in the Writings of Stanislaw Lem." In *The Art and Science of Stanislaw Lem,* edited by Peter Swirski, 104–116. Montreal: McGill-Queen's University Press, 2006.

Johnston, John. *The Allure of Machinic Life: Cybernetics, Artificial Life, and the New AI.* Cambridge, MA: MIT Press, 2008.

Kaes, Anton. *Shell Shock Cinema: Weimar Culture and the Wounds of War.* Princeton, NJ: Princeton University Press, 2009.

Kang, Minsoo. *Sublime Dreams of Living Machines: The Automaton in the European Imagination.* Cambridge, MA: Harvard University Press, 2011.

Kaniuk, Yoram. "Ha-ḥaverim shel Beni." *Davar,* 4 May 1973, 55.

———. "Ha-sipurim she-nihiyu le-sipur ḥayay." In *Me'ayin naḥalti et shiri: Sofrim u-meshorerim medabrim 'al mekorot hashra'a,* edited by Ruth Karton-Blum, 65–74. Tel Aviv: Yedi'ot aḥronot, 2002.

———. *Himmo, King of Jerusalem.* Translated by Yosef Shachter. New York: Atheneum, 1966.

———. *Ḥimo melekh yerushalayim.* Tel Aviv: Am 'oved, 2004.

———. *Tasha"ḥ.* Tel Aviv: Yedi'ot aḥaronot, 2010.

Kaplan, Arie. *From Krakow to Krypton: Jews and Comic Books.* Philadelphia: Jewish Publication Society, 2008.

Keisari, Uri. "Drishat shalom le-'Habima.'" *Ma'ariv,* 10 May 1948, 7.

Kieval, Hillel J. "Pursuing the Golem of Prague: Jewish Culture and the Invention of a Tradition." *Modern Judaism* 17, no. 1 (1997): 1–20.

Kisch, Egon Erwin. "Dem Golem auf der Spur." In *Der rasende Reporter,* 293–309. Berlin: Aufbau-Verlag, 1990.

———. "The Golem." In *Tales from Seven Ghettos,* translated by Edith Bone, 153–165. London: Robert Anscombe, 1948.

Kittler, Friedrich A. "Romanticism—Psychoanalysis—Film: A History of the Double." Translated by Stefanie Harris. In *Literature, Media, Information Systems: Essays,* edited by John Johnston, 85–100. Amsterdam: G+B Arts International, 1997.

Kligerman, Eric. "Reels of Justice: *Inglourious Basterds, The Sorrow and the Pity* and Jewish Revenge Fantasies." In *Quentin Tarantino's "Inglourious Basterds": A Manipulation of Metacinema,* edited by Robert Dassanowsky, 135–162. New York: Continuum, 2012.

Koch, Gertrud. "Béla Balázs: The Physiognomy of Things." *New German Critique* 40 (1987): 167–177.

Korrodi, Eduard. "Golem—Wegener—Poelzig." In *Kein Tag ohne Kino: Schriftsteller über den Stummfilm,* edited by Fritz Güttinger, 323–326. Frankfurt am Main: Deutsches Filmmuseum, 1984.

———. "Paul Wegener im Kino." In *Kein Tag ohne Kino: Schriftsteller über den Stummfilm,* edited by Fritz Güttinger, 322–323. Frankfurt am Main: Deutsches Filmmuseum, 1984.

Kovessy, Albert. *Der goylem: Muzikalisher legend in dray akten mit a prolog.* Translated by Max Schweid. Adapted by Max Gabel. D 59524, Lawrence Marwick Collection of Copyrighted Yiddish Plays, Library of Congress, Washington, DC.

Krasnoff, Barbara. *Robots: Reel to Real.* New York: Arco, 1982.

"Kritiken über das Filmwerk: *Der Golem, wie er in die Welt kam.*" Ufa distribution pamphlet. Schriftgutarchiv. Stiftung Deutsche Kinemathek, Berlin.

"Landsbergers Golem-Musik." *Die Lichtbild-Bühne*, 13 November 1920, 22.

Laor, Dan. *Ḥayey Agnon: Biografya*. Jerusalem: Schocken, 1998.

Ledig, Elfriede. *Paul Wegeners Golem-Filme im Kontext fantastischer Literatur: Grundfragen zur Gattungsproblematik fantastischen Erzählens*. Munich: Verlaggemeinschaft, 1989.

Leed, Eric J. *No Man's Land: Combat and Identity in World War I*. Cambridge: Cambridge University Press, 1979.

Leivick, H. [H. Leyvik]. *Der goylem: A dramatishe poeme in akht bilder*. New York: Amerika, 1921.

———. *Die geule komedye: Der goylem kholemt*. Chicago: Yiddish Culture Society, L. M. Stein, 1934.

———. "Di keyten fun mashiaḥ." In *Ale verk fun H. Leyvik: Dramatishe poemes*, 393–418. New York: H. Leyvik yubiley-komitet, 1940.

———. "Di literatur in klem." H. Leivick Collection: Manuscripts, File 10. YIVO Archive, New York.

———. *The Golem*. In *The Golem: A New Translation of the Classic Play and Selected Short Stories*, edited and translated by Joachim Neugroschel, 111–254. New York: Norton, 2006.

———. "Yossele goylem fun prag." In *H. Leyvik: Eseyen un redes*, edited by Y. Zilberberg, 60–65. New York: Alveltlekhn Yidishn Kultur-Kongres, 1963.

Lem, Stanislaw. *Golem XIV*. In *Imaginary Magnitude*, translated by Marc E. Heine, 97–248. San Diego, CA: Harcourt Brace Jovanovich, 1984.

Liebes, Yehuda. *Torat ha-yetsira shel sefer ha-yetsira*. Tel Aviv: Schocken, 2000.

Lipshitz, Yair. "Ge'ula megulemet ba-guf: 'Avar, 'atid ve-'avodat hasaḥkan be-hatsagat 'ha-golem' shel 'Habima.'" *Reshit* 1 (2009): 279–304.

Lifson, David S. *The Yiddish Theater in America*. New York: Thomas Yoseloff, 1965.

Lipson, Hod, and Jordon B. Pollack. "Automatic Design and Manufacture of Robotic LifeForms." *Nature* 406 (2000): 974–978.

———. *The Golem Project: Automatic Design and Manufacture of Robotic LifeForms*. 2000. Accessed 20 February 2016, http://www.demo.cs.brandeis.edu/golem/.

Loshitzky, Yosefa. "Kalat ha-met: Falotsentrizem u-milḥama be-Ḥimo melekh yerushalayim." In *Mabatim fiktiviyim: 'Al kolno'a yisra'eli*, edited by Orly Lubin, Nurith Gertz, and Judd Ne'eman, 247–260. Tel Aviv: Open University of Israel, 1998.

Lube, Manfred. *Gustav Meyrink: Beiträge zur Biographie und Studien zu seiner Kunsttheorie*. Graz, Austria: Technische Universität Graz, 1980.

Lukács, Georg. "Gedanken zu einer Ästhetik des Kinos." In *Kino-Debatte. Literatur und Film 1909–1929*, edited by Anton Kaes, 112–118. Tübingen, Germany: Max Niemeyer, 1978.

———. "Thoughts toward an Aesthetics of Cinema." *Polygraph* 13 (2001): 13–18.

Magilow, Daniel H. "Jewish Revenge Fantasies in Contemporary Film." In *Jewish Cultural Aspirations: The Jewish Role in American Life; An Annual Review of the Casden Institute*, edited by Ruth Weisberg, 89–110. West Lafayette, IN: Purdue University Press, 2013.

"Maḥshev elektroni 'golem' hufʿal be-makhon vaytsman." *Davar*, 30 December 1963, 8.

Markish, Peretz. "From *The Mound*." In *The Penguin Book of Modern Yiddish Verse*. Translated by Leonard Wolf. Edited by Irving Howe, Ruth R. Wisse, and Khone Shmeruk, 352–367. New York: Viking Penguin, 1987.

Mayer, Sigrid. *Golem: Die literarische Rezeption eines Stoffes*. Bern, Switzerland: Herbert Lang, 1975.

McCloud, Scott. *Understanding Comics*. New York: Harper Perennial, 1994.

M.D. "Davar ha-yom." *Davar*, 21 July 1948, 1.

"Medieval Ghetto in the Center of Action in 'Golem' Film." *New York Tribune*, 19 June 1921, 2.

Mendelsohn, Daniel. "The Robots Are Winning!" *New York Review of Books*, 4 June 2015, http://www.nybooks.com/articles/2015/06/04/robots-are-winning/.

Mendelson-Maoz, Adia. "Ba-karḥon haze yekhola litsmoʿaḥ kalanit. Ḥimo melekh yerushalayim: Bein etika le-estetika." In *Gufi he-karoʿa melavlev: ʿAl maḥala ve-refuʿa. Maʿamarim u-kitei sifrut*, edited by Yehosheva Bentov, 203–210. Jerusalem: Carmel, 2009.

Merwin, Ted. *In Their Own Image: New York Jews in Jazz Age Popular Culture*. New Brunswick, NJ: Rutgers University Press, 2006.

Meyrink, Gustav. *Der Golem*. Frankfurt am Main: Ullstein, 1991.

———. *The Golem*. Translated by Madge Pemberton. New York: Dover, 1986.

Milligan, Peter (w), Jim Aparo (p), and Mike Decalro (i). *Batman: The Golem of Gotham, Part Two #632*. New York: DC Comics, July 1991.

Mindell, David A. *Between Human and Machine: Feedback, Control, and Computing before Cybernetics*. Baltimore: Johns Hopkins University Press, 2002.

Mintz, Alan, and Anne Golomb Hoffman. "The Artist in the Land of Israel." In *A Book That Was Lost and Other Stories by S. Y. Agnon*, edited by Alan Mintz and Anne Golomb Hoffman, 79–86. New York: Schocken, 1995.

Mishnah, The. Translated by Herbert Danby. Peabody, MA: Hendrickson Publishers Marketing, 2011.

Most, Andrea. "Reimagining the Jew's Body: From *Self-Loathing* to 'Grepts.'" In *You Should See Yourself: Jewish Identity in Postmodern American Culture*, edited by Vincent Brooks, 19–36. New Brunswick, NJ: Rutgers University Press, 2006.

Mukerji, Chandra, and Michael Schudson. Introduction to *Rethinking Popular Culture: Contemporary Perspectives in Cultural Studies*, edited by Chandra Mukerji and Michael Schudson, 1–62. Berkeley: University of California Press, 1991.

Nahshon, Edna. "The Yiddish Theater in America: A Brief Historical Overview." In *The Lawrence Marwick Collection of Copyrighted Yiddish Plays at the Library of Congress: An Annotated Bibliography*, by Zachary M. Baker, xiii–xviii. Washington,

DC: Library of Congress, 2004. http://www.loc.gov/rr/amed/marwick/marwickbibliography.pdf.

Niles, Steve (w), Matt Santoro (w), and Dave Wachter (a), *Breath of Bones: A Tale of the Golem #2*. Milwaukie, OR: Dark Horse Comics, July 2013.

———. *Breath of Bones: A Tale of the Golem #3*. Milwaukie, OR: Dark Horse Comics, August 2013.

Nordau, Max. "Jewry of Muscle." June 1903. In *The Jew in the Modern World: A Documentary History*, 3rd ed., edited by Paul R. Mendes-Flohr and Jehuda Reinharz, 616–617. New York: Oxford University Press, 2011.

Noverstern, Avrom. *Kesem ha-dimdumim: Apokalipsa u-meshihiyut be-sifrut yidish*. Jerusalem: Magnes Press, 2003.

"Nyu york zet dem 'goylem.'" *Yidishes tageblat*, 24 June 1921, 12.

Oksiloff, Assenka. *Picturing the Primitive: Visual Culture, Ethnography, and Early German Cinema*. New York: Palgrave, 2001.

Ordway, Jerry (w, p), Karl Kessel (w, p, i), and Dennis Janke (i). *Superman: Time and Time Again #54*. New York: DC Comics, April 1991.

Osherovitch, M. "An alte yidishe maysele in di movies af brodvey." *Forverts*, 4 July 1921, 7.

Ozick, Cynthia. *The Puttermesser Papers*. New York: Knopf, 1997.

Papapetros, Spyros. *On the Animation of the Inorganic: Art, Architecture, and the Extension of Life*. Chicago: University of Chicago Press, 2012.

Peleg, Avraham. "Ha-'maharalim' mi-rehovot." *Ma'ariv*, 27 November 1970, 14.

———. "'Ha-maharal mi-rehovot' kiba et 'ha-golem' ha-elektroni." *Ma'ariv*, 1 January 1984, 14.

Peretz, Isaac Leib. *Far kleyn un groys*. Vilnius, Lithuania: Vilner Farlag fun B. Kletskin, 1925.

———. *The Golden Chain*. Translated by Marvin Zuckerman. In *Selected Works of I. L. Peretz*, edited by Marvin Zuckerman and Marion Herbst, 398–468. Malibu, CA: Pangloss, 1996.

———. "The Golem." Translated by Ruth R. Wisse. In *The I. L. Peretz Reader*, edited by Ruth R. Wisse, 130–131. New Haven, CT: Yale University Press, 2002.

———. *A Night in the Old Marketplace*. Translated by Ruth R. Wisse. In *The I. L. Peretz Reader*, edited by Ruth R. Wisse, 361–432. New Haven: Yale University Press, 2002.

"Picture Plays and People." *New York Times*, 9 October 1921, 75.

Piercy, Marge. *He, She, and It: A Novel*. New York: Knopf, 1991.

———. Research Files: Cyborgs, Robots, and Golem Legend. Box 17. Marge Piercy Papers. Special Collections Library, University of Michigan, Ann Arbor.

———. Research Files: *He, She, and It*. Box 17. Marge Piercy Papers. Special Collections Library, University of Michigan Library, Ann Arbor.

———. Research Files: Notes and Comments. Box 17. Marge Piercy Papers. Special Collections Library, University of Michigan Library, Ann Arbor.

Polda, Oscar. "Palast- und Reichshallen-Lichtspiele. Gastspiel Paul Wegener. *Der Golem*." *Kieler Neueste Nachrichten*, 7 March 1915.

Polland, Annie, and Daniel Soyer. *Emerging Metropolis: New York Jews in the Age of Immigration, 1840–1920*. Vol. 2 of *City of Promises: A History of the Jews of New York*. New York: NYU Press, 2012.

Presner, Todd Samuel. *Muscular Judaism: The Jewish Body and the Politics of Regeneration*. London Routledge, 2007.

Rabbinowitz, A. S. "Der Golem." *Die Welt* 34 (1901): 9–10.

"Reinhardt's Art on Screen to Be Seen Soon on Broadway." *New York Tribune*, 10 April 1921, 4.

Riegert, Kristina. "The Reagans: Fiction, History or Propaganda?" In *Politicotainment: Television's Take on the Real*, edited by Kristina Riegert, 237–266. New York: Peter Lang, 2007.

Riess, Steven A. "From Pike to Green with Greenberg in Between." In *The American Game: Baseball and Ethnicity*, edited by Lawrence Baldassaro and Richard A. Johnson, 116–141. Carbondale: Southern Illinois University Press, 2002.

Rivkin, Baruch. "Untern tsaykhen fun goylem." In *H. Leyvik: Zayne lider un dramatishe verk*, 165–170. Buenos Aires: Yidbukh, 1955.

Roberts, Ian. *German Expressionist Cinema*. London: Wallflower, 2008.

Robinzon, S. "Mit 300 yor tsurik un 300 yor shpeter: Der 'goylem' un der 'letster yid.'" *Yidishes tageblat*, 27 January 1922, 4.

Rogoff, Hillel. "'Der goylem': A dramatishe poeme fun H. Leyvik." *Forverts*, 5 June 1921, 2.

———. "'Der goylem': A prakhtfole opereta in Gebil's teater." *Forverts*, 13 January 1922, 3, 5.

Rosenberg, Warren. *Legacy of Rage: Jewish Masculinity, Violence, and Culture*. Amherst: University of Massachusetts Press, 2001.

Rosenberg, Yudl. *The Golem or The Miraculous Deeds of Rabbi Leyb*. In *The Golem: A New Translation of the Classic Play and Selected Stories*, edited and translated by Joachim Neugroschel, 1–76. New York: Norton, 2006.

———. *Nifla'ot Maharal*. In *Ha-golem mi-prag u-ma'asim nifla'im aherim*, edited by Eli Yassif, 75–139. Jerusalem: Mosad Bi'alik, 1991.

———. *Seyfer nifloes Maharal*. Jerusalem: Yudl Rosenberg, 1967.

Rosenfeld, Beate. *Die Golemsage und ihre Verwertung in der deutschen Literatur*. Wrocław, Poland: Dr. Hans Priebatsch, 1934.

Roskies, David G. *Against the Apocalypse: Responses to Catastrophe in Modern Jewish Culture*. Cambridge, MA: Harvard University Press, 1984.

Roth, Laurence. "Contemporary American Jewish Comic Books: Abject Pasts, Heroic Futures." In *The Jewish Graphic Novel: Critical Approaches*, edited by Samantha Baskind and Ranen Omer-Sherman, 3–21. New Brunswick, NJ: Rutgers University Press, 2008.

Rubinstein, Ts. H. "Di uffirung fun 'goylem' in Gebil's teater." *Der tog*, 23 December 1921, 3.

Salus, Hugo. *Ernte*. Munich: Albert Langen, 1903.

"Schauspielkunst und Krieg." *Berliner Börsen-Courier*, 9 January 1915.

Scheffauer, Herman G. "The Vivifying Space." In *Introduction to the Art of Movies*, edited by Lewis Jacobs, 76–85. New York: Noonday, 1960.

Scholem, Gershom. "Die Vorstellung vom Golem in ihren tellurischen und magischen Beziehungen." In *Zur Kabbala und ihrer Symbolik*, 209–259. Frankfurt am Main: Suhrkamp, 2000.

———. *From Berlin to Jerusalem: Memories of My Youth*. Translated by Harry Zohn. New York: Schocken, 1988.

———. "The Golem of Prague and the Golem of Rehovoth." *Commentary* 41, no. 1 (1966): 62–65.

———. "The Idea of the Golem." In *On the Kabbalah and Its Symbolism*, translated by Ralph Manheim, 158–204. New York: Schocken, 1969.

———. "The Star of David: History of a Symbol." Translated by Michael A. Meyer. In *The Messianic Idea in Judaism and Other Essays on Jewish Spirituality*, 255–281. New York: Schocken, 1995.

———. "Toward an Understanding of the Messianic Idea in Judaism." Translated by Michael A. Meyer. In *The Messianic Idea in Judaism and Other Essays on Jewish Spirituality*, 1–36. New York: Schocken, 1971.

Schönemann, Heide. *Paul Wegener: Frühe Moderne im Film*. Stuttgart, Germany: Menges, 2003.

"Screen, The." *New York Times*, 20 June 1921, 20.

Sefiker. "'Abdala ha-golem ha-briti hikhriz 'aleynu milḥama." *Yedi'ot aḥaronot*, 27 April 1948, 1.

Seltzer, Mark. *Bodies and Machines*. New York: Routledge, 1992.

Shandler, Jeffrey. *While America Watches: Televising the Holocaust*. New York: Oxford University Press, 1999.

Sharet, Moshe. *Davar davur: Dvarim she-be'al pe be-zirot pnim va-ḥuts, 1948*. Edited by Yaakov Sharet and Rina Sharet. Tel Aviv: Ha-'amuta le-moreshet Moshe Sharet, 2013.

Shepard, Richard F. "'Yossele Golem' in Its World Premiere." *New York Times*, 18 April 1982, 65.

Sieg, Katrin. *Ethnic Drag: Performing Race, Nation, Sexuality in West Germany*. Ann Arbor: University of Michigan Press, 2002.

Siegel, Jerry (w), and Joe Schuster (a). "How Would Superman End World War II?" In *Superman Sunday Classics, Strips 1–183, 1939–1943*, 186–190. New York: Sterling, 2006.

Simmel, Georg. "Rodin (mit einer Vorbemerkung über Meunier)." In *Philosophische Kultur*, 168–186. Leipzig, Germany: Alfred Kröner Verlag, 1912.

Singer, Israel Joshua. "Fun bikher-tish: Vegen 'goylem' fun H. Leyvik." *Folkstsaytung*, 1922. In H. Leivick Collection, File 40, YIVO Archive, New York.

Singer, Isaac Bashevis. "Why the Golem Legend Speaks to Our Time." *New York Times*, 12 August 1984, 1, 25.

Sokoloff, Naomi. "The Sense of Smell." In *Reading Hebrew Literature: Critical Discussions of Six Modern Texts*, edited by Alan Mintz, 109–117. Hanover, NH: Brandeis University Press, 2003.

Solomon, Alisa. "A Jewish Avenger, a Timely Legend." *New York Times*, 7 April 2002. http://www.nytimes.com/2002/04/07/theater/theater-a-jewish-avenger-a-timely-legend.html.

Solomon, Eric. "Jews, Baseball, and American Fictions." In *Jews and American Popular Culture*, edited by Paul Buhle, 1–13. Westport, CT: Praeger, 2007.

Spector, Scott. *Prague Territories: National Conflict and Cultural Innovation in Franz Kafka's Fin de Siècle*. Berkeley: University of California Press, 2000.

Stephenson, Hunter. "Interview: Eli Roth Talks *Inglourious Basterds*, Going Method to Play the Bear Jew, Nazi Atrocities, and Quentin Tarantino's Place in History." / *Film: Blogging the Reel World*, 21 August 2009. http://www.slashfilm.com/interview-eli-roth-talks-inglourious-basterds-going-method-to-play-the-bear-jew-nazi-atrocities-and-quentin-tarantinos-place-in-history/.

Sturm, James. *The Golem's Mighty Swing*. Montreal: Drawn and Quarterly, 2001.

Sturm, James, and Rich Tommaso. *Satchel Paige: Striking Out Jim Crow*. New York: Jump at the Sun / Hyperion, 2007.

Sverdlin, Nosn. "Baym forhang." *Der tog*, 21 May 1948, 9.

Tannenbaum, Eugen. "*Der Golem, wie er in die Welt kam*." *B.Z. am Mittag*, 30 October 1920. In "Kritiken über das Filmwerk: *Der Golem, wie er in die Welt kam*," Ufa distribution pamphlet, Schriftgutarchiv. Stiftung Deutsche Kinemathek, Berlin.

Tarantino, Quentin, dir. *Inglourious Basterds*. Weinstein Company / Universal Pictures, 2009.

———. *Inglourious Basterds: A Screenplay*. New York: Weinstein Books, 2009.

Thomas, Alfred. *Prague Palimpsest: Writing, Memory, and the City*. Chicago: University of Chicago Press, 2010.

Thomas, Roy (w), Frank Robbins (a), and Frank Springer (a). *The Invaders: The Golem Walks Again!* #13. New York: Marvel Comics, February 1977.

Thomas, Roy (w), Herb Trimpe (p), and Sal Buscema (i). *Hulk* #134. New York: Marvel Comics, December 1970.

Thomas, Roy (w), Herb Trimpe (p), and John Severin (i). *Hulk* #133. New York: Marvel Comics, November 1970.

Tolts, Mark. "Population and Migration: Migration since World War I." YIVO Institute for Jewish Research. Accessed February 4, 2015, http://www.yivoencyclopedia.org/article.aspx/Population_and_Migration/Migration_since_World_War_I.

Tucholsky, Kurt. "Die patriotische Synagoge." In *Gesamtausgabe: Texte 1907–1913*, edited by Bärbel Boldt, Dirk Grathoff, and Michael Hepp, 81–82. Reinbek bei Hamburg: Rowohlt, 1997.

Turner, Victor. *Dramas, Fields, and Metaphors: Symbolic Action in Human Society*. Ithaca, NY: Cornell University Press, 1974.

Turszinsky, Walter. "Paul Wegener." *Bühne und Welt. Zeitschrift für Theaterwesen, Literatur und Musik* 14, no. 2 (1912): 12–15.

Underhill, Harriette. "On the Screen." *New York Tribune*, 21 June 1921, 6.

"Vi a krist hot baarbet di legende fun goylem." *Der tog*, 17 June 1921, 3.

Webber, Andrew. "About Face: E. T. A. Hoffmann, Weimar Film, and the Technological Afterlife of Gothic Physiognomy." In *Popular Revenants: The German Gothic and Its International Reception, 1800–2000*, edited by Andrew Cusack and Barry Murnane, 161–180. Rochester, NY: Camden House, 2012.

Wecker, Helene. *The Golem and the Jinni: A Novel*. New York: HarperCollins, 2013.

Wegener, Paul. "Der Golem, Exposé." 4.4–80/18, 1. Schriftgutarchiv. Stiftung Deutsche Kinemathek, Berlin.

———. "Der Golem und die Tänzerin." 4.4–80/18, 3. Schriftgutarchiv. Stiftung Deutsche Kinemathek, Berlin.

———. *Der Golem, wie er in die Welt kam: Eine Geschichte in fünf Kapiteln*. Berlin: August Scherl GmbH, 1921.

———. "Die künstlerischen Möglichkeiten des Films." In *Paul Wegener: Sein Leben und seine Rollen. Ein Buch von ihm und über ihn*, edited by Kai Möller, 102–113. Hamburg: Rowohlt, 1954.

———. *Flandrisches Tagebuch 1914*. Berlin: Rowohlt, 1933.

———. "Mein Werdegang." In *Paul Wegener: Sein Leben und seine Rollen. Ein Buch von ihm und über ihn*, edited by Kai Möller, 13–37. Hamburg: Rowohlt, 1954.

———. Nachlass Paul Wegener: Sammlung Kai Möller. Deutsches Filminstitut, Frankfurt am Main.

———. "Schauspielerei und Film." *Berliner Tageblatt*, 15 January 1915, 2.

Wegener, Paul, and Carl Boese, dirs. *Der Golem, wie er in die Welt kam*. Projektion-AG Union (PAGU), 1920.

Wegener, Paul, and Henrik Galeen. "Der Golem: Phantastisches Filmspiel in vier Akten." In *Film-Materialien: Henrik Galeen*, edited by Hans-Michael Bock and Wolfgang Jacobson, 3–16. Hamburg and Berlin: CineGraph, 1992.

Wein, Len (w), John Buscema (p), and Jim Mooney (i). *Strange Tales: The Golem* #174. Edited by Roy Thomas. New York: Marvel Comics Group, June 1974.

Weiner, Robert G. "Marvel Comics and the Golem Legend." *Shofar* 29, no. 2 (2011): 51–72.

Weisel, Leopold. "Sagen der Prager Juden." In *Sippurim eine Sammlung jüdischer Volkssagen, Erzählungen, Mythen, Chroniken, Denkwürdigkeiten*, edited by Wolf Pascheles, 50–52. Prague: Wolf Pascheles, 1858.

Weiss, Hillel. "*Ad hena* ke-mavo lasho'a." *Bikoret u-farshanut: Ktav-'et bein thumi leheker sifrut vetarbut* 35–36 (2001–2002): 111–146.

Westheim, Paul. "Eine Filmstadt von Poelzig." *Das Kunstblatt* 4, no. 11 (1920): 325–333.

Whales, James, dir. *Frankenstein*. Universal Pictures, 1931.

Wiener, Norbert. *Cybernetics*. New York: Wiley, 1948.

———. *God and Golem, Inc.: A Comment on Certain Points Where Cybernetics Impinges on Religion*. Cambridge, MA: MIT Press, 1964.

———. *The Human Use of Human Beings: Cybernetics and Society*. Boston: Houghton Mifflin, 1954.

Wiesel, Elie. *The Golem: The Story of a Legend*. New York: Summit Books, 1983.

Winter, Jay. *Sites of Memory, Sites of Mourning: The Great War in European Cultural History*. Cambridge: Cambridge University Press, 2006.

Wolff, Kurt. *Autoren, Bücher, Abenteuer: Betrachtungen und Erinnerungen eines Verlegers*. Berlin: Klaus Wagenbach, 2004.

———. "Der Golem." *Börsenblatt für den deutschen Buchhandel*, 12 June 1915, 7632.

———. *Kurt Wolff: Briefwechsel eines Verlegers 1911–1963*. Edited by Bernhard Zeller and Ellen Otten. Frankfurt am Main: Verlag Heinrich Scheffler, 1966.

Wollenberg, Hans. "Der Golem." *Lichtbild-Bühne*, 10 October 1920, 26.

Wright, Bradford W. *Comic Book Nation: The Transformation of Youth Culture in America*. Baltimore: Johns Hopkins University Press, 2001.

Yassif, Eli. "Mavo: Yudl (Yehuda) Rosenberg—sofer 'amami." In *Ha-golem mi-prag u-ma'asim nifla'im aherim*, by Yudl Rosenberg, 7–72. Jerusalem: Mosad Bi'alik, 1991.

Yaznevich, Victor. "Problems and Dilemmas: Lem's *Golem XIV*." Translated by Peter Swirski. In *Lemography: Stanislaw Lem in the Eyes of the World*, edited by Peter Swirski and Wacław M. Osadnik, 140–158. Liverpool: Liverpool University Press, 2014.

Young, Elizabeth. *Black Frankenstein: The Making of an American Metaphor*. New York: NYU Press, 2008.

Zelikovitsch, G. "Der goylem fun prag af brodvey." *Yidishes tageblat*, 22 June 1921, 4.

Zertal, Idith. "Eyma be-khos shel zkhukhit: Siḥa 'im Yoram Kaniuk." *Davar*, 26 August 1966, 22.

Zweig, Arnold. "Der Golem." *Die Schaubühne*, 11 March 1915, 224–228.

Zyd, Marian. "Yehudim be-'esh 'ha-golem ha-me'ofef.'" *Ha-mashkif*, 22 September 1944, 4.

INDEX

Page numbers in italics indicate figures.

ABOUT THE AUTHOR

Maya Barzilai is Assistant Professor of Hebrew Literature and Jewish Culture at the University of Michigan.